"Beaver's bracing honesty makes this a Hollywood st[...] resonate. . . . It's also a reminder to cherish your own partn[...]

"[A] moving creative endeavor." —*Chicago Tribune*

"A wrenching, uplifting memoir." —*The Oregonian*

"A memorable and poignant story, written with compelling frankness. I can't wait to recommend this to everyone I know."
—Beth Henley, Pulitzer Prize–winning playwright of
Crimes of the Heart

"Reading this, I quickly learned to keep a jumbo-size box of tissues at the ready. You will cry—and laugh—as Jim unwraps his unvarnished heart and soul. It will evoke memories of everyone who ever touched your heart, and remind you to talk from your heart to the people who mean something to you."
—Russell Friedman, coauthor of *The Grief Recovery Handbook*
and *When Children Grieve*

"*Life's That Way* grabbed me and wouldn't let me go. . . . Beaver writes in the dark of night to his extended family and friends with such honesty and humor, we readers feel he is writing to us personally. This book is a husband's story, a father's story, a love story, about the dying of his remarkable wife, and the first year of raising their amazing child as a single parent. We all have our cancer stories, but *Life's That Way* is one you don't want to miss."   —Patty Dann, author of *The Goldfish Went on Vacation*

"Night after night, Jim Beaver reached into his heart and wrote e-mails that were unabashed love letters—to his wife, his daughter, his friends, and now, through this book, to the rest of us. Despite great sadness, he writes with humor and a sense of exhilaration about the gifts found in marriage and the lessons learned through loss."
—Jeffrey Zaslow, coauthor of *The Last Lecture*

"Jim Beaver, the laconic character actor best known as the appealing prospector, Ellsworth, on *Deadwood*, has written a compassionate, funny, searing, and ultimately transcending memoir chronicling a year of tragedy, grief, and survival that would send the strongest of men, even an ex-Marine and West Texas preacher's son, to their knees. As Jim puts it, 'I'm no Job—though I think we went to the same school.' That his story is so compulsively readable, inspiring, and ultimately hopeful is due entirely to Jim's bracing honesty, dry humor, and deeply felt humanity. Read this book, tell your friends about it, and then go hug your loved ones."

—Robert Schenkkan,
Pulitzer Prize–winning playwright of *The Kentucky Cycle*

"To have known and read this man over these years, reveals to me I knew nothing of what love could and should be."   —Edward Asner

"Jim Beaver has walked through the valley of the shadow, and returned with a moving testament of discovery."

—David Milch, writer-creator of *Deadwood*

"Beaver collects a series of riveting, heartfelt e-mails chronicling the courageous cancer battle of his beloved wife. . . . The revealing e-mails depict the somber travail of Beaver on the horrific deathwatch of his wife, and detail the roller-coaster ride of emotion from hoping for a speedy halt to the disease's onslaught to experiencing the dark abyss of loss. . . . While this cancer memoir often chills the reader to the core with pain and frustration, it offers countless reasons to cheer Beaver as a remarkable man, a loving husband, and a responsible single parent."   —*Publishers Weekly*

"[This] passionate book is about how we mourn. . . . Beaver treats it with uncommon honesty and a bit of wisdom."   —*Kirkus Reviews*

"A powerful document, beautifully rendered, of both loss and healing, at once tragic and uplifting."   —Kem Nunn, author of *Tijuana Straits*

"*Life's That Way* is a heartbreaker, but is also rich in hope, humor, and insight into how to survive losing the things that matter most to you, and then rebuilding your life from the ground up. I cried over this book, but I cracked up too—Jim Beaver has a profound ability to diagram the depths and heights of his own heart, and that heart is both generous and humorous. This book should be required reading for everyone who has ever loved anyone. Losing someone you love may be part of the deal when it comes to being human, but this book shows that real love is worth it."

—Maria Dahvana Headley, author of *The Year of Yes*

"An extraordinary and beautifully written piece that poetically and humorously gives an intimate view into a husband's grief, loss, and pain. What is most exceptional to me is how this gentle but courageous man reveals what is perhaps the most under-explored region of our lives . . . the truth. This is a unique and brilliant work."

—Jon Turteltaub,
director-producer of *Jericho* and *National Treasure*

"One of the most powerful, heartbreaking, and hopeful things I have ever read." —Jackie Filgo, writer-producer of *That '70s Show*

"This is a journal straight from the heart and beyond, to the guts and marrow, blood and bone of life and death."

—Ed O'Neill, Golden Globe–nominated star of
Married with Children, Dragnet, and *John from Cincinnati*

"It is not often that you will encounter a primary source so honestly and expertly written as this. Expressing what it is like to go through such a tragedy may be one of the most difficult things one can do. Yet, Jim tackled his challenges in an awe-inspiring way. 'Inspiring' is a benediction one hears frequently these days, but Jim and Cecily truly embody that which reaffirms others' faith in life. This journal is something that everyone can benefit from reading."

—Haley Joel Osment, Academy Award–nominated actor

continued . . .

"This is an incredible look into the mind of a man going through a staggering loss. Everyone's coping mechanism is different. Jim's happened to be writing. It still amazes me that while his world was crumbling around him, he was able to express himself so beautifully. This book serves both as a love letter to his wife and also as a guide for anyone going through a similar struggle."   —Will Forte, writer and cast member, *Saturday Night Live*

"*Life's That Way* is a gift of a book and one that will join Joan Didion's *The Year of Magical Thinking* as a classic exploration of love and grief. . . . I can't recommend this book highly enough."   —*The Book Lady's Blog*

"Compelling and emotionally touching . . . an uplifting look at how deeply connected people can become in times of loss as well as times of gain . . . [A] powerfully written story."   —*Eclipse Magazine*

LIFE'S
THAT WAY

A Memoir

JIM BEAVER

BERKLEY BOOKS, NEW YORK

THE BERKLEY PUBLISHING GROUP
Published by the Penguin Group
Penguin Group (USA) Inc.
375 Hudson Street, New York, New York 10014, USA
Penguin Group (Canada), 90 Eglinton Avenue East, Suite 700, Toronto, Ontario M4P 2Y3, Canada
(a division of Pearson Penguin Canada Inc.)
Penguin Books Ltd., 80 Strand, London WC2R 0RL, England
Penguin Group Ireland, 25 St. Stephen's Green, Dublin 2, Ireland (a division of Penguin Books Ltd.)
Penguin Group (Australia), 250 Camberwell Road, Camberwell, Victoria 3124, Australia
(a division of Pearson Australia Group Pty. Ltd.)
Penguin Books India Pvt. Ltd., 11 Community Centre, Panchsheel Park, New Delhi—110 017, India
Penguin Group (NZ), 67 Apollo Drive, Rosedale, North Shore 0632, New Zealand
(a division of Pearson New Zealand Ltd.)
Penguin Books (South Africa) (Pty.) Ltd., 24 Sturdee Avenue, Rosebank, Johannesburg 2196,
South Africa

Penguin Books Ltd., Registered Offices: 80 Strand, London WC2R 0RL, England

While the author has made every effort to provide accurate telephone numbers and Internet addresses at the time of publication, neither the publisher nor the author assumes any responsibility for errors, or for changes that occur after publication. Further, the publisher does not have any control over and does not assume any responsibility for author or third-party websites or their content.

The author acknowledges permission to reprint the following:
Christopher Logue, "Come to the Edge," copyright © Christopher Logue, 1983.

"One for My Baby (And One More for the Road)" from the motion picture *The Sky's the Limit*. Lyrics by Johnny Mercer. Music by Harold Arlen. © 1943 (renewed) Harwin Music Co. All rights reserved.

PRINTING HISTORY
Amy Einhorn / G. P. Putnam's Sons hardcover edition / April 2009
Berkley trade paperback edition / April 2010

Berkley trade paperback ISBN: 978-0-425-23250-7

The Library of Congress has cataloged the Amy Einhorn / G. P. Putnam's Sons hardcover edition as follows:

Beaver Jr., James N., date.
   Life's that way: a memoir / Jim Beaver
      p.   cm.
   ISBN 978-0-399-15564-2
   1. Beaver Jr., James N.   2. Actors—United States—Diaries.   I. Title.
   PN2287.B3945L43   2009   2008054497
   792.02'8092—dc22
   [B]

PRINTED IN THE UNITED STATES OF AMERICA

10   9   8   7   6   5   4   3   2   1

*Penguin is committed to publishing works of quality and integrity.
In that spirit, we are proud to offer this book to our readers;
however, the story, the experiences, and the words
are the author's alone.*

FOR MY GIRL,
CECILY APRIL ADAMS,
AND OUR GIRL,
MADELINE ROSE BEAVER

INTRODUCTION

Announcing your plans is a good way to hear God laugh.
—AL SWEARENGEN IN HBO's *DEADWOOD*
(AS WRITTEN BY DAVID MILCH)

In the dog days of 2003, we heard no hint of laughter. Indeed, God seemed to smile most beamingly on the plans under way in our little household. Family, careers, home, and security all were shaping up just as we had hoped, dreamed, and, yes, planned.

After a couple of decades toiling unnoticed in the not-so-trenchlike trenches as a character actor, I was suddenly starring as the lovable prospector Ellsworth on what was about to become the critically acclaimed television program *Deadwood*. My wife, Cecily Adams (the daughter of TV legend Don Adams, *Get Smart*'s Maxwell Smart), had her own fan following as Ishka, the beloved "Moogie" of *Star Trek: Deep Space Nine*. And she was simultaneously ensconced as one of television's most respected casting directors, responsible for such shows as *3rd Rock from the Sun* and *That '70s Show*. I was in the homestretch, finishing a long-aborning book on the life of TV Superman George Reeves, and Cecily was traveling the world, making public appearances at science-fiction fan conventions.

More important, we were the proud parents of Madeline Rose, a delicious two-year-old we had struggled through horrifically difficult fertility treatments to conceive. (Granted, most of the horror and difficulty were Cecily's.) We were building our dream house, just a block from Cecily's studio office, and she would be able to walk home to see her baby at lunch every day. The house was taking shape to Cec's most detailed and tasteful design. Life, family, home, and career. We had it all.

And then the roof fell in.

In less than two months, our child was diagnosed as autistic, and Cecily, a nonsmoking health nut, learned she had lung cancer at age forty-five.

What followed was a whirlwind of terror, pain, and sorrow. But what accompanied those horrors was another whirlwind, a whirlwind of love and generosity and unfathomable human kindness, and of wondrous gifts and invaluable lessons for living. In a tale that seemed bent on rivaling Job's, the sheer drive of the human spirit toward life ultimately overwhelmed the narrative.

Upon learning the facts of Cecily's illness, I spent fourteen hours on the phone that first day with family and friends, delivering the news and explaining what we expected the future to hold. Knowing I could not devote such time every day, I set out to write a nightly e-mail letter. At first it simply encapsulated the day's treatment and any news or change in prognosis. Soon, however, the newsletter mutated into a journal of our experiences as a family.

Initially, I sent out the e-mail to a hundred or so friends and family members. Very quickly (and to me, quite astonishingly), people began to forward the e-mails to others. Many of those people then forwarded them to still others, until the circle of people receiving and following the journal far exceeded those we knew personally. Based on feedback I received from readers, I estimate that in less than a month, more than 4,000 people, worldwide, were reading my nightly writings.

I was aware that some phenomenon was occurring with the journal, that something about the way I had opened up myself and our lives and invited people to take the intimate journey with us had registered with many souls. I also discovered an amazing gift—the astonishing healing power of the *written* word, for myself and for others. I continued writing on a nightly basis until the following October, completing my journal exactly one year after starting it. The result is a written journey through shock and terror, as well as an examination of intense love and the goodness of our fellow man that still boggles my mind.

This book, then, is that journal. Oh, not all of it. The uncut version is considerably longer than *Moby-Dick*. But this condensed version is no adaptation, nor a reflection written after consideration of long-past events. While things have been trimmed, and a few lines have been inserted here and there to more fully identify people or to ease the transition over omitted sections, what sits between the covers of this book are the words I wrote, virtually as I wrote them. The story is *immediate*, told in real time, in the moment, as things were happening. There is no twenty-twenty hindsight applied, no rewriting to fit what we learned later. And *nothing* is written with knowledge of what the future held. What I wrote for a given day is what I knew or felt or feared on that day, nothing more. Only as I reached the journal's end did I know the story I had been telling.

As my journal took shape, I developed one overriding goal: to make it as honest a representation of what such an experience was like as I possibly could. The only self-censoring I did was on rare occasions to avoid frightening Cecily, who at times was reading some of the entries. I did my utmost to be true to facts, feelings, fears, and shames, as well as to the joy and pride and blessings that revealed themselves at every turn.

And so, here it is: a story that takes place in Hollywood but also one that takes place every day in every city and village in the world. I hope my version throws a little light on the path.

*In the middle of winter I at last discovered that
there was in me an invincible summer.*

—Albert Camus, *Return to Tipasa*

Part One

NEWS FROM
CECILY

ONE

To Cecily's friends and family, and my friends and family, and our joint friends and family:

Some of you are aware of what's been going on with us. To others, this will be a shocking piece of bad news. I've gotten so many phone calls in the past few days that I cannot keep up with them, and it's difficult repeating information to thirty or forty people a day. So I'm going to attempt a nightly e-mail report, to keep all of you abreast and also to shorten the amount of valuable time I use telling people individually.

It appears that Cecily has an advanced case of lung cancer. It was discovered this past Saturday, October 25, though it is clear that she's had (misleading) symptoms for several months. We don't have a firm diagnosis yet, but the test results continue to point to the same conclusion.

For three months, Cec has suffered increasing pain in her breast-bone. We assumed it was a pulled muscle or maybe torn cartilage—not a surprise when one is picking up a two-year-old every few minutes. But the pain wouldn't go away. Then about two weeks ago, she appeared to throw her back out; this happens a lot to Cec, so it wasn't unnerving. The combination of the two "muscle" pains kept her in bed for the past couple weeks. During this time, we moved into our rental house (until the new house is finished) and Cec worked by telephone, occasionally dragging herself to the office for casting sessions.

Last week, her orthopedist said he couldn't understand why there was no improvement, so he ordered a CT scan. It showed a mass just below Cec's left lung, and some fluid around her heart. The mass was apparently not *in* her lung, but below it, and seemed to be a calcified lymph node—not much to worry about. It seemed this finding was accidental and unrelated to Cec's chest and back pain.

They decided to do a bronchoscopy—an examination of the interior of her lung—this past Thursday, October 23. This outpatient exam, under mild anesthesia, showed only a little swelling and nothing frightening inside the lung. But coming out of anesthesia, Cec awoke to excruciating pain in her lower back and chest, so bad that morphine only lessened it, so bad that the hospital refused to release her. She was admitted to Cedars-Sinai Medical Center in L.A./ Beverly Hills—still under the presumption that it was severe muscle cramping or something similar.

The next day, Friday, October 24, she was given more tests, including a PET scan, to determine what was going on. (The PET scan finds the parts of the body with the fastest metabolizing cells— either infectious cells or cancerous ones.)

On Saturday morning we got the results. There was high metabolic activity in the mass under Cecily's left lung, in her sternum, her pelvis, and her lower spine. The oncologist said it was probably cancer, but without a biopsy, no one could be certain. The biopsy, to determine what type of cancer it was and what kind of chemotherapy would be necessary, was scheduled for today, October 27, but has been postponed until Wednesday, October 29, in order to obtain additional blood tests.

There's the tiniest of tiny chances that this isn't cancer. There's a small chance that if it is cancer, it's not lung cancer. If either of these chances proves true, Cecily's outlook improves dramatically. Whatever the case, though, she's facing a difficult ordeal of chemotherapy and radiation treatment. We are told that many people, although sick and in distress from the treatment, are able to carry on their normal lives most of the time, except perhaps for two or three days a month when they receive the chemo. Time will tell if that's true for Cec. She plans to continue to work, though, and has asked some of the best casting directors in the business to be her backup when she needs help.

Right now, Cec is still in Cedars-Sinai Medical Center and will probably be there until Thursday. She needs more rest so we are *not* encouraging visitors or phone calls. We've been utterly overwhelmed with calls already, so please forgive me if I don't get back to you quickly or even at all.

Maddie and I are in the rental home. We've had some of Cec's family here to help, and Maddie has a nanny much of the time. But I know that I'm going to have to put out a call for help pretty soon, as it's terribly hard to be at my job, at the hospital, and with Maddie all at the same time. Grocery runs, sandwich runs, and babysitting are going to be invaluable, if you have the time, ability, and locale to offer them.

Cec is scared, as am I. This is the most horrible thing that has ever happened to us. But Cec is terribly, terribly brave, too, and she's ready now to do anything she has to do to survive. Even though chemo makes one very sick, she wishes she could've started it yesterday. We are praying and ask you to do the same, in whatever fashion is meaningful to you. Please don't hesitate to offer help, hope, or prayers. But please forgive us if we're not good at spending time discussing the general situation with you individually. We're in a fight for life here, and it's already taking everything we've got.

Oh, yeah. Cecily's gonna beat this. You watch.

I'll try to do nightly reports, so watch your e-mail. Feel free to pass this on—I don't have e-mail addresses for everyone who might want to know about this.

We love you all.

Jim Beaver

October 28, 2003

Cec is in a lot of pain, though it's been diminished a little with steroids. But steroids can only be used for a limited time, and they've begun cutting back. The pain will grow, therefore, but they say that radiation treatment helps diminish the pain. I hope they're right.

Cecily's producers at *That '70s Show* sent over lunch today for me and Maddie, and I realized it was the first hot meal I've had in six days. I promise to do better from now on. I know I've got to keep well in order to help Cec get well.

We have nannies for Maddie both day and evening, but I'm not sure how long we can afford it. So those of you who've offered assistance with the youngster may get your chance.

Cecily's sister Cathy came in from Las Vegas and has stayed with Cec every night in the hospital, but she has to return home today. I'm hoping one of Cecily's other sisters arrives in time to stay with her starting tonight, as I have to be home with Maddie, and the nursing staff at Cedars-Sinai responds to Cec's needs better when there's someone else running interference.

That's all for now, except that Cec and I have been deeply moved by the outpouring of love and offers of help. We are going to take all of you up on both. I'm trying to organize a list of everyone who's offered help so we can spread it around. That way no one gets called too often. Cec will probably be home in two to four days, and that's when our need will be greatest. Thank you all. Nearly every call and e-mail I've received has left me in tears. Of course, they're pretty close to the surface these days.

Jim

October 29, 2003

Not a lot of news today. Cec had a needle biopsy of her hipbone this morning (not the sternum, as expected). Surgery on her chest for biopsy purposes was postponed; the needle biopsy should be sufficient to identify the type of cancer so treatment can begin.

Some of you may wonder, as I did, whether the delay from the first scan results showing the cancer last Friday and obtaining a decent biopsy sample today (or tomorrow) affects Cec's chances of recovery. Her thoracic surgeon, Dr. Ward Houck, assured me that cancer grows fast, but fast in terms of months and years, not hours and days. I hope he's right. I never would've dreamed they could find evidence of cancer on Friday and still not know for sure or what kind six days later.

1:08 a.m. I'm off to bed. More tomorrow—and we're planning on good news.

Jim

October 30, 2003

"The best-laid schemes o' mice an' men gang aft agley."
—ROBERT BURNS

Our plans for good news today did not pan out. Cecily had a bone scan this morning, but it didn't provide immediate conclusions.

After getting Maddie up and turning her over to her nanny Maribel Elena (whose husband has cancer and for whom Cecily staged a benefit this summer), I called the hospital to find out what was up. I couldn't get anyone in Cec's room, so I called her oncologist, Dr. Becky Miller. She asked me if I could join her in Cec's room at noon, as she had a pathology report on Cec's needle biopsy. She refused to elaborate, which left me with a feeling I can compare only to having one's seat on an airliner suddenly drop out through the bottom of the plane.

Dr. Miller entered Cec's room with a grim, tight smile and all I could do was pray that there was some small part of what she was going to say that was good. I suppose there was, but not much. She confirmed most of what we already feared.

Cec has what's known as non-small-cell lung cancer. There are three types of non-small-cell lung cancers. Cec has the type known as adenoma. It has spread to her sternum, lower spine, and hipbones. There's no sign of metastasis (spreading) in her organs. They will do MRIs tomorrow (Friday) on her neck and brain, looking for metastasis in those areas, which have not been scanned.

I have minuscule knowledge of lung cancer, but my reading over the past few days gave me a bit of information. Apparently there are four types of lung cancer: small-cell and three kinds of non-small-cell. Small-cell is worse than non-small-cell. And adenoma, Cec's kind, is the best of the three non-small-cell varieties. So if my understanding is correct, the tiny bit of good news was that she had the least bad of four bad possibilities. None of this changes the fact that she is seriously ill and that the fight we are beginning is in every sense of the word a fight for her life. Cecily does not want to know the odds against her and I will not state them here. But she has one of the toughest cancers there is, and beating it is going to be a Herculean task. Thankfully, my wife makes Hercules look like Paul Lynde.

We got a second opinion tonight from Dr. Ronald Natale. Dr. Natale is one of the world's leading researchers in lung cancer and is actually the inventor of the chemotherapy technique which Cec will probably begin tomorrow. He agreed to be Cecily's oncologist if we so choose.[1] Our feeling is that this is akin to having Albert Einstein agree to be your physics tutor. Dr. Natale pulled no punches. He let us know we were in for a fight that comparatively few people win. But he also said that Cecily struck him as a woman of Unrepressible Determination, and that he would rather have U.D. on his side than any drug.

Cecily will start chemo tomorrow and then go home. Chemo will be in three-week cycles: treatment on the first and eighth days, then skip a week. By the end of the second three-week cycle we should know if Cec is among the 30–35 percent of people who show marked improvement with the chemo combination. If she's not, then another blend will be used. If she doesn't respond to that, we plan to employ new experimental drugs that Dr. Natale is an expert in. But the first line of attack is the chemo. We are great believers in alternative therapies (our daughter, Maddie, would not have been born were it not for acupuncture), and we are open to more information in those areas. But chemotherapy, as difficult as it can be, is our choice for now, in combination with radiation to diminish her considerable pain.

The prayers, calls, e-mails, and cards, as well as gifts, flowers, and food have touched our hearts beyond imagination. The offers of help will not find our pride an obstacle. We will need it. Cecily may improve her mobility with the treatments, but she does have cancer in her spine and it will be hard for her to get around. Her radiation treatments will be at St. John's Hospital in Burbank, much closer to home than Cedars-Sinai. Radiation treatments will be every day, five days a week. We hope to arrange for volunteer drivers so no one has to do it more than once or twice. Same with grocery runs, that

---

1. Due to unrelated circumstances, Dr. Natale unfortunately became unavailable and we never retained his services.

sort of thing. Our friends Nancylee Myatt and Kitty Swink will be coordinating. In only a few days this has become the transforming experience of my life. I will never forget the lessons I've learned thus far, including the one that has taught me that a friend in need is a friend indeed, and that friends indeed come out of the woods like army ants when you call them. God bless you all. Prayer, hope, and determination have won the day in greater battles than this.

I want to include something sent to me by my dear friend Beth Becka, something which rocked and moved Cec and me to our souls. I hope it does the same for you.

> *"When you get to the end of all the light you know, and it's time to step into the darkness of the unknown, faith is knowing that one of two things shall happen: either you will be given something solid to stand on, or you will be taught how to fly."*
>
> —EDWARD TELLER

Till tomorrow, signing off at 12:42 a.m.

Jim

October 31, 2003

Cecily was supposed to have her first chemotherapy today at 2:00 p.m., which is when I arrived at the hospital. By 2:50 she still had not returned to her room from a "five-minute" trip to X-ray at 12:30 p.m. I waited there for her with her stepmom, Dorothy, and Cec's sister Stacey. Cec finally arrived back in her room around 3:00. I then ordered a sandwich from Jerry's Deli around the corner, and *it* didn't arrive for two hours. I thought perhaps it was going to turn into one of those days.

It didn't, actually. Aside from the nastiness of our situation, it was a good day. Cec started her chemotherapy and seemed to tolerate it. She began with a powerful antinausea medication, and then two different chemotherapy agents were introduced consecutively through her IV. She lay there and talked with me and with her family on the phone and seemed only to have a little problem with acid stomach—a common response. Before she allowed the nurse to start the flow of chemicals, she and her sister Chris, by phone from Maryland, spent a few minutes meditating and fixing in her mind the image of these drugs as powerful friends come to wage war against her internal enemies. When she felt confident in that mind-set, she nodded and the nurse started the IV. It took about an hour and a half. Following the chemo, she spent another couple hours getting an IV infusion of a drug to help strengthen her bones against further attack.

The brain and neck scans were (again) postponed, and the late start on her chemotherapy meant she would (again) have to stay another day in the hospital. Cec wants badly to be home with her Maddie, but it simply was not practical to bring her home late in the evening, before knowing whether she might have a bad reaction to the chemo.

Cecily's sister Cathy stayed with her every night in the hospital until last night, when she had to return to her job in Nevada. Cathy was an enormous boon to Cec these first frightening days. With my own presence demanded at home with Maddie at night, Cec would otherwise have been alone at the hospital, and it's our experience that many of the nursing staff are kinder, more present, and more accommodating when a patient has a family member there to bear witness.

Since Cathy's departure, others (Stacey tonight) have been Cec's companions and guardians through the night vigil. Cec's mom has been staying at our little temporary bungalow, keeping an eye on Maddie and running up somebody's phone bill. Cec is blessed to have some family near her, and more family not too far away. My family is all quite far away—Florida, Texas—so their help and companionship are by needs telephonic. This is a hard, hard time. I've not mentioned it, but my father is in rapidly failing health and he surely will not live to see Cec's recovery nor, probably, another holiday. Fortunately, he and I have had a Norman Rockwell–esque relationship our whole lives, and we have nothing unsaid, nothing unresolved, no love unspoken, and though I've dreaded his demise since I was old enough to suspect he might someday have one, I take comfort in knowing that he's taught me well and that through faith and determination I can bear anything. Even this.

As the shock of these events has begun to shift into the dullish ache of reality, Cec and I have begun to peck at the edges of making plans for a future that might not include us both. It creates great pain to go there, but a two-year-old child forces many issues, even in good times. So wills and savings and financial planning must somehow be faced, not because we lie down before the onslaught of events, but because when a hurricane arises, only a fool doesn't board up his windows.

Cecily will, barring more unexpected delays, be home tomorrow (Saturday). I'm sorry she can't come home to our comfortable abode of fifteen years, which now houses some other family's joys and sorrows. And I'm sorry she can't come home to our new house, still being built to a design that Cecily's great good taste will surely make into this man's castle. Instead she must come home to a hospital bed in the living room of a lovely but tiny rental house which is neither truly a home nor truly ours. That said, we are grateful that we have an interim locale, and having Cec return here will make it all the home Maddie and I need.

As happens every day now, a flood of goodwill has washed over us, and the prayers, gifts, and favors of scores of people have eased our hearts and bodies. And for those of you who are in the entertainment business: the next time I hear some fellow talk about the egos, decadence, and hedonism of Hollywood, I may just pop him in the nose. Kinder, more helpful, and thoughtful people I've never met.

1:41 a.m. Good night. Say your prayers.

Jim

November 1, 2003

Today was a hard day. I've lost no hope. I clutch with a strength I never knew I had to my belief that Cecily can overcome this monster. But despair wells up nonetheless. Despair over her suffering, now and to come, and over her awareness of that suffering yet-to-be. Despair over the loss, temporary or permanent, of so many dreams and plans. Despair over even the concept of living without her, of Maddie living without her.

I went to our new house today to pick up the mail. The roof was sealed, just in time to save the newly built, newly painted interior from being drenched in our first rains in six months. I walked through the empty house, examining the work of our contractor (another gift from God—I'll fill you in on this guy at some point). There's nothing in the house, not even real floors yet. Just new walls and door frames and wires where light switches will be. The most prominent feature of this new house, however, is Cecily. She's in every inch of it. Her taste, her great good taste, infuses every corner. The windows are as high and as wide as they are because she saw them that way in her mind. The muted yellow of the walls, the balconies, the gable-esque configurations of windows, they're all her handiwork. She thought and planned and chose the look of everything, and spent hours daily telling the craftsmen how it should be. There's a twelve-foot-high built-in bookcase inside the entryway—because she knows I love my books and love for people to see them. Anyone who's known me for long knows there was a good chance I'd spend my life sleeping on other people's sofas. Until I met Cecily.

Walking through this house, empty of everything but her influence, I was ripped through the heart. The idea that something that was so much her, something that was so long and so often her dream, might not remain hers or ever even be hers hit me like a taxi. I've cried many a time in the past two weeks. In that empty house, I cried as I've never come near crying in my life.

When she's well, I'll be glad to show you where all that crying took place, and we'll smile and maybe laugh.

Cec was supposed to come home today, following that much-delayed brain scan. It took them until 4:30 p.m. to begin the scan, too late for her to come home thereafter. So she's there tonight at Cedars-Sinai, alone for the first night of her stay. Though volunteers are plentiful, we just didn't logistically pull off getting anyone to stay the night with her. It's difficult, as she's had a similarly hard day, that same creeping despair and fear reaching in and getting a handful of her heart now and then. We pray, we work to lift each other up, we visualize powerfully positive outcomes. Just because she's brave doesn't mean she's fearless.

Tomorrow she should be released from the hospital. Though she's a little intimidated by the prospect of being away from the IV with the painkillers, the prospect of being at home with Maddie far outweighs any wariness. A few weeks ago, Cec was thinking about attending a conference in Virginia this weekend. But she hesitated, as she'd never yet spent a night away from Maddie. She didn't go, of course, as life threw up a roadblock. Ironically, she's only been with Maddie two hours in the past ten days.

Cec has such pain in her chest and back that she can't hold Maddie or pick her up, so I ordered a hospital bed for the house with full-length rails, thinking that might protect Cec from Maddie climbing up onto the bed and accidentally hurting her. Today I put Maddie on the floor after her breakfast, took her bowl to the kitchen, and turned around to see her sitting on top of the hospital bed, grinning—having just clambered up the side rails. I don't call her "Monkey" because she looks like one.

As Cec leaves the hospital, there will be less news, fewer noteworthy events, as tests will be comparatively infrequent and revelations will come every few weeks rather than hours. So if these reports tend to be less actual reports and more just ramblings about our journey, forgive me. Some have suggested that this must be therapeutic for me. I feel that it must be. I don't always feel better after writing this stuff. But I feel clearer. If it helps or interests any of you, more's the good.

As always, thank you all for your generosity of spirit and effort and your willingness to let us lean on you. I will bore you with my thanks every night.

1:12 a.m. God bless.

Jim

November 2, 2003

I never particularly wanted kids. Oh, I'd play along with girl-friends and come up with names for if and when. But it never got that far, and frankly, I was too involved with my inner child to go looking for any outer ones. Cec was the same way—maybe a little more inclined toward the notion, but not much.

Then I got cast in *Thunder Alley* and began to work with Kelly Vint, Lindsay Felton, and Haley Joel Osment. What they and their parents taught me was that children needn't be rug rats. That wisdom and audaciousness and courage and love and enormous intelligence were often to be found in short packages. I fell in love with three kids (and then their siblings), and Cec and I started looking differently at the idea of having one ourselves.

I still never quite got to the point of being desperate for one, but biology tipped Cec over that precipice. To the reverberations of her inner clock, we began a long, expensive, and difficult process. I don't mean the natural part! Lots of doctors and drugs and treatments and procedures and heartbreaks were necessary before we ended up with this sweet little girl of ours. Like all parents, we had fears. I was afraid of losing the freedom from responsibility that makes an acting career a little easier to sustain. I was afraid of being an older parent and the calamitous possibilities that might force upon a child of mine. And we were both afraid of having a child with problems.

We have a perfect child. A perfect child who's autistic. We learned this in August, at almost the same time that the pain in Cec's chest was beginning to pass Irritating on its way to Worrisome. At eighteen months, Maddie was an incipient social butterfly, laughing, verbal, spouting new words every day. But six months later, she'd been transformed into a silent, staring statue. She'd lost nearly all semblance of interaction and could barely still say "Mama." In August we found out why.

The past three months have been spent in aggressive intervention, in hopes of helping Maddie rewire her brain and fend off the most difficult aspects of this syndrome. In a short time, we've had such wondrous success a casual observer wouldn't see anything but a normal little girl, acting normally. But there's a long road ahead of us, and a lot of therapy will be necessary to provide Maddie with a normally interactive future. It has been our first priority, our foremost commitment. And it's still Cecily's foremost commitment, even when she's lying in her hospital bed, hooked up to IVs and wracked with pain. If they could harness her mother-love and use it as a weapon against cancer, she would be free of the disease tomorrow.

So we're frightened. Frightened not just of the shade looming, but for our ability to care for this lovely little girl in the midst of a turmoil we never expected. We're frightened of losing all we have, even if we succeed in winning this war. We're frightened that I alone can't provide what this child needs. I trust and believe that I won't be alone, that Cec will be here struggling alongside me, but sooner or later we're likely to lose her income. I'm not ashamed to say that she's the major breadwinner in this family. My work, like that of most character actors, is sporadic—not badly paid when it comes, but even in the best of times irregular and unpredictable.

I call the pharmacy for a prescription and a stab of fear shoots through me: What if I lose my insurance? Some guy cuts me off in traffic and I quiver: What happens to Maddie if something happens to me? These things are part of every parent's emotional life, but when they are shadowed by this horrific image of real disaster, they cannot be so easily tossed off. Life is, I've discovered, much harder to live when you're afraid every moment. One still persists, perseveres, plods on into the fight, but there's a dull sickness in the gut pervading the journey. One fights not just cancer, but also the fear of cancer and the myriad other fears that seem to gain strength from their alliance with it. The operative term, though, is "one fights." We fight on.

Cec did not come home from the hospital today. She had a bad night Saturday night and her doctor agreed that it was better she stay one more day under the watchful care of the nurses rather than the much less confidence-inspiring care of her husband.

Cecily's college roommate and bridesmaid, Teresa Jones, drove sixty miles today to take over the babysitting for the afternoon and evening. Then she drove sixty miles back home. To quote the monster in *Young Frankenstein*: "Mmm . . . Friend good!"

At incredibly late notice, our friend Jane George went to spend the night in Cec's room. So she's not alone tonight, in actuality. Of course, there are now 182 names on the list to receive these late-night reports, so it's clear she's not alone in spirit, either.

Thanks be to God. Thanks be to you.

12:04 a.m.

Jim

TWO

Cec is home.

It took all day, but we got her home.

She had a good night with Jane, who, besides being a wonderful friend, is a woman with a deep awareness of the relationship between the physical and the spiritual. She helped Cec balance herself a little; Cec found her fears reduced somewhat and was able to sleep.

I didn't get much sleep, though. Maddie awoke at 2:00 a.m. and I brought her into bed with me. Somewhere in the course of her twenty-six months she's learned flamenco dancing. It was a rough night.

Cecily's mother has been staying with me. Dell's pretty cool, a former saloon singer who decided to be a doctor but couldn't get into medical school in this country, so she took her four kids to Italy and attended med school there, despite the fact that she didn't speak Italian. She ended up back in the States as a schoolteacher rather than a doctor. Smart lady. Kind heart. And about as calm as a bag of bees. She's seventy-nine now and needs an awful lot of looking after. I can't manage much more looking after. But she's Cec's mom and she should be here, whether it's manageable or not.

Cec's dad is also in poor health. He has lymphoma, and he broke a hip a few weeks back and got pneumonia, along with all his other ongoing ailments. He's eighty and not so fun to manage, either. That job has fallen to Cec's sister Stacey, who finds herself in an emotional bind similar to mine. With me, it's my wife and my dad facing either impending or imminent death. For Stacey, it's her dad and her sister. But both of hers are here and drawing her most committed attention. There are moments each day when I feel as though the tension will rip my chest apart. But I wouldn't trade with Stacey. Say a prayer for her, too. She's been a rock for us, though I doubt she feels much like a rock.

I got to the hospital around 12:30 p.m. to check Cecily out and bring her home. But she'd had a resurgence of pain late in the morning and her pain medication knocked her out, so I spent much of the next several hours waiting for her to wake up. We had a thirty-minute ride home in the world's bumpiest car, the '97 Ford Explorer, just the thing for a patient with spinal cancer. But Cec got through it fine and walked under her own power into our little temporary house.

Maddie looked up and said, "*Mama*!" Then she said, "No bye-bye." This is Cec's new watchword. No bye-bye.

A word about a fellow named Mark Sobel. He's been Cec's friend for seventeen years, and mine for a lot less time, though I knew him well all that time. I didn't like Mark at first. It took me years to tolerate him, and I don't think he cared for me, either. But we've come to be friendly over the past few years and now I'll fight anybody who says anything (too) bad about him. Despite the fact that he has an unfinished self-financed film opening this Friday at the AFI Fest, he's devoted nearly every waking moment of the past two weeks to collecting cancer information, bombarding doctors with questions and entreaties, and running errands, including taking Maddie and her nanny fifteen miles and back to therapy on days when I have to be at the hospital. Mark and Cecily go way back. He was the director of Cec's very first film as a casting director. He thought she was the greatest thing since prewrapped cheese slices, and she became his best friend almost on first sight. I think Mark has no friendship as vital to him as Cec's. He loves and needs her, I believe, more than anyone on earth. I think he would do anything for her, even die for her. His obsessive drive to save her and his devotion to the needs of her family might seem strange in another context. But this is not another context. As miserable as our lives have been at times recently, they'd have been infinitely more miserable without Mark Sobel.

Jane George came over to the house tonight and bathed Cec, dried and brushed her hair, and again calmed and soothed Cec by whatever that magic is that Janie does. It's quiet and peaceful here in the house. Even if it's an illusion.

12:09 a.m.

No bye-bye.[2]

Jim

November 4, 2003

This will be short. I'm so tired. It usually takes me about ninety minutes to write up one of these. But I need to treat myself to seven uninterrupted hours if I can get them, and I can't get them if I spend ninety minutes typing.

Let me tell you a story about Cecily. Cec was determined to breast-feed Maddie, because she wanted to give Maddie all the nutritional, immunological, and developmental benefits that nursing provides. But about three weeks after she was born, Maddie started having trouble. Cec's milk flow was too fast and Maddie would choke. The two of them struggled to make it work, but eventually

---

2. While the phrase has been largely omitted for space considerations, from this point on virtually every message in the journal signed off with "No bye-bye."

Maddie simply wouldn't suckle. Cec tried everything. She went to eight different lactation specialists. She went to La Leche League. She tried techniques that were guaranteed to work, but only ended up throwing out her back because they were so awkward. Finally, in discussion with a lactation consultant, Cecily said, "Maddie's getting breast milk. I don't care what I have to do. I'll use a breast pump and pump every meal for her."

The consultant said, "That's six or seven times a day. You can't do that." Cec asked why not. The consultant said, "I don't mean you *can't*. I mean you *won't*. Lots of people say they will, but they give up when they see how hard it is to pump every four hours around the clock *and* feed it to the baby *and* sterilize the pump after each time. You won't do it."

Cec said, "You don't know me."

Maddie had breast milk for every meal until she was seven and a half months old. Six times a day, every four hours, 'round the clock, day in and day out, at work, at home, Cec pumped and then fed. She only quit when a health issue forced her to.

Maddie's twenty-six months old and has had three colds. That's it.

I tell this story to let those of you who don't know Cec know just how tenacious this girl is. She will fight this disease with that same tenacity. And for her, it's for the same reason: Maddie. Cec was never a quitter, but the very idea of Maddie has inspired in her a commitment and determination I've never seen in anyone else. It took us five years to get pregnant. If she hadn't had a false-alarm breast cancer scare, she might still be pumping. She says she's going to beat this cancer. I believe her.

Cecily's asked me to thank everyone who's followed her situation, who's written, called, or volunteered. As am I, she's been mightily touched by the generosity and support of hundreds of people, many of whom she doesn't even know. These reports started by going out to our close friends and family, but requests to be included have swollen the number of recipients. Why, I'm not quite sure. There are millions of people suffering from this and other diseases and misfortunes. But I've always felt there was something quite special about Cecily Adams. And something about her plight and her fight has registered with people, even former strangers. She thanks you and I thank you.

She's asked that each of you spend a few moments every day visualizing the image that she and I picture many times a day: an older, healthy Cecily and her possibly decrepit husband, Jim, walking their grown daughter, Madeline, down the aisle. That's the gift we hope for and pray for. If you don't mind, keep that picture in your consciousness every so often.

12:38 a.m. Halfway through those ninety minutes I couldn't afford.

Jim

November 5, 2003

Today was the first day that our new volunteer program went into action. Kitty Swink, Nancylee Myatt, and G. Charles Wright have organized all of the volunteers and have provided a designated driver for Cec's radiation appointments and a utility helper (gofer) for each day.

Bridget Hanley drove Cec to radiation. The appointment was to mark the locations on her body where she'll receive radiation. Some of these marks are permanent tattoos. They allow the radiation to be aimed precisely at the same spot every time. They also allow me to sing "Lydia the Tattooed Lady" more times than Cec appreciates.

It turns out that no one made a radiation appointment for Cec tomorrow. (Bureaucratic missteps before now were merely enervating; now I begin to understand why so many of these places have metal detectors.) So her first radiation treatment will be Friday, shooting rays into her hip to burn out cancer cells.

A word for volunteers and visitors: Cec's immune system is being depleted by the chemotherapy, so *please*, if you're helping out or coming for a visit, don't bring a cold or the flu or anything like that with you. She won't be able to fight off even simple bugs. Please understand, too, if we ask you to wash your hands. And clean your room. And why can't you comb your hair out of your face? Don't talk back to me.

Sorry. It's late.

12:31 a.m.

Jim

November 6, 2003

When Cec got out of bed today, Maddie said, "Mommy up!" She seemed so happy to see Cec moving about. Maddie continues to say "No bye-bye" several times a day, if she even *suspects* Cec might be going somewhere. It's clear that her mom's absence affected her considerably, though her spirits seemed good throughout. This morning, I lay Maddie in Cec's arms in the hospital bed. They cuddled for half an hour. You could see color coming back into Cec's face. It was the first time Cec has been able to hold Maddie in any meaningful sense in weeks.

Cec wants people to know that she's feeling better. She says she can tell that the chemo's in there knocking off cancer cells, and that she can feel the internal improvement. She's moving more easily, even without having started radiation, and I expect her improvement to increase with that treatment. Of course she's still taking a lot of medications, but it's heartening to see how much better she looks and feels than she did even a week ago. Dr. Miller, the oncologist, said she was encouraged by how well Cecily looked, since many people seem to decline under the effects of chemo.

Cecily has a number of things on her side: she hasn't smoked in two decades, she's a woman, and she's twenty years younger than the average age of the person who gets this disease. She has strength and youth and resiliency that are not available to those sixty-five-year-old patients. People beat this disease on occasion, and the ones who beat it are the ones with advantages. And drive.

By the way, for all you medicinal potheads out there who've suggested that a few good tokes or a half dozen brownies would ease the chemo-induced nausea, thank you for the suggestion. It's quite true that the cannabinol in marijuana is a powerful antinausea agent and that it's especially effective for cancer patients. However, it appears that the weed is ineffective for platinum-based chemotherapy agents, and that's what Cec is taking. But thanks for the advice and for the surprisingly plentiful offers to help us get some.

Tomorrow is Cec's first radiation treatment. They say it's painless but produces fatigue. That seems like a fair trade, especially since radiation is the best nondrug way to overcome the pain inherent in bone lesions.

Thanks to all who've brought food. It's only in the past couple of days I've been able to eat much. I lost seven pounds the first week we learned of Cec's illness. That's only a pound less than she's lost. The refrigerator's crammed like the inside of a radio. If there's one thing I hate, it's throwing away food, so if you must bring us food (and we are so grateful not to have to worry about getting and preparing it), it's best to check with us first. For a few days there, the surprise deliveries meant not everything could be used before it went bad. So call or e-mail first.

There's a peculiar thing that happens to a man's pride when he realizes he can't do everything, and that realization usually comes just at the moment when he feels he *ought* to do everything. It's not comfortable for me to lean back and let others "bring home the bacon." But two aspects make it all right. One is the incredible warmth I get from the love and graciousness and generosity of these offerings. The other is the knowledge that my girls are being taken care of better than I can do myself at the moment. I daresay no one ever gets to understand truly what brotherly love is until they need it this desperately.

12:28 a.m.

Jim

November 7, 2003

It took a week longer than it should have, but Cecily had her first radiation treatment today. Antoinette Spolare-Levine and Carolyn Hennesy arrived at noon to transport Cec to St. Joseph's Hospital in Burbank, a little over two and a half miles from our house. Cec said the treatment was like an X-ray. It took just a few minutes.

Cec watched Maddie playing today. Maddie had a wonderful day, but it's terribly hard for Cec not to be able to get down on the floor with her daughter and play, not to be able to pick her up and squeeze her hard. She's scared Maddie will draw the wrong conclusion about Cec's apparent withdrawal. I think her fears are unfounded. No, Maddie doesn't understand why Mommy won't pick her up, but she seems thrilled with just her mother's presence.

I'm encouraged by what I read and hear of people overcoming this awful thing. Yet the fear of loss and the certainty of Cecily's upcoming travail are sad and daunting. I'll say this, though: most of my weeping the past few days has been over kindnesses done. I confess, I'm a crybaby for a nice good deed.

12:40 a.m.

Jim

November 8, 2003

Tonight's going to be real short. It's already 1:00 a.m. and it was a hard, hard day.

Cec is having some real uncomfortable reactions to chemo now. Her pain seems diminished, but the reflux and the nausea are getting worse. That said, she asked me to relay to everyone that we are feeling blessed and fortunate in many ways, despite our situation. We have a large coterie of loving friends doing everything possible to relieve our burdens. We have food, clothing, and shelter far beyond that which most people in the world enjoy. And we have each other.

Gene Pack came by with a huge dinner which he wouldn't stay to share. Cec's sister Cathy came back from Vegas to spend a few days—fortunate timing, since I'm back at work on *Deadwood* on Monday. A friend of ours, Will Forte, a company member on *Saturday Night Live,* mentioned Cec in a sketch tonight as a little personal memento.

Bed now. I'm wiped. Maddie won't be up for another hour or two, so I can get a little sleep before then. Then I'll get another two or three hours before she's up for the day. . . . I should have started this father gig in my twenties. It ain't an old man's game, I'm tellin' ya.

1:14 a.m.

Jim

November 10, 2003

Work, which has always been my great escape, was not quite an escape today. I was almost overwhelmed with emotion several times, often in the midst of shooting a scene. My costar and friend of many years, Dayton Callie, is, I believe, psychologically incapable of being warm and fuzzy, but I'll give him this: the man tried. I know lots of warm and fuzzy people, and they all like to give me big hugs and comfort me and it's easy for them. When a paisan like Dayton tries it, though, it's particularly affecting, even if it doesn't quite come naturally.

For Cec, a relatively comfortable and easy day—nothing near as good as a healthy day, but better than many recent ones.

Cec thanks everyone for their prayers and thoughts. "They're holding me up," she says. She sends love.

11:30 p.m.

Jim

November 11, 2003

We had some good news. Blood tests revealed that the chemotherapy has not significantly damaged Cecily's blood supply, which means she can continue to receive chemo. For all its difficulties (and in some cases, horrors), chemotherapy is considered the primary mainstream weapon against metastasized cancer. We've had many suggestions for alternative therapies, all of which interest us. And we've had a few suggestions that chemotherapy would do more harm than good. But life's not always about making the right decision, it's often about just making a decision and living with the consequences. I've read (or skimmed) thousands of pages of cancer-treatment documents and Web pages in the past three weeks. The unimaginable range of information, theories, and grinding axes leads Cec and me, like the majority of people in our situation, to try the conventional approaches first.

Stephanie Shayne was our utility gofer today. She wasn't asked to do anything, but on the phone Cec mentioned not knowing what time it was, since there isn't a clock anywhere in sight of her hospital bed. Steph drove over from West Hills, a good twelve to fifteen miles, to drop off a clock she'd bought which clips onto the side rail of the bed. How in the world can anything bad happen anywhere if there are this many good and kind people around?

12:35 a.m.

Jim

November 12, 2003

Somehow it's 12:21 a.m. and I haven't started this yet.

We had a good day. Maddie woke up in the greatest mood and kept it up all day. She laughed and played and talked and charmed us and everybody who saw her, and we reveled in the blessing she is to our lives.

Cec made a visit to someone who was recommended to her, an acupressurist who apparently deals in some kind of mind-body balancing. Cec said that it was an extraordinary experience, making her feel good and also giving her a huge lift in feeling powerful. She came home with her spirits soaring higher than I've seen them thus far in our adventure. Nancylee Myatt took her to this encounter and to radiation and even on a short trip to the grocery store. Cec seemed to enjoy the day very much, though she was quite tired by the end of it.

Our friend Michael Osment brought Cec her dinner and also brought along a friend who had survived cancer, a man who was able to talk with her and answer a number of questions. Cec enjoyed the conversation, and it's always wonderful to see Michael. He goes by Eugene now as an actor, but he was Michael when I met him and Michael he remains. It's kind of weird when a friend changes his name. Anyway, I should talk. Half the people reading this aren't used to calling me Jim, since I was James until I left home at seventeen.

The other day Tina Carlisi gave Cec a stuffed red heart-shaped pillow. She said that it held all the prayers and hopes and good wishes she had expressed on Cec's behalf, and that Cec could hold it to herself and think about all the love therein. Cec loves it—says it's just the size of her lungs—and she holds it close at all times. Today, Maddie came over to Cec's bed and grabbed the pillow. "Mommy's heart!" she said. Then she said, "Maddie kiss," and she kissed it and put it back on Cec's chest. If you think it was hard to get it away from Cec before . . .

I probably seem more of a sentimentalist in these e-mails than some people thought me to be. I don't know. I'm capable of being rough around the edges, I think, but all my life I've enjoyed the fact that whatever I'm showing the world, my emotions bubble not far from the surface. I would never want any of this stuff I write to seem cloying or artificial. It might be cloying, to the observer, but there's nothing artificial about it. What's working for me is just opening up and letting each day fall onto the page the way I saw it and felt it, and hoping that all of you who've asked to be kept up to date are being informed not only about what happens, but how what happens affects us. Part of me wonders why anyone would care what happens with us on a daily basis, but another part of me says, "Stop asking questions." What I hope is that anyone reading this will have a sense of Cec's fight, of her humanity, her beautiful soul, and of what this kind of experience is like—without, God willing, ever having to go through it. Additionally, I hope that these writings will continue to draw from people who read them the kind of loving and encouraging remarks, wishes, stories, and deeds that we have experienced thus far.

You're rambling, Beaver. Go to bed.

12:50 a.m.

Jim

November 13, 2003

Thursday was draining.

I went to our new house and took videos of the flooring going in and the bathroom tile work being installed. Cecily had waited patiently for so many months while the gross structural part of the building was completed and was panting with anticipation for what she calls the "fun" part: decorating and picking out the detail work. But she was immobilized just as that part was getting under way, and she's felt depleted, not being able to approve the tile and paint and moldings. But by seeing the video, she was able to participate. I'm not sure I've ever seen her more happy than when she called the contractor tonight and said, "That floor tile in the master bath is *wrong!*" It made me happy, too.

My sister Denise says to look for the gifts in this situation, and one of them is the passage in and out through our door of more friends than we could have counted. I do look for the gifts, and I find them.

12:52 a.m.

Jim

November 14, 2003

Cec fell asleep early tonight. The cumulative effects of the radiation are knocking her out. I spent the quiet time after Maddie went to sleep doing things I might have done anyway, but which now have this awful edge of morbidity and doom about them: putting together information for wills and living trusts and powers of attorney and guardianship instructions. I was working on all this stuff long before we knew Cec was sick. Back then it just seemed like something any middle-aged couple with a child should get done. None of that has changed, nor has our intense hope and confidence in a happy outcome in this battle. But it's so hard not to think about all the "what ifs" when you're filling out forms that repeatedly ask what you want to do "if." As positive as we are that things will go well, as trusting in miracles (medical and otherwise) as we are, there's always a fearful darkness nearby.

12:37 a.m. Shortened nanny hours tomorrow. I'd better get some sleep.

Jim

November 16, 2003

Like almost everyone in Cec's family, Maddie loves the ponies. Unlike almost everyone in Cec's family, Maddie prefers riding on them to betting on them. Up until a few weeks ago, it had been our routine to take Maddie to the farmers' market in Studio City, a couple of blocks from our new house, to let her enjoy the pony ride and the petting zoo. It was a beautiful day today, cool with bright blue skies. Although Cecily was tired, she decided that Maddie ought to get on a horse, so she threw on some street clothes and we drove to Studio City. It was a bit of a struggle for Cec, walking the block from our parking spot to the farmers' market, but she lit up when she saw Maddie mounted on a sorrel filly. Maddie has gone horse crazy. I know most girls do, but I thought it was around ten or so. Maddie says, "I ride pony" about sixty times a day.

After a few minutes in the petting zoo, where Maddie petted a lamb and a goat, but ran from a pig and a rabbit, we left the market and went to the new house, where Cec inspected the offending floor tiles and their intended replacements. (The replacement tiles were "*wrong!*" too.) Worried about the effect of paint fumes, drywall dust, and open insulation on her lungs, Cec has refused to go into the house since getting back from the hospital, so she hasn't been able to see the progress. I feel so bad for her, when everything it will be is really, in a sense, her handiwork. And my heart breaks when she wonders aloud if she'll ever really get to live in it. She will get to live in it—our move-in is only a little over three weeks away. But I know what she means by "really." I can't bear more than a moment's contemplation that she might not have that house as her home for many, many years. Try as we may, we can't always shoo that elephant out of the room.

I don't know how to express what this girl means to me. We've been together for eighteen years. Married for fourteen. All but two of that was just us two together. We've been all over the map emotionally, days when we stalked around looking for opportunities to smash a bottle over the other one's head, and days, many more of them, when the anticipation of getting home to see her was almost more than I could stand. There's almost nothing she doesn't know about me, and she loves me even so. She's as determined and hardheaded as a safe full of rocks, and she makes me nuts hourly. And she's touched my heart and brought me to astonished, joyous tears so many times I can no longer count them. Every Christmas, every birthday, while I flounder in a sea of incompetent, inconsequential last-minute shopping, hoping to find something that might possibly interest her, she staggers me every time with some perfect, deeply considered, inventive gift. She pops my every bubble of pomposity, but nine times out of ten, she makes me laugh when she does so. She needs way too much affirmation and approval from others, but she gets it and deserves it. She's as sexy and flirtatious as the day we met and if she did again what she did that day, I'd chase her down the street one more time.

She's fearful, afraid of almost everything. I've given her a hard time over the years about that, stupidly trying to talk her out of worrying, assuring her over and over that the odds of any of her fears coming true were astronom—. And now look at us. Of course her fears were always rooted in something real, in the awful instability of her young childhood, shuttled between an exotic and overburdened mother, grandparents, her famous father's new family, and a series of Dickensian Catholic boarding schools where abuses were rampant. I always understood this, but nonetheless foolishly believed that logic could overcome her Pavlovian responses. And here's where all my reassurances have led us. To a place where the fear is palpable and present in every moment, where no reassurance assures either of us, and where we each cling to the other, not to be told everything will be all right, but in order to be as completely together as possible at a time when our conjoined fears are not of events but of separation.

She tells me I can survive without her, if it comes to that. For Maddie's sake, I tell myself the same thing. But were it not for Maddie, I'd find the notion highly debatable. More than doctors and medicine and various healing arts, this child she fought so hard to create may prove the most valuable thing of all in saving Cec's life. And mine as well. There's no pain, no ordeal, no struggle Cec wouldn't go through with all her might for Maddie. And that same little girl will force me to bear whatever comes my way. She may save my life. If she saves Cecily's, I won't need her to save mine.

This sounds despondent. I don't mean to convey that idea. We hope. We expect. We have confidence and trust in all our resources, be they spiritual, medical, familial, or social. Faith and hope banish much of the fear. Not all of it. But much.

1:18 a.m.

Jim

November 17, 2003

I don't know what to write about tonight. Except for the fact that my wife has cancer, it seemed like a normal day. If I'm remembering correctly what those were like.

Cec continued to feel better today. She ascribes it to the work of Joseph, the healing therapist she saw on Saturday. Perhaps. It's also true this was her first week without chemo, so perhaps that's why. I don't care, as long as she feels better. Don't confuse my skepticism with cynicism. I'm open to almost anything, even if I don't understand it. If it can't hurt her, then I'm all for trying it, because *"there are more things in heaven and Earth, Horatio, than are dreamt of in your philosophy."* If it's good enough for Hamlet, it's good enough for me.

We just got the hospital bill for Cec's eleven-day stay. It was for more than one hundred thousand dollars. The hospital. We haven't seen a doctor's bill yet. Now before you all run off starting a telethon for us, somebody, the hospital I guess, wrote off seventy-two thousand dollars, leaving a mere twenty-eight thousand for insurance to pay. Screen Actors Guild insurance has suffered some in recent years, but it's still amazing. We should come out pretty well on the hospitalization. I'm not sure what coverage we'll have on the doctors. But what amazes, bewilders, infuriates, and astonishes me is the markup on things, just because they're provided in a hospital. Cec had a CT scan as an outpatient just before we found out what this illness really was. It was about nine hundred dollars. The CT scan in the hospital was eleven thousand dollars. They charged a hundred dollars to put an IV in her arm, then charged $15,600 for the drugs they ran through it. Is there something going on here I don't understand? They charge these incredible sums, and then, if you've got the right insurance, they tell the insurance company, "Hey, just forget the first seventy-two thousand dollars of that."

I spoke with my mother the other day. My parents are sort of stoic types, not given to yakking about their problems. Numerous times in recent years I've found out that somebody fell off the house or had something amputated or was diagnosed with Glaubner's disease not when it happened, but days, weeks, even months later, when it just happened to come up in conversation. Usually followed by my mom saying, "Oh, didn't we tell you about that?" So it was a note from my mom's sister, my Aunt Jo, that informed me that my dad's downhill slope had steepened. I called home, talked with my mom, and then she put the phone to my dad's ear. For the first time since the onset of his slow loss of speech, he was unable to make a single sound. It's been a couple of weeks since I spoke to him by phone on his seventy-ninth birthday, and he then could make some small sounds. It's been months since I've heard him say a word I could understand. It's been years since he's been able to speak without difficulty. And it probably hasn't been ten minutes since he thought of something funny to say, if he only could.

I wish all of you who don't could know my dad. He's a good man, a very, very, very good man. Not because he's perfect, but because he isn't, and yet he tries so hard to grasp the goodness he reaches for. He has the kindest heart of anyone I've ever met, and one of the quickest wits. He was a preacher for many years—not a swaggering Jimmy Swaggart or puffed-up Pat Robertson, but more like the kind of preacher you'd imagine Jimmy Stewart or Joel McCrea playing in a movie. As a kid, my friends used to say, "I wish your dad could be my dad." And I knew enough not to be mystified by such a statement. I wouldn't have traded mine for any dad in the world.

I've spent at least some time, every day of my sentient life, dreading, fearing the loss of my dad, knowing that I would not be able to maintain my composure or even my sanity in the face of losing him. Now he lies in Texas, half a continent from me, unable to speak or rise or care for himself, and I sit here uncannily peacefully, pained but functioning, knowing anything I could ever do for him has either already been done or won't be, and knowing that I cannot give myself over to grieving his impending departure, knowing that he's going and I must let him go and stay the course here where I can still make a difference. How incredibly far our lives drift from where we knew with all certainty they would go. How little today resembles what yesterday thought it would look like.

Cec is feeling better (relatively speaking), and has even managed to sleep on her side a little bit—a position she has longed for futilely for months now. Every morning, I lay Maddie in her arms and she feeds her daughter her bottle and snuggles her back to sleep. It's a pretty picture, but prettier far, I suspect, from where Cecily lies.

12:49 a.m.

Jim   (

November 18, 2003

Cec went to radiation today; then she and I and Mark Sobel (armed with reams of his own cancer research) went to Cedars-Sinai to consult with Dr. Edward Wolin. He was recommended by Cec's friend Frances Miller, whose brother Dr. Wolin had brought back from a dire lung cancer diagnosis nine years ago. Dr. Wolin works in the Cedars-Sinai Cancer Center, an adjunct establishment devoted not only to the care but to the comfort and ease of cancer patients. We waited two hours past our appointment time, but, we are told, that's the way it is with Dr. Wolin. He's too giving of his time to the individual patient and gets far behind. But he makes it up by giving you all the time you want.

Wolin is well informed on treatment and quite open to combining traditional with alternative therapies, when benefits outweigh disadvantages. His demeanor is warm and human, he talks straight, and he answers any questions. But just as Cecily doesn't want to know statistics, Dr. Wolin doesn't want to tell them. He explained that statistics do not address the individual patient, but only mathematical averages. He said that statistics are based on old data, and that the changes in therapy occur too fast for improvements to show up in statistics. Add to that the fact that the majority of the statistics contain the cases of many more eighty-year-old lifelong chain-smoking males than they do young nonsmoking health-nut women, and he concludes that we can extrapolate no expectations for Cecily's survival from statistics. So why consider them? He says many patients live fairly normal lives twelve years after they were told they had three months to live and he would never ever tell a patient what to expect in terms of survival.

He not only discussed the various therapies and chemotherapies, he also gave us a good idea of what to expect during the process as a patient in the cancer center. Everything about it seemed more human, humane, and personal than what Cec has been experiencing with her current oncologist. So Cec decided, and I agreed, that we would ask Dr. Wolin to take over her case. We are still planning consultations with other institutions, but in the meantime, someone has to be treating Cec, and we want it to be Dr. Wolin. We'll make the change tomorrow, which means that Cec will not begin her second three-week chemo cycle tomorrow with Dr. Miller, but with Dr. Wolin, probably on Thursday.

For the first time since this started, I've been wise with my time. I've been typing for an hour, and it's only

11:03 p.m.

Jim

November 19, 2003

I helped Cec take a shower tonight, and her obvious weight loss was troubling, saddening. It's not that she's not doing well—in fact, she's feeling better and better every day. It's just that she hasn't regained her weight yet, even though her appetite is back and, in fact, huge. I'm not sad about Cec's chances, I'm sad about all she has to go through. I can't stand to see her in pain, to see her nauseous, or weak, exhausted. Cec said the other day that this illness had been a crushing blow to her illusion that she could control the universe. What it has crushed for me is the illusion that I could fix anything

I tried to fix. I suppose that both of us are grieving for, among other things, our illusions.

Dr. Wolin said that we need to adjust our thinking about this disease, that we should deal with it not as a monster that either we conquer or it devours us, but as a chronic illness like diabetes, something that we control rather than eliminate. Barring miracles (which nonetheless we plan to have in our arsenal), the cancer Cecily suffers from is going to be part of the rest of her life. The question's not how to cure it, but how to keep it under control. A cure may come, but until then our mission is to keep it from increasing in size and threat. A task like that is perhaps easier to encompass mentally. We don't have to do something no one's ever done, devise a cure for this cancer. We just have to stave off its effects until either someone does devise a cure or Cec turns ninety-eight and says the heck with it. I think we can do that.

Cec told me tonight as she prepared to sleep that she was scared, that she'd had a difficult evening. Another sketch-comedy pal, Leslie Dixon, came by and fixed some healthy natural food for Cec and spent a lot of time with her. Cec enjoyed the visit immensely. But after Leslie left, Cec began to feel her fears welling up. We held hands and prayed for a bit, then she asked me, when I would write this, to remind everyone how much strength she's drawing from your cards and calls and the evidence of your love and especially your prayers. She said that when she wakens in the middle of the night, alone in her hospital bed in the living room, she's often frightened, but that the knowledge of all of your great good will and prayers and hopes helps her "push the darkness away." She thanks you.

Speaking of thanks, enormous gratitude goes to one of the best human beings I've ever met, Ken Jenkins, for the gift of a *lot* of gift certificates to Whole Foods, the semihealthy grocery store. Please watch Ken's show *Scrubs* so he can earn back what he spent on us.

11:56 p.m.

Jim

November 20, 2003

Long day here. Cec left at 7:30 a.m. for Cedars-Sinai to get her arm catheter installed, which they'll use to give Cec her chemo. Maribel, the nanny who takes care of Maddie in the daytime, had to take her husband to the hospital; they've got their own cancer saga to deal with. So Maddie's nighttime nanny, Zully, whom we hired part-time to reduce Maribel's burden, worked both shifts today, from 7:30 a.m. to 10:00 p.m.

Neither Cec nor I got to see much of Maddie today; either we were gone or she was. Debi Derryberry, who rents us our house and lives a few houses down the block, has been the most incredible friend and neighbor. She's got a boy around Maddie's age, and Debi has taken on Maddie almost as a second child. Talk about a friend in need.

Tomorrow is Cec's next chemo. It's a long one, six hours. She gets two drugs, consecutively. One of them is so toxic it has to be administered extremely slowly to avoid immediate painful reaction. So we'll go together, pop a DVD or two into the cancer center's one-per-patient DVD players, and have a chemo date.

Bedtime for Bonzo.

12:03 a.m.

Jim

November 21, 2003

Sign over hospital toilet: IF YOU ARE RECEIVING CHEMOTHERAPY, PLEASE FLUSH TWICE.

That's so the next occupant doesn't get injured by splashed droplets. I now have a clearer idea how toxic these chemicals are.

Cec started her second round of chemotherapy today. She hasn't lost any of her hair yet. And even her nausea—the worst part of chemo—hasn't been debilitating. But I sense that it's already a touch worse than the first cycle. They say it tends to get worse, cycle by cycle. I hope not. But Cec says if this is what it takes to be here for her daughter, then bring it on.

That's my girl.

2:09 a.m.

Jim

November 22, 2003

A pretty bad day. Maybe not as bad as the one JFK had forty years ago today, but nonetheless we didn't like it.

Cec broke my heart in jagged pieces this morning when she started apologizing to me for getting sick, for "doing this" to me. I told her I could take just about anything this situation had to offer, but not her blaming herself. I don't know if I actually can take anything this situation has to offer. But I'll push through, somehow. If Cec is willing to take anything she has to in order to survive this, what right have I to question my ability to stand up to what's ahead?

She's so worried about Maddie and what will happen to her if I'm the only one left to look after her. She wants so to be part of Maddie's world, to get down and play with her, to pick her up and hug her, but because she can't do those things, she's finding it hard to see Maddie. Cec spent the day in her own bed in our bedroom rather than the hospital bed in the living room, because Maddie's play is noisy and rambunctious, but also, I think, because it lessened the ache she feels for Maddie if she couldn't see her. I think she believes she does a disservice to Maddie if Maddie runs to be picked up and Cec doesn't do it. I think she's wrong about that. I think Maddie adores her and brightens visibly whenever Cec is up and about, but I think she also understands that Mommy loves her but can't pick her up even though she wants to. Lots of times when Cec says, "I'm sorry, I can't pick you up," Maddie says, "Mommy have boo-boo." In my estimation, Maddie senses that something is preventing her mommy from being as close as her mommy would like to be. I don't think Maddie's hurt by it at all.

I keep getting notes from people crediting me with being "so honest" in these e-mails. Well, I'm not honest, not to the extent that people think. There's a lot that goes through this old cowboy's head in the dark, dark night when pondering the future, the present, and the past, stuff that won't ever see the light of these pages. I'd love to journalize in unfettered style, spontaneously revealing any thought that passed through my mind. I think it would have some value, in a way. But I'm not honest enough to be that unafraid. Or maybe I'm too afraid to be that honest. In any event, anyone who's ever been in my boots or in boots like them will know that there are fears and imaginings and speculations and even hopes that pop up uncalled for in the night that you don't even voice out loud to yourself, much less share with the world. So in the interest of full disclosure, this ain't Honest John you're dealing with.

1:07 a.m.

Jim

November 23, 2003

Wonderful, clear moments of brightness today: I had understood that the writers and producers of *That '70s Show* had arranged for ten hours of babysitting from a nice lady named Roseanne Rozier. I thought that was a lovely gift. But Roseanne informed me that I was wrong. The gift was for ninety-six hours of babysitting. Please watch *That '70s Show* and tell your friends to watch.

Another terrific moment today: I talked to our contractor, the aforementioned Best Contractor in the History of the Universe, T. J. Miller (who's working seven days a week to get the house ready in time and who drives long, long distances to sit and pray with Cec). He informed me that the ultra-high-quality air filters we have to install in the heating/cooling system of the house (since Cec's lungs now need extra protection) will cost fifty-six hundred dollars. I almost needed Cec's antinausea drug. Within a *minute* of that revelation, I went to the mailbox and found a California state income tax refund check for $5,550. (Amateur dramatists: don't try this at home. In fiction, nothing happens this dramatically.)

It's quiet in the house. Cec must have fallen asleep. All I can hear is my little girl breathing noisily in her crib. Sometimes, even in the midst of a storm, there's peace.

Those of you who pray, pray for my girls today. Those of you who don't, hum along.

12:44 a.m.

Jim

November 25, 2003

Today was tearful for everybody. I dropped off Maddie at her therapy session, then headed to Beverly Hills to pick up Cec and Cathy at Cedars-Sinai. Along the way I talked with my sister Denise in Arizona. She's been my strong right hand, my comrade-in-arms, ever since we left off pulling each other's hair forty years ago. Today, she called to offer me support but found herself overcome with her own emotion. Denise cried because she felt powerless to lessen my burdens. It was odd, with a whiff of irony, comforting her when she'd called to comfort me. But she needed to know what I've told several people since this adventure began: we don't need people to be perfect, we just need them to be there.

Cec cried, too, after we got her home. Her emotions have been pitched high through all this, but particularly so the past three or four days. You may recall that I ended last night's missive with "Those of you who pray, please pray for my girls. Those of you who don't, hum along." This morning, Cec's brother-in-law, Pascal, for whom religion is not part of daily life, wrote an e-mail to Cec with words to this effect: "I'm humming at the top of my lungs." Cec found this willingness to offer whatever he personally had to offer so moving that she was reduced to tears. A few minutes later, her sister Cathy had to return to her home and family in Las Vegas, and between them the place got pretty soggy. I got fairly verklempt myself later in the evening. Cec was lying in bed feeling awful and I was sitting in the rocker at the end of the bed talking with her about the this-and-thats of our mixed-up life. Suddenly I was overtaken with grief—not grief for the idea of losing her, but for the suffering she's going through and must continue to go through. I've never gotten caught up in the notion that this turn of events isn't "fair." I don't believe in "fairness." Good things happen to bad people and bad things happen to good people and all the possible permutations of those happenings, and there's nothing fair or unfair about it—it just is. Cancer's no more unfair than gravity. And yet . . . there's my Cecily, the girl I spent four years asking to marry me before she'd even acknowledge the question!— the one who quit smoking eighteen years ago because I asked her to—the one who has fought for her health and pummeled me to fight for mine since the day I met her—the girl who wouldn't take an aspirin while she was pregnant for fear it might hurt the growing child inside her—here she is, lying there, losing weight, losing the thick and luxuriant hair I love (and envy), feeling like a gut-sick dog, too weak to sit up without help . . . and suddenly all I could feel was the vast, cosmic, unfathomable unfairness of it all. Even as I told myself that the blessings and travails of this life fall like rain on the just and unjust, I couldn't help but think that even the unconscious science of nature should have *something* fair about it, and this wasn't it.

I believe in God, don't get me wrong. I simply believe that His hand moves as He sees fit, and that the unthinking nature of our world, without fairness or unfairness, is how He chooses to allow it to run. I believe in prayer and in answered prayers. But I don't believe in saying this shouldn't have happened to us, that it's not fair for it to happen to Cec, when the world is filled to overflowing with sorrows and illness and death, most of it happening to people who don't "deserve" it. The world also contains multitudes of beauty and happiness and glorious occurrence, and that too falls on the heads of the deserving and the not-so. What's happened to Cec—we're allowed to hate it, to wish it gone or never come, but it's fruitless to feel we've been singled out. And still, it seems so unfair.

Maddie knows something's up. What it is, she can't know, nor, fortunately, can she understand. But it's become plain in the past few days that she understands something is rotten in the state of Denmark. (I think that's the third or fourth time I've quoted *Hamlet* in these letters. Sorry. It's just that everything that ever needs to be said is already said better somewhere in *Hamlet*.)

What a beautiful, happy little girl Maddie is. There are a lot of little kids, babies even, that I don't like. Don't like the way they look, don't like the way they talk or act or crawl. But if I had written down every aspect of a child that I would want in one of my own, they all show up in my Madeline Rose. Oh, I thought I wanted a boy, but now I see that the glorious thing that is a little girl simply has no comparison. Also, a little boy would have killed me by now.

Cec said again today that she wants everyone to know that she feels the strength from your prayers and loving wishes, that they hold her up when she's weak, that they cradle her in the fearsome dark parts of the night. And, yes, she cried when she said it.

1:12 a.m.

Jim

November 27, 2003. Thanksgiving Day.

What I am thankful for:

I am thankful this day is over.

I may not be the first to express thanks for the conclusion of another Thanksgiving Day, but I am sure I'm among the most fervent.

Maddie's having a difficult time. For quite some while, it seemed that she was aware but unaffected by the changes around her. But yesterday and today it became clear that her equilibrium has been thrown off. She's been waking earlier and earlier, and several times in the past two days, she's had periods of hysterical anxiety. She's normally calm and enjoys life and is compliant. When we tell her not to play with something, she puts it down and plays with something else. She always smiles and laughs.

But today, she had two or three major freak-outs. The first occurred in the morning, but seemed to dissipate when she got some breakfast. The second occurred as we were getting ready to shoot a family portrait. She went berserk, crying, squirming away from any-one who tried to hold or comfort her—mainly me, since Cec can't hold her. She was completely lost as to what she wanted. She cried, "Maddie, up!" and I picked her up, at which she screamed, "Maddie, down!" I put her down, and she reached up, calling, "Maddie, up!" I picked her up and she tried to throw herself out of my arms. She tried to climb into her crib, but when I helped her get in, she screamed, "Maddie, out!" In desperation, despite her nice Thanksgiving outfit, I gave Maddie a lime Popsicle. She stopped sobbing and gasping long enough to give it a tentative taste. (We don't usually give her any-thing with refined sugar, so she wasn't real sure what this thing was. She called it a "cold lollipop.") She sucked contentedly and calmed down. We ran to the doorway and our photographer pal Michael Helms shot some quick family portraits, which ought to look brilliant photographically and a bit odd, content-wise. Cec is standing, I'm sitting, and Maddie's in my lap, with green slime covering her face, hands, clothes, and father. Well, at least in years to come, we'll have an excellent conversation starter in these photos.

We are thankful for so much, of course. Cec feels a little better every day further from her last chemo treatment. We are blessed with loving friends and family with the kind of generosity I thought only bona fide saints possessed. We love each other, we have food and clothing and shelter and no real fears or worries beyond the big one we face. We have more than most people, even most people we know.

I'm still glad the day is over, though.

12:54 a.m.

Jim

THREE

November 30, 2003

Today I decided I need more life insurance.

That's not a joke. Today I began to have real concerns about how I'm going to get through this. The issue revolves, in an immediate sense, not around Cecily's illness but rather Maddie's situation. The daily meltdowns continue, and I've gotten better at dealing with them. But Maddie's waking up two and three times a night, instantly going from a dead sleep to screaming hysterics, and I've gone from five to six hours of sleep a night with maybe one interruption to two to four hours with two or three interruptions. I've always thought I was pretty tough and resilient, but two to four nonconsecutive hours of sleep doesn't seem healthy, and I don't feel healthy anymore. Knowing that Cec is being awakened too, even though she sleeps in a different room, concerns me too, for she needs rest even more than I do. If Maddie doesn't start sleeping through the night—something she's never done consistently anyway—we are in deep trouble. Like we weren't already.

While I was drying off Maddie after her bath tonight, she said, "I love you" to me for the first time. It sounded like "All lub boo," but I didn't care. To reciprocate, I showed her what an ex-Marine looks like when he cries.

Tomorrow, if Dr. Wolin thinks her blood platelet count will

support it (or can be made to support it), Cec will get her next chemo. We pray that her platelets will allow it and that God will make it effective. The process will take at least four hours. Maddie has three hours of therapy. I have to pick up sinks and faucets for the new house, pick out toilets, order carpet from somebody who can install it on time, and somehow talk SBC Pacific Bell out of turning off the phones ('cause I've let paying the phone bill get away from my attention too long. Time, not money.). Other than all this, we'll probably just be lying around, eatin' grapes all day.

12:24 a.m.

Jim

December 1, 2003

Hamlet again: *"To die—to sleep, no more; and by a sleep to say we end the heartache and thousand natural shocks that flesh is heir to. 'Tis a consummation devoutly to be wished."*

Can't say that one hasn't fluttered through my head a number of times today.

Maddie's hysterical night-wakings continue. Her pediatric neurologist feels that the radical changes in her little life, coupled with the sensory overload that is symptomatic of autism, lie at the root. In addition to the therapy, her doctor has prescribed antiseizure medication, as Maddie has shown seizure-like symptoms. If the medication helps, we'll know. If it doesn't, it won't hurt her.

Last night I finished the e-mail and was asleep by 1:15. Exactly two hours later, Maddie flared into frenzied crying. Struggling to control my own hysteria and, most damnable, my own anger, I tried for forty minutes to calm her—a task made more difficult by my own complete lack of calm. Finally I took her outside, neither of us with a coat in 49 degrees, and drove her around town. Within another half hour, she was asleep. I put her back in bed, and, thinking perhaps I was snoring and waking her, I went to sleep on the floor of my office, ten feet down the hall from the bedroom. Ninety minutes later, on the baby monitor, I heard her crying and clambering over the crib rail. I ran to catch her before she fell, and we were off on another round then, sometime around 5:45 a.m. I found a technique that kept her from going into total paroxysms of turbulence. Instead of trying to give her whatever she wanted, only to be greeted by tearful protestations that she *didn't* want it, I tried just saying okay to everything she asked for, but *doing* nothing. Somehow "okay" seemed to allow her the permission or autonomy her mind wanted, yet by making no action I didn't infringe on her confusion as to what it was she really wanted. It kept her from flying around the room like a berserk balloon, but it didn't stop the problem. For two hours we went through this pattern, until Maribel the Magnificent showed up at 8:30. Maddie's hysteria stopped like the plug had been pulled. She had a great time the rest of the morning, and at 9:30, after her medication, I was able to catch a nap. From the time Maddie went to bed to the time she was up for good, I had three and a half hours of nonconsecutive sleep. That's on a par with the past four days. I know that despite the additional changes that are coming and the deleterious effect they may have on Maddie's emotions, things should be better once we've settled into the new house, with room to move and bedroom doors that lock and toddler beds instead of cribs and separate sleeping quarters and playrooms that don't have hospital beds in them. But that's still two weeks away. I cannot tell you how seriously, how closely, I relate to Maddie's hysterical confusion. I'm not a tough guy, but I play one on TV. I'm beginning to think I'm a better actor than I realized.

1:36 a.m.

Jim

December 2, 2003

Cec and Maddie had a wonderful meeting with Dr. Susan Schmidt-Lackner, the child development psychiatrist who diagnosed Maddie as autistic. The doc was extremely impressed with Maddie's development over the past four months. Her prognosis: with continued therapy, we can hope to get Maddie back to or near 100 percent of typical development levels. She also recommended some things to deal with Maddie's outbursts and her night waking. These are either nightmares or night terrors (a distinction I'm unable to elaborate on), and it's unclear whether they are autism-related or perhaps the result of a kind of mild, nonthreatening seizure. In any event, hope abounds.

Cec and I headed for a 7:00 p.m. meeting in Santa Monica at the Wellness Community support group but ran into thick traffic on the 405 and watched as the clock hit 7:15 while we still had ten miles of creeping freeway to traverse. So we gave up, turned around, and went to a movie.

I know, I know, shame on us. Don't we know we've got cancer and need support? Well, we'll go next week. Tonight, for the first time in about six months, Cec and I were alone together, holding hands at the movies. We picked a really lovely choice, *Love Actually*. There's a sequence where Liam Neeson deals with the death of his young wife, and I thought we might be in for something way too dark. As we watched Neeson's character grieve and try to comfort his young child, it seemed way, way too close to home. Cec leaned over to me and said, "I'm sorry." I asked what for, and she said, "For bringing you to see this." I was surprised since the movie was my idea. But we held hands and shook it off and had a wonderful romantic, funny, touching evening.

At the car, before we left the movie theatre, our fears and sorrow came to the surface briefly, and we held each other next to the world's bumpiest ride, the 1997 Ford Explorer, and cried into each other. Then we renewed our vows—the ones about kicking and pummeling this disease into submission.

There's more, but you'll have to tune in tomorrow, same bat time, same bat station (now I'm dating myself) to find out.

Love and thanks.

1:14 a.m.

Jim

December 4, 2003

I promised some background a while back. Here's some.

Cecily April Adams was born on a February 6 not so many years ago in Queens, New York. Her mom, a cabaret singer-dancer, was Adelaide Adams, née Adelaide Efantis, the daughter of Greek and Italian immigrants who lived in Chevy Chase, Maryland. Cecily's father, Don Yarmy, was an actor and stand-up comedian known professionally as Don Adams. Cecily's parents split up before she was born, and she grew up with her mother and three older sisters. She spent much of her childhood shuttling between grandparents, other family and friends, and, from the age of three, rather gothic Catholic boarding schools. (Cecily is the only person I've ever heard of who ever *literally* was locked overnight in a belfry as punishment. She was four at the time.) She spent some summers with her father, who remarried and became world-famous as Maxwell Smart on *Get Smart* in quick succession. From her father's subsequent marriages, she got two more sisters and a brother. She spent part of her childhood in Italy, where her mom took the family in order to attend medical school in Rome. She also spent some summers in Costa Rica with the family of Ida Lee, who started out as a caretaker for the kids, but who quickly evolved into a true member of the family. (More about Ida—St. Ida—in future reports. She's a novel and a movie and a TV series unto herself.)

Cec's mom moved to L.A. in time for Cec to attend Beverly Hills High School. Cecily became interested in theatre there, doing plays and then going on to the University of California at Irvine as a theatre major. After college, she waited tables and looked for acting jobs. Her aunt, Alice Borden, then an actress but now a respected fund-raising director for candidates such as former L.A. mayor Richard Riordan and current governor Arnold Schwarzenegger, recommended Cecily to the apprentice program at Theatre West, the oldest membership theatre company in Los Angeles. While she was there, she acted in plays and on television. A recommendation by another Theatre West member got her an internship with Reuben Cannon, a major film and TV casting director. Casting took over her career direction, and she worked steadily in the field and gained a terrific reputation. She continued to act, including a stint on the TV series *Star Trek: Deep Space Nine*, as Moogie, the colorful mother of popular character Quark.

In 1985, not long after joining Theatre West, she met me and shamelessly flung herself at me until I decided I couldn't live without her. Four years and many, many proposals later, she finally answered one, with a yes, and we got married in '89. Our daughter Madeline Rose was born twelve years later. And that's how she got here. I've left a couple of things out, but this isn't A&E's *Biography*.

Cec and I had a lot to do today, taking care of business for the new house and getting Cec ready for her appointment with a nutritionist specializing in cancer patients. We had things lined up from 8:30 onward, tasks stretching across the day in neat succession. All that went out the window when Maribel, the day nanny, didn't show up. After half an hour of waiting, I called and learned she had fallen and possibly broken her ankle. On top of this, she was starting to suspect she had chicken pox.

If I'd had a moment or two, I'd have gotten out my Bible and reread the Book of Job, just to see what was next.

Oh, yeah. Last night I climbed into bed and lay next to Maddie, who was asleep. I must have jostled her getting into bed, for as I settled, she started singing the tail end of the "Alphabet Song" (you know, "*Q, R, S . . . T, U, V . . . W, X . . . Y and Z . . .*"). I realized she was singing in her sleep. She finished the song (*"Now I've said my ABCs. Next time won't you sing with me?"*) and then there was the briefest of pauses, and then this angelic little pipe of a sleeping voice said, "Yay!"

That warmed up the room pretty good.

12:03 a.m.

Jim

December 5, 2003

Maddie alternates between periods of hysteria and periods of absolute deliciousness. But even the delicious moments are hard for Cecily, since she can't hold Maddie or even let Maddie kiss her, since Cec's low white count is no match for the world of germs that exists in a toddler's kiss. For that matter, I haven't had a real kiss in a month or so, either. From Cec, I mean. Maddie's good about giving them to me, but I kinda miss gettin' 'em from the wife. Call me old-fashioned.

There's an interesting circumstance going on here. I am more likely to get caught feeling sorry for myself than is my dangerously afflicted spouse. She has her moments, I suppose, of evident doubt and fear, but the only one I catch whining about it is me. I'm so proud of her, so amazed at the equanimity she brings to a situation which defies equanimity. I know her well enough to know that on the best day of her life she was wracked with fears, and that she must be living with the mother lode these days. But I stalk around the house pulling my hair out in unattractive desperation; she makes jokes as hers *falls* out. It's a lucky man who can both love and admire the woman in his life. I've always been lucky.

11:51 p.m.

Jim

December 6, 2003

Every day I get e-mails from many of you, far too many for me to answer. But I read every one and share them with Cec and we take great comfort in the fine, beautiful words that come with such frequency and with such love. If this weren't the worst thing that ever happened to us, it would be the best thing that ever happened.

11:09 p.m.

Jim

December 7, 2003

I called home to Texas tonight. I talked to my sister Teddlie, who lives with my parents and looks after my dad. It was a painful but wonderful conversation. Throughout this entire process with Cec's illness and Maddie's mood swings, I've not had a chance to see any of my birth family. As is clear from these nightly reports, I've got a support team second to none. But somehow there's something about your first family, the people you grew up knowing they could never get rid of you, nor you them. Talking to my sister Teddlie, who is herself God's proof that miracles happen, talking about what our world is like now—me as the person most responsible for the well-being of Cec and Maddie, and Teddlie the primary caregiver for our gently fading father—talking with her broke down whatever barriers I've had holding back the tide of emotion, and I sat in the dark on the floor of the kitchen with the dishwasher rumbling against my back, sobbing across fourteen hundred miles.

Maddie went to sleep easily. Cec and I got a few sparse moments together while I helped her dress for bed. She's so afraid, so frightened of what may come, yet her strength arose like a lioness and she tried to take care of me. It makes no sense, I know, but I think she would gladly give her life to save Maddie and me from the pain of losing her. That logical quandary leaves us with no place to go, but to fight. Today we fight. Tomorrow we fight. The day after, we fight. And if this disease plans on whipping us, it better bring a lunch, 'cause it's gonna have a long day doing it.

And that's the end of this day.

12:12 a.m.

Jim

December 8, 2003

Cecily needs a blood transfusion. Her red-cell count is down. We've got a few volunteers from the clean-living types among you. A good match should be available from within that group.

Dr. Wolin is concerned about Cec's growing cough and congestion, despite all indications that her lungs are clear and functioning well. He's put her on a second round of antibiotics, in case there's some bacterial infection.

At 8:00 a.m. we were visited by several people who specialize in Christian prayer for healing. They prayed with Cec twenty minutes or so. They had flown in from Chicago at the behest of Cami Patton, with whom Cec used to work in casting *3rd Rock from the Sun*. Cami paid for their trip! They returned in the afternoon to pray for Cec, and will come again in the morning before catching their plane back to Chicago. Cec felt a strong spiritual power during their ministrations, and we were both touched by their devotion and the generosity of spirit that accompanied them.

Maddie had her therapy session. She gets speech therapy, to help her improve her communicative interaction; occupational therapy, to enhance her physical skills and diminish problems of sensory-input hyper- or hyposensitivity; and floortime, which is a therapy aimed at getting the child who has interactivity problems to invite others into her play. From the child's point of view, it all looks like play. But the therapist is actually directing the play in a manner which will improve the child's abilities and sensitivities in the pertinent areas at issue. Maddie loves it. I like it, too, though I wish there were more army men.

11:51 p.m.

Jim

December 9, 2003

Cec feels tired and depleted. But she's grateful for the number of people who donated blood today, and for those who offered to do so if needed. She feels better knowing she'll have some of her friends' corpuscles swimming around in her on Friday.

Believe it or not, I'm done. And it's only

10:50 p.m.

Jim

December 10, 2003

Today, Cec went to see her acupuncturist, Dr. Daoshing Ni. He was, once upon a time, largely responsible for Cecily's ability to get pregnant. We had struggled for a long time with Cec's low fertility numbers. But after a few treatments by Dr. Dao, augmented by herbal teas that tasted like water out of an old tire, Cec's numbers climbed, and now we have a two-year-old keeping us up nights. Dr. Dao is also a noted cancer specialist in the area of Chinese medicine, and it was a foregone conclusion that she would see him.

Maddie had a poor night. She woke only once, around 1:45 a.m., but my first reaction to her sudden screaming scared me. I got angry.

It took great effort to stifle my knee-jerk reaction and to shake myself awake enough to remember that Maddie is a victim herself of whatever is waking her. For just a moment I was so incensed at being yanked awake in the middle of one more night that I yelled at her. When I yelled, she cried louder, and her crying was so pitiful that I instantly realized how innocent and tortured she is in these circumstances. It astonishes me that I could ever be angry with Maddie, because I'm addled with love for this little monkey. But, oh, how I wish she'd sleep quietly through the night. Even after she goes back to sleep, she tosses and cries out so that I wake up more tired than when I went to bed.

12:24 a.m.

Jim

December 11, 2003

I don't know how far I'll get tonight. There's lots to talk about, but Maddie's been throwing up since 6:00 p.m. with the stomach flu. I'm sitting here at 11:20 in my third shirt, and even it's got puke on it. She's asleep right now, but she's been asleep four other times tonight and each time woke up with the Technicolor Yawns. Good thing I got plenty of practice not sleeping last night. I should be well prepared for tonight.

Tomorrow: transfusions, blood tests, and today's CT scan results. All three are important. Pray for shrinkage.

12:12 a.m.

Jim

December 12, 2003

Good news: Maddie stopped throwing up around midnight last night and has been fine ever since.

Bad news: now I've got it.

No news: Cec is, even as we speak, at Cedars-Sinai getting her transfusion. However, there's no word on the results of her CT scans, so we'll have to wait the weekend to learn whether there's been any tumor shrinkage.

We move to our house next Thursday: volunteers to help pack and move on Wednesday and Thursday are not needed, as professional packers have been hired by Cec's former and current producers at *That '70s Show*, Mark Brazill and Jeff and Jackie Filgo.

Today I reluctantly did an interview with the *National Enquirer* about Cec's illness. They had gotten the story from one of the *Star Trek* fan websites after a remark I'd made to some fans, asking them to pray for Cec. Since the *Enquirer* had already put together a preliminary story with a number of inaccuracies, I talked to Cec and we decided it was better to try to manage the story than to let something go out that was totally off base. Some of the things the *Enquirer* reporter said made me glad I could head some of his notions off at the pass. Nonetheless, believe none of what you read and only half of what you see.

11:04 p.m.

Jim

December 15, 2003

First the news: Cec's scans showed that her primary lung tumor is about the same size it was before chemo started. Her oncologist, Dr. Wolin, states that he's pleased that there has been no growth, and that he would not expect much shrinkage from only two cycles of chemo. As I've mentioned before, disappearance, shrinkage, or stability were all things we hoped for, in that order. Stability is not the best we'd hoped for, but it will do. Patients often live for many years with stabilized cancers.

Cec is having a difficult time tonight, not having gotten the bright news she hoped for. And the changes, deadlines, uncertainty, and chaos are no less severe for her than they are for Maddie, and Maddie's certainly having a difficult time. Me, I'm sailing through without a care in the world.

11:26 p.m.

Jim

December 20–24, 2003

Trying to catch up, but it's 11:30 on Christmas Eve, so who knows?

Saturday, December 20, was one of the greatest days of my life. It had all kinds of crummy things about it, mostly Cec's illness, Maddie's lingering flu, and whatever the heck this cough is I've developed. But Saturday nevertheless overflowed with blessings, and Sunday was a close second.

At 11:00 a.m. I went to the new house to find Melanie Patterson, producer of *That '70s Show*, leading a crew of volunteers in decorating the house for Christmas, inside and out. They hung lights, they put up a tree, they covered furniture in ornaments and wreaths, they put out cookies and candy canes—it was a Hallmark card come to life. And then they, and a dozen other volunteers from various parts of Cecily's life, took scores of boxes from our garage and unpacked us. They washed dishes and linens, polished glasses, and lined cabinets. They scrubbed toilets and floors. They plugged in lamps and computers and TV sets and VCRs, installed shower curtains and sconces, organized the pantry, made the beds, folded clothes, and refilled filing cabinets.

The next morning, more people showed up and did more of the same. My sisters were part of it. (My sister Denise at one point asked me, "Who was that cute little redheaded girl I sent upstairs to fold laundry?" I told her that was Jackie Filgo, Cecily's boss. Denise, unflummoxed, said, "Well, I sure guess it's a good thing I didn't know who she was!") Cecily felt too weak to spend much time at the house Saturday, though she tried to show up for a while to express her gratitude. For my part, I was overwhelmed. I've been overwhelmed a lot lately. But this weekend takes the cake. There are far too many participants to thank by name, and the truth is, there were an awful lot of people we don't *know* by name. If you've ever gotten a thrill up your spine at the ending of *It's a Wonderful Life*, you will have an inkling of what I felt as the last volunteer left Sunday night. My contractor, T.J., was there, and he said, "You and Cecily sure have a lot of friends." He paused a moment and then said, "You're a lucky guy." I haven't often felt lucky in the past couple of months, but that's how I felt that evening.

There were some technical glitches that kept us from moving into the house that night—a wiring problem on the heater, in particular. Also, with Maddie sick, it was just too tough to move on a night with no one to watch her. My sisters went back to their homes in Texas and Arizona, and I went to Cec's Aunt Alice and Uncle Russell's, where we are staying since we moved out of the rental.

Monday, December 22, Mark Sobel told me he'd talked to an outside oncologist who recommended against some of the treatment regimen Cec has been getting from Dr. Wolin. Mark said that the oncologist thought Dr. Wolin's current protocol would cause more harm than good. Mark hoped I would urge Cec not to have the chemotherapy scheduled for the next morning. Mark has opinions based on his conversations with this other doctor, but nothing I've heard suggests that anyone else has better recommendations than Dr. Wolin's. Cec was having a gastric attack and was in no position to discuss the matter, and neither was I. So Mark left and we all went to bed with the issue unresolved.

Tuesday morning, December 23, still at Alice and Russell's, I awoke late, as Maddie had slept later than usual. We had little more than an hour before Cec's scheduled chemo at Cedars-Sinai when her Aunt Alice woke me with word that a drama was unfolding that needed my attention. Cec was on the phone with her sister Cathy in Las Vegas, and Cathy was hysterical, begging Cec not to have the chemo. Cec's mom arrived at Alice's, too, and she also was pleading with Cec to cancel the chemo. Mark had talked to both of them, enlisting them in an "intervention" to stop what he considered a dangerous step. After a lot of turgid back-and-forth, we agreed that if the oncologist Mark championed, Dr. Leo Orr,[3] could tell me or Cec *directly* that he considered the morning's planned chemo to be dangerous and give substance to the concerns being expressed by the freaked-out family members, then we would postpone the chemo. Additionally, if we could discuss Dr. Orr's concerns with Dr. Wolin and if Wolin didn't refute these concerns, we would wait.

We paged both doctors to our cell phones and left for the hospital with Frances Miller, who was supposed to be Cec's driver and companion while I took Maddie to therapy, but who ended up serving as a sounding board for our own worries about the decision. At Cedars-Sinai, the nurses began hydrating Cec and prepping her for the chemo, though we told them we might not do the treatment. We sat there for a couple of hours, waiting and debating. Neither doctor called us. Dr. Wolin, it turned out, was out of town until Monday. His on-call doctor, a physician at UCLA Cancer Center, did call. He said that he concurred with Dr. Wolin and refuted the notion that the planned chemo could be a problem. With no direct word from Dr. Orr, and with Cec fearful of delaying treatment, we proceeded with the chemo. Cec had the treatment and has responded well, in terms of side effects. Other than fatigue, she's not made any mention of new discomfort.

---

3. Dr. Orr, "coincidentally," had been Cec's mom's personal physician and idol for many years, a fact which actually served for a time to make us unnecessarily skeptical of him.

Obviously, Cec's mom, sister, and Mark were disappointed in our decision. But the decision had been made primarily because there were so many doctors who had, at one time or another, concurred on Cec's current chemo regimen, and therefore, we felt, the difference made by a decision one way or the other could not be too definitively good or bad. If it were clearly the wrong wrong wrong choice, we thought, so many reputable doctors would not be supporting it. And we had not been able to get a clear, firsthand opinion from the one doctor who opposed it.

I was to have moved Maddie and our "overnight bags" from Alice and Russell's to our new home during the afternoon while Cec had chemo. But because of the turmoil, I stayed with Cec. So when we got back to Alice's, our stuff had been packed by Cec's mom and Alice and Zully (the fill-in nanny). We all traipsed the eight blocks to our new house, and finally, on Tuesday night, December 23, after owning this house for eleven months and sixteen days, and seven months and ten days after starting construction, we moved in. I was worried about Maddie, who'd been shuttled from house to house for three months now. But she took to the new place well. The only difficulty was in sleeping. Our bedroom has no curtains yet—only temporary paper shades. There's a bright streetlamp outside that casts a steady glow into the room, and the sunrise fills the room from the big east-facing windows. Maddie tossed and turned more and more as the night turned to morning, occasionally calling out in her sleep, "Bye-bye, light!" She awoke for good at 7:00 this morning—a normal, realistic wake-up time in most families, I know, but *way* too early for this bunch of night owls.

Today, as promised, Cec and I went to see Dr. Orr, to hear what he had to say. In a nutshell, Dr. Orr believes that most cancer treatment is too conservative and bound by old successes. He feels that there are too many new possibilities available just to rely consistently on tried-and-true methods. And he did something no one else we've talked to has: he talked about how Cecily's treatment should be based on her own specifics and not on generalized trends. For example, he believes the treatment she's been getting from Dr. Wolin is fine for the typical victim of non-small-cell adenocarcinoma: male smokers. But, he says, women, and especially women who've never smoked or, like Cecily, quit many years ago, have different reasons for contracting the disease and thus need different treatment. This coincides with the research that we've done ourselves, particularly that of Mark Sobel and Lisa Jacobs-Pontecorvo. I know it's potentially dangerous to decide what treatment should be and then go looking for a doctor who'll provide it. But Dr. Orr was complimentary about Mark's research and stated that it was quite well-founded.

Cec and I have concurred that his approach is aggressive in the way we want her treatment to be, that it's open to innovative and recent developments that seem promising, and that it's fitted to the specifics of her case rather than to a "typical" case. So, now that her current cycle of chemo is over, we'll be turning over to Dr. Orr the responsibility for Cecily's case.

Love thy neighbor and *Do unto others as you would have them do unto you* may sound like slogans embroidered on your grandma's pillows, but there's power in them when they're brushed off and used as real ideas and not just clichés. This week, this month, this year, I've seen those two credos worked out in real life. To all of you who've restored my faith in my fellow man—a faith that wasn't all that shaky to begin with—the thanks of me and my sweet wife Cecily and our daughter Madeline Rose, and the wish that this holiday will forever be a high mark in how you feel about *your* fellow man and how you feel about yourselves. In the words of at least two better men than I, "God bless us, every one."

1:17 a.m. Christmas morning

Jim

December 25, 2003. Christmas Day.

Merry Christmas to all, and to all a good night.
12:29 a.m.

Jim

December 26, 2003

Every couple knows, if they've got a brain between them, that they are joining in a compact in which each of them agrees to out-live the other, if that's what it comes to. And if they stay together, that's what it always comes to. But there's a fantasy version and a real version. The fantasy version nearly always involves very old peo-ple, lots of sadness, but very little ugliness or debilitation or horrific pain or terror. The real version sometimes has all those qualities and happens years and years before you ever imagined it might. I've been an actor for thirty years or more, and I've played every kind of emo-tion you can think of, and I've watched other actors play levels and kinds of emotion that are beyond what you can think of. As an actor and as an audience member, it can seem so real that you can fall into the trap of believing that's what these things would be like if they actually happened. I'm of the belief that acting is a great and noble art that can illuminate human life like nothing else, no other art. Yet I've never seen a sorrow onstage, never played a fear or an anger, never watched someone portray a loss or dread that comes anywhere remotely resembling the depth of what I feel inside me when I look at Cec and wonder how long I'll have her, wonder if her daughter will grow up with a mother, wonder if she'll have a fraction of the splendid life she's struggled so hard to create for herself.

I go through most hours and days acting as best I can as if those emotions were not careening through me like water through a mountain gorge. Acting as if what color shirt I put on today matters, as if the electric bill matters, as if things were still just as funny and interesting and charming and innocuous as they once were. I'm sure Cec feels the same way. She's compelled to be as upbeat as she can manage, putting on the best smile she can muster, because the sense is that even the people who care most about you have to be protected from the enormity of your fears and despair and fury. So we have Christmas dinner and try to laugh and kid about old times and maybe once in a while someone notices that we look a little distant, but we don't really come out and say out loud that we're so scared we could scream, and so hurt by this cosmic pummeling that every moment we manage without vomiting is a tiny victory. The most we allow ourselves is some discussion of how bewildering it is that such a thing should have come to pass, and how hopeful we are that some process or another will make things better.

Between Cec and me there's far less talk about our own fears, because, I think, we feel that same need to protect the one we love. And so, as intimate as we are, as privy to each other's secrets as we've become in eighteen years, we rarely ever poke at the elephant in the room. We know he's there, we even acknowledge his presence, but we don't prod him. Some part of me feels things would be better if we could express to each other, Cec and me, the truth and depth of feeling. And yet, another part of me fears that the solution to our desperate problems lies, if anywhere, somewhere else than in baring our terror.

I'm out of words. Words don't touch what's going on here. And what good these words of mine will do for anyone other than me is hard for me to say.

O God, Thy sea is so great and my boat is so small.

12:55 a.m.

Jim

December 27, 2003

With Maribel taking the day off, we had no scheduled help with Maddie today, but Uncle Russell came over and devoted his entire day to watching her with Grandma Dell. Russell Friedman is a good guy. My snap judgments rarely turn out right, and when I first met Russell over a decade ago, I had a doozy of a bad snap judgment.

Russell's a terrifically intelligent man, and he's a mensch of the first order. (My Texas relatives should scurry to a dictionary at this point.) Russell codirects the Grief Recovery Institute, an amazing institution that has helped many, many people cope with the tragedies and emotional baggage of life. He and Cecily's Aunt Alice are a couple, and they are among the brightest spots in our lives these days.

1:01 a.m.

Jim

December 28, 2003

A beautiful day for riding the ponies. Maddie was up at the crack of dawn—me, too, then—and Uncle Russell showed up for the second day in a row to save the day. After Cec and I caught a little mid-morning nap, she and I and Russell, on the first Sunday we've lived in this house, took advantage of the fact that the pony ride we take Maddie to every week is now within walking distance. We piled Cec and Maddie into the wheelchair and all of us traveled three blocks to the farmers' market and the ponies—which were, apparently, spending the holidays in the Caribbean, because there was no sign of them. After mollifying Maddie for several hours about going to ride the ponies, we couldn't very well say, "Whoops, no ponies for you today." So we all walked and rolled back to the house, piled in the car, and went to Griffith Park. There Maddie rode the ponies (along with approximately 67,400 other kids) and the little train and the wonderful huge merry-go-round with the calliope. Maddie had ridden the merry-go-round once before, but she was less nervous this time. She had a great time and fell asleep on the way home. She and I both napped at home, then I got her up so she could have dinner and go to bed(!).

It was a fun day and if it weren't for the wheelchair and the elephant, it might have been a perfect day. At the park, even with thousands of smelly kids and an arena full of ponies, I caught a whiff of the elephant and broke down for a few moments. I managed to pull myself together—when you play as many cowboys as I do, you can't let the ponies catch you crying. But it crimped the edges of an otherwise swell day.

I've been short-tempered lately. I've snapped at Cec's mom several times and even at Cecily. After eighteen years, some things are on automatic pilot and it's hard to catch and disable them before they happen. I always get a sick feeling in my gut when I'm snappish or rude or curt to someone. My first reaction afterward is always a guilty awareness of how bad I must have made that person feel. But there's nothing that compares to the guilt you feel when you snap at someone with stage IV lung cancer, especially when that someone is the love of your life. I know, I'm only human, blah, blah, blah. I can excuse it, but I don't have to like it.

The *National Enquirer* story came out this weekend. The article focused not on Cec's illness, but on her dad's reaction to it. They barely mentioned her own claims to fame and the huge number of fans she has from *Star Trek*. The last thing Cec needs is to see herself treated like an afterthought in a story about her own fight.

Three more days till this year's over. I can't wait, because the way I see it, 2004's the year Cec goes into remission.

12:35 a.m.

Jim

December 29, 2003

Cecily's mom fell in our bathtub today and broke her wrist.

Dell was in the ER only about twenty minutes before being seen by a doctor. They took X-rays of her wrist and put a splint on it and sent her home. It was all pretty smooth—if you don't count the broken wrist part.

Astonishingly, the rest of the day went casually.

Yesterday, Maddie made her first joke. She looked at my hand and touched my wedding ring. I said, "That's Daddy's ring." She said, "Daddy have a ring. Mommy have a ring." Then she got this funny look on her face and she said, "Bathtub have a ring!" and she laughed hysterically. Now I don't claim she was making a play on words with "bathtub ring." That double meaning was just coincidence. But she clearly put two normal things together and then threw in a third completely incongruous thing just to be funny. The fact that she saw the absurdity of the third item and laughed at it was exciting. And she seems to have learned early the basic comedy rule of threes— two setups and a punch line. I'm proud. But if she goes into stand-up comedy, I'll put her in a convent.

10:26 p.m.

Jim

December 30, 2003

Oh, Cecily. I tell you, I am so in love with this girl, so intricately interwoven with her, that I want to scream whenever the prospect of losing her pushes up through one of the grates of the dungeon in my mind where I keep such thoughts. It seems a betrayal to even mention that I'm scared to death of losing her, when she needs so very much to know that I believe to the utmost in her survival. The dichotomy is ironic; I write things here that she might read or have read to her, yet they are things I would never say to her. That's a bizarre aspect of this entire endeavor, that I can write for public consumption what I could never say to anyone. I bury as much of this terror as I can, stuff it back where it came from, but it always finds a way out, if only for a moment, and in those moments, life is unutterably hellish, with only my belief and my love for my two girls keeping me putting one foot in front of the other. How much worse must it be to be the one in the actual dire straits, the one faced with the possibility of losing not just some but all of life, and the one who must face great pain throughout the process?

12:49 a.m.

Jim

December 31, 2003. New Year's Eve.

The last day of the worst year of my life. It's my fervent hope that 2003 remains the worst year of all of our lives.

Cec and I used to spend each New Year's Eve with two other couples, and we would always write cards to ourselves envisioning the next year and describing what we'd like it to look like. Then we had an arrangement where we would receive the cards back on the following New Year's Eve, to see how much had come true. For years, Cec wrote about wanting the next year to see her pregnant or having given birth to a child. So tonight, we're contemplating the glorious child those hopes engendered, and counting our blessings, and visualizing 2004 and 2024 with all three of us happy, healthy, and together. We invite you to join in.

11:48 p.m.

Jim

January 1, 2004. New Year's Day.

I wrote yesterday that I hoped 2003 was the worst year of all of our lives.

I hope today was the worst day of 2004. It was certainly an awful start.

The phone rang. It was Cec's sister Stacey. She said that Cecily's brother, Sean, had had a severe brain seizure in the night and had been hospitalized with serious swelling and edema. Sean was awaiting an MRI of his brain, but because it was a holiday, MRI technicians were not going to be available until tomorrow, January 2. Stacey and her husband and her mom had driven in from Palm Springs, and Sean appeared to be doing better. He was conversing and joking. Eventually, it was arranged for him to go elsewhere to have the MRI, but a few minutes after arriving at that other location, he had another seizure and was rushed back to ICU. The preliminary opinion of the hospital staff was that the problem stemmed from one of three possibilities: a parasitic infection, a blood clot, or a tumor. The infection was considered the least likely.

So we spent our New Year's Day at home, waiting for further word. Sean is thirty-three, the second-youngest of Cecily's six siblings. He's quick-witted, ironic, self-deprecating, and quite lovable. But there was no consideration given to going to be with Sean, as Cecily's immune system is so depleted that she could not risk picking up something from Sean or other patients.

Some hours later we learned that Sean recovered somewhat from the second seizure, though his speech was now slurred. He returned for another attempt at the MRI. By evening, a preliminary diagnosis was reached: a viral infection of the brain. Stacey said this was good news, at least on the scale of possible diagnoses. It will be tomorrow before a course of action is instigated.

So that's how 2004 started. We managed to get out with Maddie for a short visit to Nancylee Myatt's to get some "good luck" black-eyed peas for New Year's. We couldn't physically eat all we felt we needed to eat in order to stave off the string of bad luck that's come our way, so we made a symbolic effort and hoped for the best.

Somebody said to Cec today how they envied her for this lovely new home. Cec said, "No, don't envy me." The person said, "Oh, no, I meant your house." Cec said, "No, you gotta take the whole package." As she said to me when relating this, it's a great house and we're happy to finally live in it. But, she said, they can take it all, house, clothes, cars, all of it, if she can have her health back. All she needs, she said, is me and Maddie and a street corner to plop down on, if she can just be well.

Keep prayin' and hummin', gang.

12:44 a.m.

Jim

FOUR

January 2, 2004

No news is good news, I suppose.

My dearest friend and brother, Tom Allard, came by with a bunch of movies for Cec and me to watch, and we were able to visit for a while. Tom and I have been through the wars together, friends for thirty-one years now, and although I can say this about several people these days, I mean it in its most emphatic sense about Tom: I don't know how I'd have made it this far without him. He has the greatest drive toward life, and he's faced and overcome the most staggering obstacles with that drive. I draw from his strength and encouragement every hour. Also, it amuses me to let him think he's funny.

I stole away for a few minutes' shut-eye around 5:00 p.m. and ended up sleeping four hours. Cecily and our substitute nanny, Zully, put Maddie to bed, and all I had to do was watch the first half of *About Schmidt* with Cec—a relaxing end to a day when the elephant slept pretty soundly. He snores, he snuffles, but at least today he slept.

1:16 a.m.

Jim

January 3, 2004

Our niece, Rebecca, has taken Cec's mom into her home, as Dell needs more attention than we can spare around here. That's a generous undertaking for our young newlywed niece—and would be even if Dell weren't recuperating. My mother-in-law has a dynamic personality and a vital, knowledgeable nature, and I enjoy her a lot. But having her stay with us is a lot like having the Battle of Bunker Hill stay with us.

No news as regards Cec's brother, Sean, except that he's now gone more than twenty-four hours without another seizure.

Nothing else to report, and too tired to rhapsodize.

1:00 a.m.

Jim

January 4, 2004

Today I was changing Maddie out of her pajamas and I noticed they were covered in hair—hair darker and longer than Maddie's. There are strands and knots of hair all over the house these days. From what's on her clothes and pillow and in her hairbrush, one would think Cec would be bald by now. But she's always had thick hair, and you wouldn't know to look at her that she's lost any. At the rate she's losing it, though, I believe it will soon become obvious. Cec is philosophical about it. One of her nurses suggested Friday that she cut her hair short. I think the conventional wisdom is that patients don't want to see their hair fall out, so cutting it short reduces the trauma of the experience. So far Cec hasn't shown any huge concern about losing her hair. I know she'd prefer not to, but I think she looks at it as a tangible sign that her treatment's having a good effect. If the chemo's killing her hair cells, then it should be killing the cancer cells, too.

Dr. Orr called tonight to tell Cecily that she won't have chemo this next week; her blood counts are too low. She was scheduled to start the new chemo protocol under his supervision on Wednesday. Of course, being Cec, she's afraid to commit to a decision and tell Dr. Wolin that she's going with a different oncologist, so she hasn't, and Dr. Wolin and his staff still think she's starting the next round of the old chemo protocol with them tomorrow. I know that Cec is also reluctant to leave the cancer center at Cedars-Sinai, because it has comfortable rooms with TVs and food, and the staff's there twenty-four hours a day, ready to deal with any problems a patient might have during or because of the chemo. Dr. Orr's chemo treatment will be in a more typical venue: his office at Good Samaritan Hospital. There won't be much in the way of amenities, and there's not the same kind of twenty-four-hour help available at Good Sam as there is at Cedars-Sinai. But my belief, as I told Cec, is that when confronted with the choice of crossing the Atlantic on a rusty tramp steamer or in a luxurious stateroom aboard the *Titanic*, the decision should be pretty easy.

Maddie conked out an hour earlier than usual tonight, so Cec and I were able to watch most of the true-story movie *Monster* (Cec has a thing for serial killers—maybe that's why she married a guy who looks like one). But she was so worn out that we couldn't finish it. It's nice, though, that we've been able to have some relaxation and downtime together lately. The intimacy of our lives has either disappeared or been radically altered, and a few shared moments together watching part of a movie (even one about serial killers) is treasured now even more than before.

12:41 a.m.

Jim

January 5, 2004

I had a blowup with Cec's mom today. She's staying with her granddaughter Rebecca, since her needs and illness were beyond our capability here. But Rebecca has to leave town for a few days and Dell wants to come back to stay with us. Well, that ain't happenin'. She could go home to Las Vegas and be tended by Cec's sister Cathy, but she prefers to be here where the action is. Also, she likes the bed in our guest room. She told me today that she would be no trouble whatsoever, because she's "got a twenty-pound plaster cast on her arm and can't even get out of bed by herself," so how could she possibly be any trouble to anyone, stuck in her room like that. . . ?

Look, I apologize to Dell and to all her brothers and sisters and family who are reading this. The fact is, she has many legitimate needs and there aren't many options she likes. But despite the fact that, under normal circumstances, I would bend backward to help her in her difficulty, I just can't do it now. My father is slipping away in Texas, and I ignore it. Cec's brother is in serious medical straits and we deal with it from a distance, doing nothing (except praying). With Cec desperately ill and in constant discomfort, with doctor trips and therapist trips for Maddie, and an unfinished house the wind still whistles through, as much as I might like to provide room service for people who need it or maybe just want it, we can't. Right now my nerves are stretched so taut I'm ready to punch Mother Teresa right in the snot-locker.

Please forgive the ranting. There's a terrible anger that underlies most of what's been happening with us these past couple of months, but I try to sublimate it, perhaps turn it into humor. Most of the time, it's an impersonal anger, not directed at anyone but just at the situation. It's most rapidly triggered when too many things happen at once or when there's great pressure to resolve some problem in too short a time, but most especially when someone suggests, in word or action, that their need is more important than mine.

These days I'm feeling pretty self-centered when it comes to who deserves the most consideration. Excluding Cec, of course. So when our need for peace and support runs into someone else's need for attention and care that could be provided elsewhere, I can get pretty snitty. Or isn't that obvious by now?

Your many kindnesses—cards, e-mails, gifts, errands, all these things continue to remind us that dark clouds really do have silver linings. We'd have preferred to continue knowing about that only from Hallmark cards, but if this cloud had to form over us, we're happy that it has such a fine lining.

11:50 p.m.

Jim

January 6, 2004

Frances Miller showed up to help out today. She lightens Cec's spirits in a way I can't because, frankly, Cec is more positive, determined, and confident with other people than with me. Perhaps it's because I'm the one she can let her guard down with, or maybe just that we're so close that there's no hiding behind propped-up good spirits. I don't know. I just know that when Fran arrived, Cec was soon smiling and even occasionally laughing.

Cecily's grown quieter these days, possibly from fatigue, possibly from reluctance to approach the speculation that inevitably arises during conversation with me. I know that she's afraid, more so with this worsening pain across her shoulders. It's always been her nature to be afraid, to worry. And with a worry as big as this one, it's harder to convince this melancholy baby that all her fears are foolish fancies.

She's been oddly forgetful lately. The past few days she's asked me something two or three times within the space of a few minutes, forgetting that we'd already gone over the subject minutes earlier.

Tonight I came home from my doctor's appointment and met her in the hallway. Ten minutes later, I walked into the kitchen and she asked me how long I'd been home. Half an hour later, she asked me when I had come in and why hadn't I spoken to her before now. I started getting a little nervous after this last, but Zully, the fill-in nanny, who was trained as a nurse, told me that morphine causes memory lapses and to expect more of these. Zully warned me that I should take particular care to help Cec keep track of her medications, since her morphine-affected memory may cause her to make mistakes.

Apparently Cec and I got pretty well bad-mouthed throughout the U.S. last night, following my minor contretemps with Cec's mom. I hope Dell got it out of her system after burning up the phone lines with her tale of woeful treatment. I hope she doesn't feel too badly. I love her, but—well, you know how when the body gets too cold or goes into shock from injury, the blood rushes to the core of the body, maintaining at all costs the warmth and sustenance of the heart and central organs—even if it means the fingers and toes turn black and fall off? Well, right now, our blood is rushing to the core. I love my fingers and toes—most of them, anyway—and I love my mom-in-law. But I can't keep everyone alive right now. I've got to focus on where my heart is. And my heart is with Cecily and Maddie.

Thank you for your support. In particular, the people I heard from today.

12:14 a.m.

Jim

January 7, 2004

A difficult day for Cec. She was in great pain, both in her back and in her stomach, which she said felt like it was burning. Despite

Cec's severe nausea, she and I and Mark Sobel went to Dr. Orr this afternoon. Orr's exam room is a cramped little compartment with an ancient exam table with upholstery held together by duct tape. But Dr. Orr is extraordinary. He suggested some new pain and nausea medications, and within half an hour, Cec was amazingly better, more comfortable, and in greater spirits. Dr. Orr discussed what he felt was the right protocol and Cec surprised me by suddenly committing to—and in fact suggesting—an immediate start to the new chemo. So following some hydration and some bone and blood medications, she started. She'll go back tomorrow for the second half of the dose.

Listening to Dr. Orr converse with Mark Sobel was nothing short of amazing. The two talked almost as medical colleagues, and listening to the conversation, one would never guess that only one of the two has a medical degree. As recently as three months ago Mark knew no more about cancer than I did; his transformation into a knowledgeable resource is astounding. A couple of times today he made technical suggestions that Dr. Orr listened to, considered, and then acted upon, congratulating Mark on the excellence of the idea. Mark gets on Cec's nerves through his rather frantic enthusiasm and his talent for noodging, but she's several times said that his help has been a godsend, and in that I concur. He eats and (occasionally) sleeps this case, devoting as far as I can tell every waking hour to Cec and Maddie and finding a way to beat this disease.

I think some of the encouragement I felt is due to seeing Cec feel better by the end of the day. When she's lying in bed too sick and too pained to move, dragging herself agonizingly up to retch, it's hard for me to feel great hope. But when she sits up easily and laughs and jokes a few hours later, I suddenly see that the appearance of a painful descent doesn't mean a descent is really happening.

12:53 a.m.

Jim

January 8, 2004

The lab report came back on one of the four cancer markers in Cec's blood. It has more than doubled since it was last tested, on December 15. Now that doesn't mean the cancer has doubled, but it makes clear that the old chemo was not working. Had we not changed doctors, we would have been continuing that old chemo regimen. I talked to Dr. Wolin's office today and officially pulled the plug on him as Cec's oncologist.

I've gotten some amazing and helpful e-mails from people in the past couple of days. My spirits and Cec's are up and down like a toad on a trampoline, and it seems that every time they get particularly down, someone finds a new and touching way to say "Keep your chin up." I'm not so good at responding individually, but I want to express how much these messages mean to me and Cec. Thank you.

Thassall.

12:32 a.m.

Jim

January 9, 2004

Maddie's been having a tough couple of days. She's in good spirits, but Cec and I and some of her therapists have noticed that she seems to be a little disorganized in her thinking and her speech is a touch more imprecise than usual. All the doctors have told us that she will not regress, that every step forward is permanent. And I wouldn't be surprised if her current uncertainties are due to the multitudinous changes in our recent lives more than any mental or physiological condition she might have. Most of the time she seems fine, but, well, we've gotten hypervigilant and thus notice subtle changes.

There's more—always more—but I can barely hold my head up.

So I'll leave you with the last noteworthy event of the day: just as I got Cec into bed and on her way to sleep, and had sat down to write this report on the day, we were startled and a little frightened to hear the phone ring, at two minutes to midnight. Cec bolted upright and grabbed the phone and I ran in to see what fresh hell this was. Not to worry. It was just Cec's mom, calling to say Cec would feel better if she just relaxed and tried not to stress out.

That's all, brother.

12:27 a.m.

Jim

January 11, 2004

The only news of the day is old news we just learned about Cec's brother, Sean. His seizures and brain swelling are not due to a viral infection. An MRI a few days ago revealed a blood clot. A number of specialists have seen him and they are all amazed that he's alive. He's being given blood thinners in hopes of dissolving the clot. He's awake and alert and quite conversational, I hear—also a source of amazement to his doctors. Apparently death or coma are the only usual outcomes of this sort of blood clot in the brain. We're all happy that he was not a typical victim of this kind of cerebral event, but we're also praying hard for better news.

That was the extent of the day, other than visits by Ann Melby and by David Burke to bring over a lot more of his amazing cooking. I ran into Elmarie Wendel, my old *3rd Rock from the Sun* co-star, at the grocery store. She didn't know about Cecily's illness, and I hated to ruin her day by telling her. I always hate to tell people, because invariably it makes them sad and quite upset. Yet I honestly don't know how to pretend it isn't happening, to ignore the elephant when people ask how we are. Maybe I just shouldn't go to the grocery store.

12:59 a.m.

Jim

January 12, 2004

Cecily spent three hours today encased in a giant magnet.

She had an MRI that we hope will, within the next twenty-four to forty-eight hours, tell us whether the pain in her upper back is something awful or merely something irritating.

I had my own doctor's appointment today, following up on the pulmonary exam I had related to my cough (which has pretty much disappeared, by the way). The doc thinks there may be a slight chance of asthma, or maybe just overreactive lung tissue clenching up whenever I breathe deeply. Either would explain my frequent coughing spasms even when I'm otherwise healthy. But he wants me to have a CT scan tomorrow to rule out such things as emphysema or scar tissue.

It was immensely saddening when he told me he wanted me to have the CT scan, and I'll tell you why. He said my chest X-ray showed no sign of disease. But, he said, X-ray is only good for certain kinds of problems. He said a CT scan can pick up anomalies months before they would ever show up on an X-ray. And he said that he always recommends a CT scan for former smokers, no matter how long ago they quit, as it's never too late to have smoking-related lung problems crop up. He said that for a former smoker, he would never rely just on an X-ray.

I quit smoking twenty-four years ago. Cecily quit eighteen years ago. If our family doctor had felt the same way about CT scans for former smokers, I can't help but wonder if Cec's cancer wouldn't have been caught earlier. Granted, he offered to give Cec a CT scan when she visited him a year or two ago, worried that she had something bad. But with a clear X-ray, he didn't see much sense in going to the trouble and expense of a CT scan, and he offered the scan most probably as a sop to her fears, with which he was quite familiar. And Cec, thinking maybe she was being childish, never got the scan.

"If you can look into the seeds of time, and say which grain will grow and which will not, speak then unto me." Would that we could have looked and seen then what is so clear now.

11:23 p.m.

Jim

January 14, 2004

I haven't felt like writing about the emotional highs and lows of this thing—mine or Cec's—for a few days. Those highs and lows haven't gone away, but sometimes I just want to get away from talking-writing-thinking about them. Cec and I had dinner at the hospital cafeteria tonight after our meeting with Orr, and after we'd chatted awhile about various things, she said, "It's so nice to talk about something besides cancer for a while." Well, I can't very well not talk about cancer in these nightly reports, but sometimes I just need a break. On those nights, I'll just stick mainly to reporting the day and letting it go at that.

Putting Maddie to bed tonight I thought about some of the junk that's going on in my head and some of the things Cec and I have lost and found in this trip, and I thought maybe I'd write about them tonight. But somehow a Dr Pepper and a *Tarzan* movie seem infinitely more meaningful to me right now. Believe it or not, it's only

10:15 p.m.

Jim

January 16, 2004

The night of January 16.

Maddie had a good day. She's the only one. Cec had an emotional day, and for a while I kept pace with her, step for step. We went out to look for light fixtures, but ended up sitting in a parked car crying. What do you say when your wife says, "I don't want to die!"? I've always had an answer or at least a response to any question, even if the answer was only a glib one, or a stab in the dark. Today as she wept next to me in front of a lighting store, I couldn't come up with a single word. I just sat there and cried with her. And it wasn't even a clean, cathartic moment such as commonly fills dramatic moments in movies. In the midst of our grief for what might be lost, we were also ragged around the edges from anger—at each other, at ourselves, at this whole bloody whirlpool of horror we've fallen into.

Alfred Hitchcock said that drama was life with the dull bits cut out. Well, I'm telling you that drama—at least the kind we see on-screen or television—also cuts out most of the clutter, even if that clutter isn't remotely dull. Catharsis on *ER* never seems to include the fact that two people who love each other desperately and who face a dread disease together may also be two people who, right through the midst of it, continue to gripe at each other over the chore ignored or the task forgotten. A sudden desperate illness and the more desperate fight for survival doesn't change the fact that one of you may occasionally be boorish or stupid and the other occasionally picayunish or illogical. At first, of course, the horror of what's overtaken you and your desperation to hang on to your life and love wipe away all the petty concerns and baggage of years together. But if time permits, you find that even the pettiest concerns rise up through the quagmire of fear and exigence to nibble at your heels and make you bleed from little vulnerabilities you'd thought crisis had lifted you above. Ah, and then there's guilt. How could you? How could I? How could I possibly say and do something so small when something so large looms? How does one conceivably snap at someone who has every right to fear the close hot breath of death? If not patience and forbearance then, then when?

Cecily's tears were not simply for herself. She's so tormented by the notion that she fought so hard to bring Maddie into the world only to leave her to fend for herself, and without the necessary resources. I think she has little confidence in my potential ability as a single parent, and no more than that in my longevity. She's afraid that Maddie will bear the greatest burden in all this, and all because Cec wanted so badly to have a child and to show her that a happy childhood was possible. I don't share the level of fear Cec has on these counts, because I think Cec will be here, that I will be here, and that Maddie will do well with either or both of us. But fear can sabotage the bravest heart, and brave though she is, Cec's fears are palpable and not quickly wiped away with casual reassurance. Or even thorough and reasoned reassurance. How do you promise someone in her condition that everything will be all right and not, by doing so, convince her that you're either a liar or an idiot? How do you show her there's no bogeyman when you can't find the light switch and there's a breathing sound in the closet?

1:01 a.m.

Jim

January 17, 2004

My back went out yesterday and I woke up with the same harpoon stuck in my lower back I'd gone to bed with. Only today I got to carry Maddie around a lot.

Cec had a hard afternoon. Physically, she seems to be feeling better, but she's awfully scared and walking a shaky emotional wire. People keep telling her how important and useful a positive attitude is in her recovery, but it appears that she hears this more as a warning that she's doomed if she doesn't lighten up. That's not what any of us mean, but I think she hears it that way, and it merely serves to frighten her more and to chip away at any positivity she's able to muster. Such was the gist of a conversation with her sister Chris today, and she was, for a time, quite demolished and demoralized with fear—all from urgings that she strive to see herself beating this thing. Cec needs encouragement from other people; she's not nearly as good at pumping herself up as she is at doing it for others. I sense unutterable bravery in her; I sense little of what one would call optimism.

Years ago, she gave me a book called *Learned Optimism*, because she felt I was pessimistic and negative in my outlook. I wish I could find that book now, and that I could infuse its lessons in her. She may be an optimist in normal life, but this thorny path would be a happier, easier one for her if she could recharge that optimism here in the face of the great natural enemy of optimism. I'd give anything to hear her boldly say, "I can beat this and I'm going to beat it!" more often than I hear her say, "Do you really think so?" when someone else tells her she can beat it. I know she can beat it, but it would make her feel better and more empowered if she could bellow that belief from her heart every so often.

The opinions expressed here are not necessarily those of the management.

12:09 a.m.

Jim

January 19, 2004

Sean has been transferred to University of California at Irvine Hospital. He had another MRI last night and today it showed that although the swelling in his brain hasn't diminished much, the blood clot shows signs of dissolving. He's on big doses of blood thinners, antiseizure meds, and other stuff to reduce the swelling. Tomorrow he's having a spinal tap, as the docs aren't 100 percent certain that the swelling is caused by the clot—it's possible both are symptoms of something else.

Cec and I had joint appointments with the lung specialist Dr. Patel. The initial feeling is that her cough was, most likely, just the same old bronchitis that many of us are having this winter. And he informed me that my CT scan was normal, with no sign whatsoever of lung disease, disruption, or other problem. All of my tests were A-OK.

I got plenty of exercise tonight. Uncle Russell dropped by to play with Maddie. Then Zully gave her a bath and Maddie turned into the toddler equivalent of a Roman candle fired in a closet. She had been up long past her bedtime, with no nap, and there were a lot of people running around the house today. Those factors, plus a bad reaction to the noise from a blow-dryer (a common event with kids on the autism spectrum), led us to the worst meltdown in weeks.

She screamed and cried for what seemed like hours. Nothing would calm or relax her, and no matter what she asked for, two seconds later she didn't want it. She was so tired—her little head kept lolling around—but she just couldn't calm herself enough to go to sleep. It was horrible, but eventually she just collapsed in my arms with her head on my shoulder from sheer burnout. By the time she conked out, I knew how she felt. Cec and I were both fried by the time we got Maddie down for the night. Cec was there right with me throughout it, even though she couldn't hold her daughter. Maddie was kicking and thrashing far too much for Cec's current capabilities.

I talked to my mom earlier in the evening. She didn't have much new to report, but it was clear that though my dad's decline proceeds at a crawl, it proceeds inexorably. Listening to my mom describe what my dad's condition and care are like nowadays broke my heart—as if it weren't already in small enough pieces. I ended up lying on the bed holding on to Cec's arm—the only way I can really hold her anymore—and sobbing. I don't enjoy telling a few hundred people every night about how much I cry. I'm not afraid of crying, but it's not something I like to breeze around. But sometimes the depths of feeling one experiences allow no other response, and I can't be as honest in these reports as I feel compelled to be without copping to the tears.

When I was a kid, I wanted to grow up to be like two people: my dad and John Wayne. In some ways, I did, though hardly in the ways I had planned or preferred. Years ago, I read that when John Wayne was dying of stomach cancer, he begged his son to bring a gun to the hospital so he could end his own suffering. That's when, if I didn't know it before, I learned that not even John Wayne was John Wayne. I find a lot to admire and emulate in the image of the strong, silent type. But it's an image, not a reality. I don't measure up to that image, and I don't mind not measuring up, because no real person does. I try not to whine, but you'd never believe me if I said I was going through this without tears. So I won't try to convince you I am.

11:55 p.m.

Jim

January 20, 2004

I called M. D. Anderson Cancer Center in Houston today and arranged for an appointment for Cec to be evaluated there. This isn't a shift in plans or doctors. It's just groping for more information, more insight.[4]

---

4. M. D. Anderson is one of the country's leading cancer treatment centers, and Cec wanted to see if they might have different opinions or options.

Going to Anderson will be a somewhat complicated procedure, as Cec would have to leave Maddie and me behind to go to Houston for a couple of days. We'll arrange the scheduling so that her sister Cathy can accompany her. Among the great things we've uncovered in our research are Angel Flights and Corporate Angels, organizations that provide free air transportation on private or corporate aircraft for cancer patients going to distant treatment centers.

Even on her worst days, Cec insists on trying to do a little work for *That '70s Show*. Part of it, I'm sure, is gratitude for everything the people of that show have done for us. But mostly I think it's a deep vein of responsibility and duty that runs through her. Even if it's only a phone call or two from her sickbed, she feels better knowing she hasn't let anybody down. As if anybody thought that.

Our much-loved friend Jeanne Dougherty has been with us a few days. She cooked another terrific dinner tonight. She leaves us tomorrow to go back to her island off the Washington coast. We love her husband, Bill, and know he would miss her, but we wish she'd stay here and just phone him every once in a while.

Big day tomorrow. Cec finally gets the word on her MRI at her meeting with Dr. Orr. She also meets with Dr. Robert Audell, a bone specialist. Maddie and I have a long day in therapy. Jeanne leaves. My sister Denise arrives.

Nothing more.

12:33 a.m.

Jim

January 21, 2004

Dr. Orr finally had the MRI results: although there's evidence of bone damage in her spine, there doesn't seem to be any evidence of additional cancer there since the initial MRI in late October. This is good news.

Mark Sobel drove Cec and conferred with Dr. Orr, who continues to be impressed with the research Mark's doing. Mark learned of university studies showing promising results from a Chinese herb combination. Unable to obtain samples from the research institute, he did an end run and bought some directly from a supplier in China. The FDA stopped the shipment at customs and wanted to know what it was. Mark informed them that it was something to make his hamburgers taste better, and they let it through. Now get this: Mark has been testing it on himself. Although there's no clinical evidence of adverse side effects, Mark wanted to make sure before providing it to Dr. Orr to give Cec. He's been taking increasing doses, with no ill effects other than a tingling numbness in his mouth. Though he turned down Mark's request to have him inject the herbs into Mark intravenously, Dr. Orr showed great interest in the research documentation. I've seen it myself and it seems promising. Cec is skeptical, though.

Tonight Cec lay for a while on our bed and we put Maddie to sleep between us. Before she dozed off she said, "Mommy not going anywhere." Hear, hear.

12:05 a.m.

Jim

FIVE

January 23, 2004

Cecily is afraid and deeply melancholy. She and I spent an endless hour or two going over wills and guardianships and stuff like that—things that every couple has to confront at some point but which now are so fraught with fearful supposings. We're trying to think of it as being like earthquake insurance: something you don't expect to need but don't want to need and not have.

Somehow in the past few days, reorganizing the kitchen and pantry, we lost a box of pain-relief patches that Cec wears for time-release of a morphine-like opiate. We've torn the place apart and can't find the box, so we called for a refill on the prescription. Since it was only a few days since the original prescription, insurance wouldn't pay for the replacements, so Cec went back on the morphine pills for pain relief. Today we caved in and bought the patches anyway, rather than wait another two weeks for the prescription refill to be insurable. If I ever decide to make steady money instead of act for a living, I'm going into pharmaceuticals. It costs $183 for five patches. Something tells me it doesn't cost $183 to make them.

11:53 p.m.

Jim

January 25, 2004

Sometimes I wonder if I'm cut out to be a father. Don't get me wrong, I love Madeline more than breath itself. But just chasing her around the house and keeping her fed and happy for one afternoon makes me feel as though I'd lugged a 10' × 12' Moroccan rug up and down a tree all day. Maybe it's my age. The only toddlers most of my peers have to deal with are their grandchildren. But, frankly, I don't think I had the necessary energy when I was twenty. And I've only got one kid. My granny had ten kids and never once killed her husband.

Cecily's brother, Sean, is home from the hospital. They're watching and waiting. I know he's nervous about being away from his professional caregivers, since another seizure is not impossible. But insurance companies don't like to pay for people to stay in the hospital "just in case."

Thanks for the visit today, Tom Allard. Maddie said, "Hi, Uncle Tom," and made Tommy Lee cry. First time I've ever seen him cry that didn't involve the University of Oklahoma losing a football game.

1:06 a.m.

Jim

January 27, 2004

Cec is still having a good response to this week's chemo. She had blood drawn for an update on her cancer markers, so we are praying and visualizing those numbers being much lower. This will be the first small evidence that the new chemo regimen's working, if these numbers come down at all. Prayer groups, hummers, meditators,

friends of the cosmic consciousness, and (my specialty) regular old
bowed-head-and-bended-knee folks, join in if you will.

Today we got our appointment for Cec's evaluation at M. D.
Anderson Cancer Center in Houston. The appointment's for next
Tuesday morning, so I guess Cec and whoever's accompanying her
will fly to Houston on Monday.

High hopes and low markers!

11:19 p.m.

Jim

January 28, 2004

No word on the cancer marker scores yet.

Cec had a painful day. Dr. Orr says the severe pain she's feeling is a direct result of the shot she had yesterday to boost her red
cells and the shot she had this afternoon to boost her white ones.
The chemo's hitting her a bigger blow than usual this time, too. She
feels sick and aches all over, as with a severe flu. On top of wearing
an opium-based pain-relief patch, she's also taking over-the-counter
Aleve, on Dr. Orr's orders. She seems so uncomfortable it's hard to
tell if the extra medication's helping.

After her trip to Dr. Orr, I took her to Joseph, the Eastern therapy
specialist she's been to a few times. This time I stayed in the room
with her. Even being there, I can't quite see or understand what he
does, but it's something perhaps related to acupressure. The process
is peaceful and gentle, and Cecily always reports feeling better after
a session.

12:00 midnight

Jim

January 30, 2004

Things are very difficult—on the scale of difficulty I'm used to measuring with. Things are terribly stressful—as I'm used to counting stress. I try to take comfort by reminding myself that most people on this planet are in far worse straits. Here, in our home (complete with roof and doors and water that arrives without being carried from a stream in buckets), we eat when we feel like it, either because we can afford it or someone has been generous enough to cook and deliver it to us. We wear clothes that we picked out and purchased, rather than found in someone else's garbage. And even though one of us is sick with a deadly disease, we go to doctors and take medicines and receive treatments, all rather than simply suffering and saying good-bye. So one might ask us, quoting that little kid in *An Affair to Remember,* "What are ya crabbin' about?"

I hate whining. I despise complaining. But on the worst days, it's so difficult to maintain dignity and composure and to refrain from crying out in unseemly lamentation. Cecily weeps occasionally from fear or regret, and begs sporadically to know *Why,* but by and large she's more stoic than I ever dreamt she could be. I, on the other hand, am guilty of far too much complaint, especially complaint that falls on her ears and, thus, on her shoulders. She's been my confidante all these years, the one who first heard my news of good fortune and my wailing over misfortune. Old habits die hard. Despite a wealth of friends, she's the one I always turned to. How not now? I am worn out; my head and heart are threadbare. For the third night of the past four, Maddie awoke an hour or so after I'd gone to bed and the two of us were awake all night. I don't know if I can do another night like the past few. I mean, I guess I can if I have to, but each one leaves me feeling increasingly likely either to pop a blood vessel or to jump in my car and drive at top speed through the nearest indoor shopping mall.

We've decided to postpone the M. D. Anderson evaluation in Houston until next week. We've received a half dozen or more offers of frequent-flyer miles, of free travel vouchers, and of out-and-out gifts

of tickets. We are beholden to you all, so beholden. The postpone-
ment of the trip allows us to have a better chance at a free trip via
Corporate Angels, but if that fails, someone's generosity will be taken
advantage of, I assure you.

You are a kind and special breed of people, you friends. God bless
you all.

11:25 p.m.

Jim

January 30, 2004—Addendum

I forgot the only actual news of the day. Dr. Orr called to say that
Cecily's cancer markers were slightly up, not down as we'd hoped. This
was disappointing, but Dr. Orr said that he actually took encouragement
from it, as the increase was so slight as to be insignificant. He feels certain that the next test (at the next chemo cycle in two and a half weeks)
will show a downturn in the markers. That would be grand news.

Sorry about leaving that out. It's probably the only part some of
you cared about.

11:37 p.m.

Jim

January 31, 2004

Cec slept all day again. This chemo's really knocking her out.
She's increasingly nauseous, even as the day of treatment recedes.
She hurts and generally feels lousy. I can't say for certain whether
her long hours of sleep are due more to exhaustion or to medication.
But she's been sleeping eighteen hours a day or more for several days.
Tonight she came downstairs and had dinner with me and her mom

and our niece Rebecca, and we were joined by Aunt Alice and Cec's cousin Claudia.

Maddie's cold seems much better.

Uh-oh, Maddie's waking up. Time to go.

1:26 a.m.

Jim

February 2, 2004

Can't do it tonight.

12:51 a.m.

Jim

February 3, 2004

I didn't get a chance to call them to tell them in person, but happy fifty-fifth wedding anniversary to my mom and dad today. I'm happy they got married. It's made them happy over the years, and it made my life less embarrassing as a result, too.

Cec's blood was tested, and her white cells were way up, happily. Her red cells were down, but not too significantly. However, Cec has started coughing blood, and she's still nauseous nearly a week since her last chemo treatment. This led Dr. Orr to suspect she might have an ulcer. He gave her a medication that only works if the patient actually has an ulcer, and Cec's nausea and stomach pain went away almost immediately. He recommended an endoscopy to confirm the suspicion of a bleeding ulcer. We tried to schedule one with our longtime gastroenterologist, Dr. Soraya Ross, but it looked like it would be more than a week before it would happen. Dr. Orr said he would call Dr. Ross himself to expedite things.

Every time I talk to Dr. Orr, I come away more encouraged, despite the fact that he's far more forthcoming about potential difficulties than any of our previous oncologists. He said that Cec's cancer is not smoking-related, but is almost certainly viral in origin, and that one of the chemo drugs she had been getting at Cedars was excellent for smoking-related cancers but had no use at all in viral-origin lung cancers. Dr. Orr is doing daily research in an attempt to design a treatment that works specifically for Cecily's cancer and her own unique biochemistry. He seems appalled that individualized treatment is so hard to come by at large institutions, and that patients who don't fit the profile for clinical trials are left, by and large, to treatment based more on classes of disease than on individual factors. I think we are fortunate to have him.

Dr. Orr spoke to Dr. Ross and was unable to get Cec's endoscopy scheduled earlier than next week. And then today she began coughing up more blood. So he decided to admit her to the hospital, since in-patients get first call on tests like endoscopies, and he can get her one tomorrow. We put Maddie to bed and then Uncle Russell drove Cec to Good Samaritan Hospital, where she is now. She should have her test in the morning and be home later in the day.

1:00 a.m.

Jim

February 4, 2004

"I will lift up mine eyes to the hills, from whence cometh my help."
                                                        —PSALMS 121:1

Today was one of those rare days in Los Angeles when one could lift up one's eyes to the hills and actually see them. I hope the help of which the psalmist wrote is on its way. We can use it.

Things took a slight downward turn today. Cecily was in the hospital all day for her endoscopy. She does not have an ulcer. She has something not so good as an ulcer. Severe gastritis has left her entire stomach lining, in Cec's word, "shredded." Dr. Orr seems quite concerned about her condition. Cecily is unable to digest her food and though she hasn't eaten in a couple of days, food's still sitting in her stomach. Dr. Orr believes this condition somehow relates to the likely viral cause of Cec's cancer. He's asserted and reasserted that the kind of cancer Cec has doesn't spread to the stomach. But her weakened immune system may have allowed a viral or bacteriological infection to wreak havoc on her stomach. If it's bacteriological, I would think that it should respond quickly to antibiotics. If it's viral, then who knows? I've not had a chance to talk to Dr. Orr. Apparently, he gave Cecily a lot of information, though she didn't (or wasn't able to) relay it to me. I have not seen her today. Having expected her test to be done by midday, I also expected to bring her home this afternoon. But things took so long she couldn't come home tonight. So Maddie and I are here alone again, and Cec is at Good Sam, really alone. Tomorrow Dr. Orr wants to give her another CT scan. I don't think this is related to her stomach problem. I think he figures that as long as she's in the hospital, he might as well find out how the tumor's doing. (This is all guesswork on my part.)

Cecily's in severe pain tonight. Her stomach hurts her a lot, even with the medication that worked so well the other night. Her neck and back are out again, a result of being in bed continuously for the past two days, she thinks. When I spoke to her last, about 11:00 p.m., she was about to get some additional pain treatment. She sounded spirited but very uncomfortable.

Maddie had a mixed day. She's had meltdowns at therapy two days in a row. It's clear that the rapidly shifting ground is unnerving her and either causing or exacerbating her emotional uproar. This is a little girl who scarcely ever cried in her first two years, who never had a hysterical moment. I don't mean that she was abnormally unaffected by things, but that she was mellow. Man, was this kid mellow. These meltdowns (I can't call them tantrums, because there's almost no anger evident in them—just fear and sadness) began within two weeks of our move to the temporary house and within a week of Cecily's diagnosis. It's certain, of course, that she's a two-year-old and that this sort of thing has been known to happen with two-year-olds. But today was a day in which she seemed to spend as much time hysterical as she spent being calm and happy. It's exhausting to her, and I feel as if I've fallen down a particularly nasty rabbit hole. My heart breaks into powdered glass to hear her cry so piteously. At the same time, I want to jump in my car and drive to Manitoba. Nonetheless, if Maddie and Cec are trying to get rid of me, they're going to have to try harder than this.

This is our nineteenth year together. Our fifteenth wedding anniversary is in May. Cec's birthday is Friday. Valentine's Day is next week. I want her home. I want her next to me. It doesn't matter that we sometimes fight like the crassest of teenagers. It doesn't matter that I find her devoid of logic and that she finds me devoid of, oh, so very, very much. She's my girl, and I hurt to have her away from me. Our daughter doesn't like it much, either.

I'd better go to bed before I do irreparable damage to whatever's left of my tough ex-Marine, hard-as-nails image. Okay, who laughed? Come on, who was it?

11:59 p.m.

Jim

February 5, 2004

Cecily's still in the hospital. Her CT scan was scheduled for this morning but it was nearly 9:00 p.m. before she got it. In the meantime, she lay in the hospital alone for half the day with severe stomach pain and nausea.

I went to the hospital and sat with her for four or five hours. She kept calling and paging Dr. Orr, and I waited and waited, hoping either the doctor would show up or the scan would happen. Neither occurred. Cec and I had some good quiet time together, but not long after I got there they gave her a medication for nausea. Within one minute, she'd gone into a near-stupor, slurring her words and barely able to keep her eyes open. She was that way the rest of the time I was there.

I knew that I'd be filming tomorrow, on location up in the mountains northeast of Los Angeles and that in all likelihood I'd need to leave for work before dawn. Which meant that I needed to be home in time to learn my lines and arrange for someone to be with Maddie. So around 6:30 tonight I reluctantly left the hospital.

When I got home, Cec called and said that Dr. Orr had finally come. An hour or so later, she had the CT scan. I talked to Cec again after Maddie went to sleep, around 10:00 p.m. Dr. Orr had seen the CT scan and compared it to the previous scan in order to determine whether there'd been any change in tumor size.

But he wasn't able to tell, because Cec has pneumonia and her lungs are too full of fluid to allow a good visual of the tumor.

Pneumonia. I don't know how serious it is, but I suspect Cec won't be coming home tomorrow. As to how they are going to treat this, or her stomach problem, I don't know. I've wanted badly to talk with Dr. Orr, but have only been able to get secondhand reports, mainly from Cec, who was groggy during most of them.

This is a heck of a time to be out of touch, as I will be tomorrow. There's no avoiding it, though. The life of a character actor pays well—*on the days he works.* But it's dreadfully irregular and unpredictable and we're in no position now to wave off any income. So as deeply as it pains me to be away for the day, I will be. We're way up in the mountains shooting, far from cell phone coverage. So getting word from back in civilization will be arduous and require information to be relayed. I'll certainly be back home by early evening, but I'm not happy about being so difficult to reach.

Cec is in good hands, though. Mark and Russell and Alice and our dear friend Bridget Hanley have all promised to be on top of the situation and ready to provide any service needed.

I should have been in bed long ago, considering when I have to get up for the sixty-mile drive to work. I'm in the last shot of the last day of shooting on the last episode of the season of *Deadwood*, and I gotta get some sleep beforehand.

Pneumonia. Criminy. Let's crank up the volume on the prayers and humming, okay?

12:09 a.m.

Jim

February 6, 2004. Cecily's birthday.

Cec spent her birthday in the hospital, and she's still there. She has a fever, and while not seriously high, it is enough that they wanted to keep her another night. She's happy about that, as Dr. Orr's out of town and she's nervous about going home and having only an untrained amateur (me) to tend her. As I've said for several days now, she should be home tomorrow. She's feeling achy from the fever. Other than that, she made no complaints to me. Though it was her birthday, I didn't get to see her once today.

12:30 a.m.

Jim

February 7, 2004

Saturday. Cecily's still in the hospital. She'll be there until at least Monday. She's still running a fever, but she's getting heavy doses of antibiotics to fight the pneumonia.

She's extremely uncomfortable. The fever gives her flulike aches and chills. Her stomach is painful and uneasy. The pain from the cancer in her bones is increasing. She's quite miserable and terribly unhappy and scared.

I have not seen her since Thursday. Today Maddie and I were alone together for the entire day, except for when I took her to a birthday party at a nearby park and a couple of times when friends dropped by. She had a wonderful day, which not everyone who's spent a day alone with me can say. But with my duties with Maddie, there was no practical way to get to the hospital to see Cec. I'm unwilling to take Maddie into a hospital unnecessarily, and Cec won't stand for my bringing her to the neighborhood in which Good Samaritan is located.

I miss her. I feel impotent and angry at this disease, this fluke, this chance mutation that has thrown a multispiked monkey wrench into a rich and lovely life. And I'm so afraid.

But as my comrade Tom says, we "soldier on," right foot after left, cursing the mud that sucks at our feet to drag us down, and praying that our steps lead us out of and not deeper into the valley of the shadow.

I'm all in. Now I get to lie next to my daughter and dream of lying next to her mother. Sweet dreams.

11:57 p.m.

Jim

February 8, 2004

Cecily remains in Good Samaritan Hospital. I didn't see her again today. I haven't seen her in three days—a thoroughly disturbing fact. I'd planned to see her today, but Cec preferred that I stay with Maddie. So I stayed home. Maddie and I have had a couple of terrific days together—lots of fun for me and, I think, for her as well. But she misses her mommy and so do I.

I'll have Maddie to myself again tomorrow. As happy and content as she's been the past few days, that's no problem at all.

Cec's hospital room and our house are full of birthday flowers and cards. Thanks from her to all of you.

11:22 p.m.

Jim

February 9, 2004

I finally saw Cec at the hospital tonight. It was a short visit, as she'd been doped up with painkillers and she fell asleep within minutes of my arrival.

Dr. Orr visited her earlier in the evening. They've determined that Cec has pericarditis, an inflammation of the heart lining. There's a considerable buildup of fluid around her heart (pericardial effusion). Tomorrow they will do an EKG and an EEG to determine the exact status, and then perform a pericardiocentesis, in which a needle is inserted into the heart lining and fluid is drawn off. Whether there's a causal relationship between the pneumonia and the pericarditis, I can't say. Once again, I've only been able to get my information from a woozy Cecily.

The rest of the day was uneventful. Maddie had her therapy sessions. I dropped in on the wrap party for *Deadwood* but couldn't divest myself of the elephant, who followed me in and inserted himself into every conversation. I thought the party would be a fun diversion, but all I could think about was Cecily. I want my girl back home, and I want her well. I've gotten about everything I've ever wanted. Why can't I get that?

2:37 a.m.

Jim

February 10, 2004

Cec is still in the hospital and will definitely remain there at least through Thursday. She had her EKG and EEG today. Detailed results aren't known, but the pericardiocentesis was put off. Evidence suggests Cec doesn't have a serious infection causing her pneumonia, but rather a comparatively tame infection.

I finally got to spend some real time with Cec. I was there all afternoon. We had a good time together. The visit almost didn't happen, as there was a new emergency just as I was walking out the door to go to the hospital. Cec's dad, who was staying at a hotel while repairs were being made to his condo, accidentally started a fire in his room. As I understand it, he awoke to a substantial blaze and fell getting out of bed. He got a good dose of smoke, but after the paramedics arrived and took him to the hospital emergency room, it seemed that he was in good shape, all things considered. The last I heard, they were observing him for a while and then sending him home.

That all sounds mild, but it didn't seem that way at first. I got a call from my commercial agent, who's also Don's. The agent had been called by the hotel in search of a family member. I was the only contact the agent had. Unfortunately, the hotel manager didn't have a lot of information, other than that there'd been a fire and the paramedics had taken him to the hospital. She told me which hospital, but she was wrong and it took me an hour to find out where he was.

By then, though, I'd put Cec's sister Stacey and her husband, Pascal, onto the situation. Poor Stacey. It's not enough that her sister's terribly ill and her brother has swelling in his brain causing seizures, all just as she takes on a complicated and demanding new job. Now her dad has another accident, which, if nothing else, scares the wits out of her. I've gotten a lot of commendation and encouragement and kind words from people during this journey, but that's due in major part to the fact that I tell people about it every night. I find the ordeal Stacey's going through to be every bit as difficult and traumatizing and more heroic than my experience. If she had my dual talents for self-promotion and logorrhea, she'd have metric tons more respect and approbation than I've gotten. Stacey's a brick. She's the best.

Ed Asner called from the set of *The Practice* to put me on the phone with a friend who had some suggestions for powerful cancer-fighting herbal supplements. I was touched by the willingness of Ed's friend to participate in our crisis, and by Ed's tireless efforts to support us. Ed's a brick, too, and possessed of one of the great good hearts in human history. He's a little right-wing for my taste, but I love him nonetheless.

11:59 p.m.

Jim

February 11, 2004

Long day, this one. Lots of turns and detours.

I went to the hospital around 2:00 p.m. for Cec's pericardiocentesis, but they took her down earlier than expected, and I missed her. I feel bad, because I know how scared Cec gets and how much she hates being alone during any important procedure. But Kitty Swink was with her when they came to take her to the procedure room, so she wasn't completely alone. Finally, around 6:00 p.m., they called me down to the recovery room. Kitty went home and I went down to the third floor to be with Cec.

Cec was woozy from anesthesia and could barely stay awake. One of her doctors talked to me about the pericardiocentesis. He said the fluid drawn off Cec's heart was clear instead of bloody. He said that was unusual and he didn't know what to make of it. The lab will analyze the fluid to see what information there is to be gleaned from it.

Tom Allard, Drew Katzman, and Teresa Jones all dropped by CSU to see Cec, and I was surprised we were all allowed to stay. I'd been told that not even I would be allowed in with her. We hung out there until 9:30, at which time I headed home to put Maddie to bed. Drew brought his sleeping bag and planned on camping out in the waiting room overnight, in case Cec needed anything. Cool friends we got.

1:36 a.m.

Jim

February 12, 2004

Cecily's still in the cardiothoracic surgery unit (CSU) in the ICU at Good Samaritan. She was to have the pericardiocentesis drainage tube removed from her chest today, but in the twenty-four hours since the procedure, over a hundred more cc's of fluid had drained out (four or five ounces), so Dr. Guy Mayeda, the thoracic surgeon, opted to leave the drain tube in for another night. I arrived at the hospital just before they were to take the tube out, and Cec was nervous and frightened. She asked for a good deal of sedation before the removal, and, boy, did they give it to her. She calmed down and then went out to dreamland. Then they decided not to take the tube out. They did, however, remove the vein catheter she's had in her arm since October. They suspect it may be the source of her fever, as these catheters (called PICC lines) often get infected. They put her on a regular IV and sent the PICC line to the lab to be tested for infection. They may put another one in at the time of her next chemo.

Her chemo was supposed to be today, but has to be postponed until she's in better shape. Another development is that the fluid drawn from the pericardiocentesis is being analyzed for cancer cells. If it contains cancer cells, they will be treated with a wide variety of chemo drugs to see which ones are most effective in stopping the cell growth. As a result, Dr. Orr may be able to switch to a chemo regimen *proven* to be effective against Cec's specific cancer.

More details emerged regarding Cec's dad's accident. As I understand it, Don fell and couldn't get up and fell asleep on the floor. He then awoke to his bed going up in flames from a fire caused by a shirt hanging too close to a lightbulb. If he hadn't fallen, he would have been in that bed. The docs say he doesn't show any soot in his lungs, but he does have pneumonia, which is the actual source of his breathing difficulty. He'll be in the hospital another few days.

It's getting easier to count the members of Cec's family who *aren't* in the hospital than to count the ones who are.

10:28 p.m.

Jim

February 13, 2004

I spent most of the day at the hospital with Cec. She was scheduled to have this opening made in her pericardium to allow constant fluid drainage without a tube, and she was extremely nervous. She was working herself up into a mild panic by the time I got there. Fortunately, four doctors in succession (Dr. Orr among them) came in and each explained the procedure. Cec responds well to reasoned explanation—or at least she does if the explainer has enough letters after his name. From me, she responds . . . less well. Cec calmed down after talking with Dr. Orr. Dr. Mayeda, who performed the procedure, told me afterward that all had gone well.

Just to make clear: Cec got a rather common buildup of fluid around the heart, as a result of inflammation of the pericardium by random cancer cells. The drainage and the pericardial "window" installed today should cure that problem permanently. Cec has pneumonia and a lingering infection—probably from the catheter in her arm these past four months—but both are responding well to treatment. *None* of these situations is life-threatening with the treatment she's received. Most of the pain and fever and lethargy and tremors and shortness of breath she's been experiencing are due to one or more of these *non*-life-threatening problems and not to the cancer. In all likelihood, once the pneumonia and infection are gone, Cec will be back on her feet and as active as she was two or three weeks ago. That is to say, tired, achy, in pain from her bones, but able to walk and get around and climb the stairs and conduct business and boss me around. I've gotten the impression that some people think she's on her last legs, and that's absolutely *not* the case. She has no organ failure nor, for that matter, any organ metastases. And her new chemotherapy regimen clearly shows signs of halting the advance of the cancer. And we are barely at the beginning of this fight. In the upcoming weeks, more specific chemo agents will likely be revealed, agents that target Cecily's specific tumor cells rather than generic tumor cells. And new drugs are on the way within days, including the new cancer drug Erbitux that put Martha Stewart in the headlines. We have reason to expect that the new chemo in combination with a cocktail of nonchemo drugs such as Erbitux will put Cec into remission, and that remission will last long enough for her to benefit from even newer drugs that are not far down the approval pipeline. I want to encourage everyone to recognize that this fight has only begun and has a long, long way to go. Nobody's on their "last legs" around here.

Cec's dad remains hospitalized—stable, but still being treated for his own pneumonia. Cec's brother Sean, who had another seizure the other night, is back home again from the hospital. They don't yet know what's causing the swelling in Sean's brain, but it's beginning to seem like there might be a small, deep tumor.

Ida comes tomorrow. Ida Lee, if I haven't described her before, was Cecily's childhood nanny. She's like a second mother to Cec, and in fact, she's like a second mother to everyone she meets. She's a little bowlegged fireplug with more energy than any other five people I know. She's about seventy (I don't think even she knows for sure), but to see her run around the house cleaning and cooking and handling babies and gardening and mowing the lawn, you'd think she was a twenty-five-year-old on speed. She is, in Cec's words, "pure love." I love her as much as anyone I have ever known, and not just because she makes my life incredibly easier when she's here. She lifts spirits wherever she goes. Ida lives in Maryland, where Cec grew up, and she tends her own extended family tirelessly. But when Cec has needed her, she's dropped everything and come to California. She spent two weeks with us right after Maddie was born, and I don't know how anyone copes with a newborn without an Ida. She was also here last summer, when we were so wrecked by Maddie's autism diagnosis. And though she's recovering from knee problems and surgeries, she's coming back to us for a whole month starting tomorrow. For a week now, Cec and I have been cheering each other up by saying, "Ida's coming Saturday!" I can't tell you how grateful I am to her, and to her family for giving her up. I know that it's a real sacrifice for her husband, Steve, and the kids and grandkids. But it will make a real difference in Cecily's spirits. And I guarantee you it will make a difference in mine.

12:28 a.m.

Jim

February 14, 2004. Valentine's Day.

I picked up our wonderful Ida at the airport and brought her to the hospital. Cecily's spirits soared when she saw her, just as I knew they would.

I got to kiss Cec's forehead and tell her how much I love her, and that was about it for Valentine's Day. Not exactly dinner on a moonlit balcony overlooking the Amalfi Coast, but we take what we can get these days.

2:32 a.m.

Jim

February 15, 2004

After taking Maddie to her Sunday-morning pony ride, I went to the hospital to see Cec. We had a good time together alone, although she's in great pain. She made some jokes and shot down some of mine, so she must be a little better. It's so weird. She looks normal and healthy, yet she feels just awful. She's still a bit discombobulated by the painkillers. She asked when they were going to take the tube out of her chest. I said, "Yesterday." She was surprised and had to look, to see if I was telling the truth.

Cec's brother, Sean, came up to see her today. She loved having him visit. They have more in common these days than ever before. I'm just sorry that ill health and fear are the most prominent of those commonalities.

11:40 p.m.

Jim

February 16, 2004

The rumor mill's grinding away at top speed, it seems. Time for me to set a few things straight.

1. Cec is doing well. She's feeling lousy, because she's got bone pain that she's not yet been able to have radiated, and she sometimes seems a little delirious because her pain medication and her nausea medication make her woozy. But none of these are indications of her survival capabilities or of her longevity. Having recently heard a number of people, directly or indirectly, talking about her situation as though it were tenuous, as though she were close to giving up the fight, I asked her tonight if she had any inclination toward giving up. She said, emphatically, "No!" She said that what she's dealing with at present is, in her words, no worse than someone who's been in a car wreck and broken both legs. It feels awful, but nobody gives up and wants to die because of it. I asked her if she was tired of the fight. She said sure she was, the same way she was tired of getting up at 4:00 a.m. to make Maddie a bottle. It's exhausting, but you still do it. This girl's nowhere near quitting. And it won't help her if she thinks anyone thinks she ought to quit.

    And there's no reason for anyone to think that. I asked Dr. Orr tonight if he was anywhere near giving up on Cec, and he guffawed. Dr. Orr, I should make clear, is a soft-spoken man whom I've never heard chuckle out loud. When he's cracking up, he only smiles. And he guffawed when I asked him that. He said, "Good lord, no, we're just getting started. The things we've just begun using are already showing promise, and in the next couple of weeks we're going to have some wonderful new tools. And we're growing Cecily's cancer cells in the lab and will be able to develop drug combinations to specifically target Cecily's cancer. We're nowhere near giving up."

Let me be clear. Cecily has not been in the hospital for the past twelve days because of the cancer, per se, nor because any part of her body is shutting down. She has no sign of tumors in any of her organs. She's in the hospital because she had a couple of peripheral problems that were side effects of either the cancer or her treatment. To put it another way, the car was in the shop because of a couple of blown tires and another that was about to blow. The rest of the car, while it may have some long-term problems, runs fine.

2. The procedure involving the fluid around Cecily's heart was, contrary to some stories that have been floating around, completely successful. Furthermore, the problem is resolved and is no longer a matter of concern. The doctors fixed the pericardial sac around Cec's heart so that fluid couldn't build up there. The fluid now drains harmlessly into the chest cavity where it's reabsorbed into the body. Cec *never* needs to worry about this problem again.

3. The pneumonia's almost gone. One can never be certain, but it seems likely that it developed as a result of an infection in Cecily's vein catheter. These vein catheters almost always develop infections, and it was way past time for hers to be removed. It has been removed, the infection source is gone, and the antibiotics Cec has been taking have almost wiped out the infection and the pneumonia. Dr. Orr expects her to be off the antibiotics tomorrow.

4. There's some fluid buildup under her lungs, but not enough to be of concern. It is *not* life-threatening.

5. Cec will be coming home from the hospital in the next day or two—not because there's "nothing more that can be done for her," but because she's not all that sick, and Dr. Orr thinks she'd be better off up and around than lying in

bed all day. Granted, she feels crummy, but most of that relates to bone pain that will, once she's up and around, be treated and presumably palliated by radiation.

6. Her stomach is responding to treatment. She's eating food instead of relying on intravenous nourishment. She's not complaining, at least to me, nearly as much about nausea or stomach pain.

I wanted to click off these items, because I sensed a growing (and unnecessary) concern among many of Cec's friends and family that her situation might be becoming more grave. That's not the case. And I wanted to halt any increased fears in that regard, not only because people shouldn't worry unnecessarily, but also because Cecily's sense of confidence and well-being is unfortunately easily swayed by her sense of what other people think. If she gets the notion that people around her have, however inaccurately, decided that she's no longer benefiting from treatment or is otherwise headed for the last roundup, she will suffer greatly. As I've said before, her determination is phenomenally strong, and it's completely self-empowered. But her confidence, on the other hand, bends and sways (and might break) with every breeze of other people's opinions. She has a radar ear for the note of hopelessness. Neither she nor I is interested in false hope, but we've not come anywhere near running out of true hope. I am convinced that whether she's at home or in the hospital, she is surrounded by angels of mercy, both earthly and heavenly. But I am also convinced that none of those heavenly angels is calling her home yet.

I won't lie to you people. If I tell you this hospitalization is but a ripple in an otherwise encouraging process, it's because that is the case. Despite the fact that she has a dangerous disease, she's still in the thick of a promising battle, one with tough odds, but one she has more weapons to fight than many people get. Please know that if the time comes when she clearly is fighting a losing and torturous battle, we will stack our arms and make her comfortable. But don't anybody suggest to her that day has come.

Except for a fifteen-minute break at 8:30 a.m. when Maddie awoke and I turned her over to Ida and Maribel, I slept straight from 2:00 a.m. to 4:15 p.m.—fourteen hours. Funny thing is, I could do it again.

1:33 a.m.

Jim

February 17, 2004

There was much to write about today. A lot of turns of events, a lot of emotion, a lot of stuff worth mentioning.

And I just can't do it. After three hours of trying to get Maddie to sleep, I'm just clobbered, and I have to sleep.

Suffice it to say that Cec's MRI today showed no spread of cancer to her brain—always a worry with lung cancer. She's feeling just lousy, but at the same time, better.

From a diminishing vocabulary of two words last August, Maddie, according to her speech therapist, now has the vocabulary of a four- or five-year-old. Since she's only two and a half, that's pretty good news. That's all I can get written tonight. I gotta get some sleep.

Funny how short a time that fourteen-hour nap sufficed.

12:37 a.m.

Jim

February 18, 2004

Cec's sister Carolyn ("Big Sister" to one and all—"Aunt Big Sister" to her nieces and nephews) had flown in from Hawaii and was at the hospital with her daughter, Rebecca, when I arrived. Cec was in dis-comfort, but her spirits were higher than usual, and with the bright spots that are Carolyn and Rebecca around us, my spirits rose, too. After they left, Cec and I spent some time together. Today was the first time since she's been hospitalized that she said she was ready to go home. This is a good sign, because before now, she's always said she felt too sick to go home. She's weak in her muscles and having a lot of back and chest pain, but she's also more energetic and clearheaded.

Have I mentioned the wonderful thing being done by our friend Glenn Morshower? Glenn is an actor of uncommon prolificity and he's been close to Cec's heart longer than I've known her. Glenn is a dynamic and motivational spirit who energizes anyone who comes into his sphere. He has, for some time now, been doing seminars at colleges and acting schools, talking about the audition process for actors and how they can invigorate and empower their work, their employability, and their daily lives. He's put together a special edition of his seminar as a benefit for Cecily, to help offset the costs associated with her ill-ness and hospitalization. Glenn has spent two or three seasons on the show 24 as the head Secret Service guy. You'd also recognize him as the sheriff on *CSI* and as the national security adviser on *The West Wing*, among a hundred other things. Glenn has arranged for three of the stars of 24 to join him in this benefit, which takes place this Sunday, February 22. I got a call today from my home theatre, Theatre West, which is hosting the event, informing me that the event is sold out. This is all pretty amazing. Only seven months ago, Cecily joined Glenn at the same theatre, doing a similar benefit, as a fund-raiser for our nanny Maribel's husband, Mario, who also has cancer.

I've got to sleep. Cec keeps telling me, "That baby needs one func-tioning parent." And I keep telling myself that as ill-functioning as I feel, I'm not the one on the fuzzy end of the lollipop.

12:23 a.m.

Jim

February 19, 2004

Cec had an uncomfortable night. Dr. Orr came by at 5:00 a.m.(!) and ordered an increase in her pain medication. Later, when Cec came back from her procedure (having a new drug-introduction catheter, a VAP, installed), she was in tremendous pain in her chest and back. Her nurse had trouble turning on the IV machine controlling her pain medication, and when it was finally operating, the dosage was set too low. Cec asked for an increase to the level Dr. Orr had ordered, but the nurse said that there was no such order in Cec's chart. She lay there for several hours in great pain, far exceeding anything I've seen her suffer for any length of time. Despite pleas to the nursing staff and calls to Dr. Orr, no substantial changes were made in her medication levels until tonight. Cec consistently described her pain level as 8 on a scale of 1 to 10, 10 being the worst.

At one point I held her hand and began to cry for her, but she ordered me to stop because my crying made her cry, and her head ached and she had difficulty breathing if she cried. So I pretended I wasn't crying. We went through the same routine late tonight on the telephone.

She's terrified of her illness, but she's so brave. Down the halls of the hospital roll the moans and sobs of other patients. But Cec never whimpers. She may cry out at a sudden jolt when she's being helped up, but she doesn't whine. She's suffering more today than I've ever seen her suffer, suffering not silently, but bravely and strongly.

There have been moments in the past day or two, despite all the promising aspects of this case, that have been as dark and disconsolate as anything in my life. Some of it relates to my down-but-not-out fears of losing her, and much of it relates to seeing her in pain. If she were to get well next week, she'd still be in torment tonight, and the pain and pity and impotence I feel torment me as well. The loneliness of not being with her, not being able to protect her, not even being able to hug or kiss her envelops me. With all the thousands upon thousands of people suffering from this disease, how can I find her pain and mine so surprising, so unexpected? How can we not all know about this stuff on a daily basis, if so many go through it? Are we all really so isolated from the trauma and torment around us? People in my own family have gone through this. I've sat by the deathbeds of friends who lived every moment of this. Yet this is all so utterly unexpected and so much more than I believed it could be. It's like having lived all one's life in a cavern, only to have the harsh light of a thousand suns blasted in upon you. Except this light is dark, pitch-dark, and throbs rather than pierces. How can I not have known what so many people have gone through? The only answer I can conjure is that a kind Providence keeps us blind to the intensity of suffering so as to keep us sane, until that day when the suffering is our own or that of someone we love beyond imagining.

Psychobabbling. I don't know what I'm talking about. I'm just fumbling with the keyboard trying to write something that's not only unwritable but inexpressible. Nothing I write comes near to what lies tonight at the bottom of my heart.

I pray, I pray, I pray that Cec feels better with the morning light. I'm sure she will. It's not that her pain is increasing, but that it was allowed to get ahead of her medication. An improvement in the medication will reduce her distress. But it's a dreadful thing to go through in the meantime, and a dreadful thing to watch.

Our three-ring circus of sorrow goes on. Cec's brother Sean had a multiple biopsy of his brain today, in the hopes that a reason for his seizures and cerebral swelling can be uncovered. He came through the exploration well but conclusions cannot be drawn until the biopsy results are available next week. And Cec's dad had an MRI and a biopsy of his throat today. His pneumonia seems about the same, but he's sleeping far too much, the doctors believe.

This is a sad state of affairs. I'm not going to send this tumbling further down the chute of depression by elaborating about my own dad, other than to say that nothing has changed. That's depressing enough.

I'm sorry to be so grim and glum tonight. There are many blessings to be grateful for, and exciting and promising possibilities in the near future. But the emotion of the day was overwhelmingly sad, and it's hard to be as cheerful as those blessings and possibilities warrant, when hurt is so abundant.

Mark Sobel picked up Cec's three targeted cancer drugs today. A month's supply of each. Total cost after insurance: $1,086.10. Thank God I have insurance to cover the other 75 percent.

Pray, hum, and give a ferocious hug to the ones you love most. You never know when you might want that hug with all your soul, and not be able to give it or get it.

1:52 a.m.

Jim

February 20, 2004

Cecily felt much better all day. Dr. Orr visited her and chastised her for having the nurses cut back on her pain meds. It seems Cec was concerned about becoming addicted to the morphine, and about being non compos mentis from the drugs. So she had told the nurses to reduce her painkillers, which allowed the pain to build to the point where her normal dosage wouldn't allay it. Dr. Orr said something to her that I think no one has ever said to her, or at least gotten away with. He said, "Cecily, you're not in charge anymore. I am." Glad it was he and not me.

My day was a mess, running around all over the San Fernando Valley trying to get things done that no one could do for me. I had to sign documents in front of a notary (including one stating that, as my father was no longer capable of handling his affairs, I was taking over as trustee of his living trust). I dashed about in the rain, trying to get to the notary, to a smog check, and to the DMV before each of them closed. It was frantic and agitating, but I made it. It kept me from seeing Cec, though, until late in the evening. When I did see her, she was full of her normal spark and clearly in less pain than yesterday.

There's still much to pray for, but tonight I go to bed feeling weightless compared to the anvil strapped to my heart last night. We ask for more, but we count our blessings.

1:44 a.m.

Jim

February 21, 2004

I'll be brief.

Cec stayed in the hospital again tonight. She had fluid drained from her chest this afternoon and was feeling pretty rough afterward. She was agitated all day, fretting about the procedure and lots of other things. Ida was there with her throughout the day. Kitty Swink and Dinah Lenney were there, as was Cec's mom and Big Sister Carolyn. Ann Melby arrived in the evening to stay overnight with Cec and allow Ida an "off-duty" night. It's arguable whether Cec will come home tomorrow, simply because it's hard to get anything done on the weekends. I don't know of a medical reason for her not to come home.

2:13 a.m.

Jim

February 22, 2004

No e-mail tonight other than to say that Cec is still in Good Samaritan, having a lot of back and chest pain. We're hoping she'll be home tomorrow (Monday).

I just got back from the benefit at Theatre West, which deserves paragraphs I can't give right now. Suffice it to say that it was wonderful, that love and generosity filled that theatre to bursting, and that Glenn Morshower and his guests and the staff of the theatre are saints, who, I hope, received as much joy in their giving and helpfulness as I did in witnessing it. My one regret was that Cecily couldn't be there to experience it firsthand.

I'll elaborate later. But it's

2:28 a.m.

Jim

February 23, 2004

Cec is home. Can't write tonight. Too busy with her. Also, I spent half the night in the emergency room getting an apparently broken index finger splinted. Not broken, though. Just a little crushed. Note to self: when having trivial but intense argument on the phone with sick spouse and smashing telephone on desktop five or six times, make sure fingers have clearance.

3:29 a.m.

Jim

February 24, 2004

Hard to type with this splint. As Maddie would say, "Silly daddy."

I wanted so for Cec to come home, but it has been nightmarish for her, for me, for Maddie, for Ida, for everyone here. Cec is panicky, desperately fearing, from the moment she left the hospital, that she wasn't getting enough air. Her chest hurts so that she breathes shallowly, and her blood-oxygen saturation hovers around 82 percent without supplemental oxygen. That's where it was all last week, but if she got short of breath in the hospital, she could take oxygen. Once we got home, she began to panic that she wouldn't be able to survive without pure oxygen. Finally, after a few frantic calls, Dr. Orr sent over an oxygen pump, despite his belief that it was not necessary to her physical well-being. She calmed somewhat, though she gets frightened every so often even with the oxygen. Her pain medication's playing badminton with her brain, and everything panics her. She has trouble coming up with the right words and then gets panicky and angry if you can't figure out what she's saying. Last night she kept saying "Chinese food" when she meant "flashlight," and got angry when I couldn't figure out what she wanted. It's a temporary thing, and it's only right after she's awakened. Once she starts getting more radiation, her pain level should diminish and the meds can be cut back. But for now, she's in great discomfort without the trained nursing staff able and available to look out for her needs.

There've been a few times in my life when I was depressed—usually over some girl or, in the early days, over some job I didn't get. But that was simple stuff and it passed quickly. The past few days I've had, for the first time, an inkling of what clinical depression must be like. It's like a fog that settles over you until everything you see seems not just gloomy, but part of the gloom itself. I feel as though I had bags of rocks tied to my shoulders. I want to run, but there's nowhere to run, and I couldn't run anyway. Responsibility and love have unbreakable chains around my legs (though it feels more like my throat). I never dreamed intense love could feel like a burden or a shackle, but it does. This is naked and off-putting stuff, I know, but what's the point of writing these offerings if I'm just going to pretend that we are happy in our gallant march against the foe? What's the point in having truth if you're not going to tell it? But, of course, even now I leave out truths, because some are too painful to tell, some are too painful to hear, and some are too painful to acknowledge.

It's weird—Cecily has moments when, though tired, she functions well. I hear her on the phone trying to do a little work for her job, or talking with a friend. Then she'll hit a rough spot and moan for an hour in pain while Ida or I try to find the sore muscle to massage or help her adjust and readjust on the bed. Then she'll pass through a frantic, hyperfrenetic period of panic or near-hallucination. For now though, she's recuperating from the pneumonia and infections, albeit more slowly than I in my ignorance had anticipated.

My sister Denise, whose stay here for the weekend was a soaring lift to my heart, returned to Arizona yesterday. She makes frequent trips to Texas to look in on my dad, whose spark dwindles imperceptibly every day but never seems quite ready to go out. Cecily's sister Carolyn returned to Hawaii this morning after a brief but wonderful time here. Some people take a lot of light with them when they go, yet seem to leave things brighter nonetheless.

I love my Cecily, with all my heart, even with her head of titanium steel and the bristles that pop out whenever she's in distress or out of a sense of control. I honestly believe I can survive and prosper through whatever challenges this brings to me. Where I am plunged into bleakness and despair is in watching her suffer and knowing that, whatever the outcome, I am powerless either to change her lot or make it easier. Love hurts, man.

1:49 a.m.

Jim

SIX

Freaky day. I was awakened by Ida telling me that Cec was flipping out and calling for me. I arrived at her bedside to find Cec in the midst of a major panic attack. Despite the fact that she was receiving supplemental oxygen, she was convinced that she couldn't breathe and that she was suffocating. She was in excruciating pain but she kept trying to get out of bed, clawing at her chest catheter and trying to rip it out. She was also having trouble talking intelligibly, and it was clear that she was hallucinating somewhat. I tried to get her to take a Xanax for her anxiety, but she refused. Finally she agreed to follow Dr. Orr's recommendation, so we got him on the phone. He ordered her to take three Xanax and come in to the office (she already had an appointment for chemotherapy this afternoon). She took the Xanax and began to breathe more regularly and to lose the near-berserk look in her eyes.

It was a painful ordeal for her to get out of bed. Ida and I gave her a sponge bath and got her dressed and out to the car. Getting her into the car was difficult, as the world's bumpiest ride, the 1997 Ford Explorer, is high off the ground, and her hip's so shot she can't easily climb in. Mark Sobel helped me and we took her to Dr. Orr's office. Ida also came along.

A blood test at Dr. Orr's revealed the true difficulty. I thought, as did Cec, her painkillers were causing her hallucinatory behavior and difficulty speaking coherently. And she's suffered from suffocation-fear panic attacks on and off for years. But it turns out that her red-blood-cell count is way down, which means her brain is getting substantially reduced oxygen. Not reduced enough to cause brain damage, but enough to cause hallucinations, difficulty speaking clearly, and a sense of suffocation. Dr. Orr indicated that her white-cell count was fine and that chemo could proceed. But immediately after the chemo, he wanted her to have a blood transfusion.

Cec was in a new room on the same floor where she'd spent the recent stay at Good Samaritan. She was in horrible pain, the worst I've seen her suffer since the first day she was diagnosed. Every movement was like a knife wound. They gave her increased pain medication, which relieved her somewhat. But Cec has the fortitude of a musk ox when it comes to clinging to consciousness (and control). On numerous occasions I've heard tales of her waking up in the middle of surgery or a root canal. She had enough painkillers, anxiety relievers, and sleep agents to send the Dutch army into a coma, yet she was still tossing about, talking and muttering, and trying floppily to control the scene around her. She got a couple of units of blood. Dr. Orr, witnessing firsthand how difficult it was for her to move, ordered her to remain hospitalized for the foreseeable future, so she can begin her radiation treatment tomorrow at the hospital and not have to travel to and from the hospital every day for the duration of her radiation. Also, her panic attacks and pain can be moderated and observed better if she's there.

I have not told Cecily this news, and don't want her to know it just yet.

Cec's sister Stacey called me tonight to tell me the news regarding their brother's biopsy and the cause of Sean's seizures. He has a malignant brain tumor. It's a stage II glioma, diffused. I don't know much except to say that it's inoperable because it's diffused, apparently meaning that it stretches through various parts of the brain, rather than being a single (possibly removable) mass. Stage II isn't nearly as critical as Cecily's cancer, which is stage IV (meaning it has spread). Sean's doctors feel that the tumor's too small to attack well with radiation, and chemo's not indicated. They believe he can go on with his life, living normally (with antiseizure medication) and being closely monitored. When the tumor grows (and it will, they say) and reaches stage III, it will be more responsive to radiation and/or chemo. It is a slow-growing tumor, and there's more opportunity in Sean's case than in Cecily's for numerous new drugs and techniques to arise to counter the disease. Simply put, Sean has a good deal to be hopeful about, more so (in terms of time for new treatments to develop) than Cec has. I have great confidence in his chances to beat this.

Life in this family is beginning to take on a Jobean aspect, with two fathers near death and two siblings afflicted with deadly diseases. But just to make clear: I do not believe that I, or my family, have a corner on trouble or pain or despair. I am quite aware that the difficulties we face are no more singular or painful than those of thousands or even millions of other families, and I'm especially aware that we are blessed to face those difficulties with resources and help that most people can't imagine.

If I write about my fear and impotence and despair, it's because I need to express it and also because I've discovered that some people place a value on the fact that in doing so, I am doing something that usually isn't done. I didn't start out thinking I was helping anybody with these journal entries, but I'm both surprised and happy to learn that some people think that I am. I'm just trying to recount this experience in my own terms and to be as truthful and as self-revelatory as I can bear to be. I'm not out to convince anyone that I'm the only one who's ever had a hard time of it.

I'm back at the hospital tomorrow. I've got an audition in the late afternoon for a movie. I can't imagine I'll be in position to go off on location for a movie, but I'm trying to change my outlook and not shoot my horse until he actually does go lame.

I'm all for shooting elephants, though. At least this big fella sittin' next to me.

2:27 a.m.

Jim

February 26, 2004

Cecily slept all night and all day. She was twitchy and uneasy through the night, but by morning the painkillers and relaxants had kicked in sufficiently that she slept calmly through the whole day.

While Cec slept, I decided to spend some time with Maddie, whom I've been feeling quite separate from while I run around like a pinball. She's the best. She lifts my spirits so. If I didn't have her, I don't know what I would do.

I'm in bad shape these days. I can maintain the outward appearance of good spirits around others, but alone I keep finding myself sitting and staring at the floor. I've never been one for that sort of behavior, yet I can't find much to steal my attention from my troubles. I can't read or watch TV, even when I have time, without sinking into melancholic rumination. There are blessings abounding, but so little happiness where I am right now, and what happiness there is is diluted by Cecily's absence. What good is happiness if you can't share it? Every minute brings something I want to talk to her about, or show her, or just experience with her. So much of that is of our little girl—the dream of Cecily's life, which she now gets so little chance to experience. The only time Cec smiles anymore is when I tell her of Maddie, and nowadays it's hard for her to lift her face in a smile even for that. What will I do if she doesn't come back to me? What will Maddie do?

How awful this is. How I long for this current situation to reveal itself as a bump in the road that is passed over quickly and without lingering consequences. How I hope for Cec's pain to be controlled or eradicated and her bright wit and twinkling eye to be back in action. She's a tough girl, and I know she has lots of fight left in her, so it's a shame to see her so quelled by pain and by medication that leaves her either asleep or delirious. I miss her laugh. She's got a great laugh.

2:28 a.m.

Jim

February 27, 2004

Today, Friday, Cecily slept all day and night again. I went to an audition, for a show called *Crossing Jordan*. I don't think I got the job.

They didn't start Cec's radiation today, much to my chagrin. Bureaucracies. They did a CT scan in order to pinpoint the areas most in need of radiation, but even that wouldn't have happened if Mark Sobel hadn't pretended to be a doctor and called Radiology and told them to come pick up Cec. None of it happened fast enough for Cec to make it to radiation therapy today—and that means Monday at the earliest.

I fell apart this evening. I was on the verge anyway, but Cec's associate at work, G. Charles Wright, delivered a package from a little girl who had acted in an episode of *That '70s Show*. The little girl wrote in a kindergarten scrawl how sorry she was that Cec was sick and that she loved her and prayed for her and was sending a dollar to help pay for her medicine. She also sent a little plastic tiara for Cec to wear "so she could feel like a queen." I'm coming apart again thinking about it.

That's all. I haven't got the steam for more.

12:54 a.m.

Jim

February 28, 2004

Saturday. Hard news today. Cecily has pneumonia again. There's a good chance that it was caused by her aspirating liquid (water going down the wrong pipe). If so, then it may be milder than the previous case. But she's on antibiotics again, and she's been moved to the ICU. She's still asleep, though she's roused herself a few times just long enough to yank out her catheters. She now sleeps with her arms in restraints.

Mark Sobel came to the house with Cec's mom to watch Maddie while I went to the hospital. I think it was the first time he'd been away from the hospital since Wednesday, and he went right back after I came home. Ida has been there all this time, too. As difficult as it is for someone to be with Cec around the clock, it's even more difficult in the ICU. Special permission was granted by Dr. Orr for me, Ida, and/or Mark to be there continuously, but there are just two chairs and no cot available. So Ida and Mark are sitting up in chairs all night tonight. Mark looks like roadkill after his days and nights there, but Ida the Magnificent (who's got twenty-five years on Mark!) looks and acts as though she just got up from the best night's sleep of her life. She's a miracle.

Besides Mark and Cec's mom, today I had the priceless help of Uncle Russell and the ubiquitous Ann Melby, without whom I might never get a shower anymore. (I don't mean she gives them to me, I mean she often watches Maddie while I'm taking one.) I had a great time with Maddie, but it's hard to do anything else when alone with her. She's just not quite old enough to leave to her own devices. Thanks to good friends, I feel a bit less gritty.

I'm hoping tomorrow brings nothing more unusual than a Sunday-morning pony ride and the Oscars. If it does bring something more unusual, I hope it's good unusual.

Big prayers and hums tonight.

1:13 a.m.

Jim

February 29, 2004

Maybe the worst day of them all.

It didn't start out that way. Maddie and I got up early, played till noon, went for a pony ride at the Studio City farmers' market, and then for a four-hour walk (she was in the stroller) around the local neighborhoods. Russell went to the hospital to bring Ida home for the first time in three or four days. The ubiquitous Ann Melby came over to help me watch Maddie and the Academy Awards. And Ida, instead of taking a nap after sitting up for days on end in a chair in ICU, ran around, cleaning house and cooking Maddie's dinner.

Then the phone calls started. I'd had a couple of calls earlier in the day and everything seemed to be going well, under the circumstances. But around 7:00 p.m., I got a call from Mark. He said that Cec was having trouble breathing. The nurse got on the line to get my authorization to temporarily put Cec on a ventilator. Both Mark and I were astonished and upset that they would have to get my permission to keep her breathing. (More about that later.) I told them to do whatever they had to do and then headed for the hospital, leaving Maddie with Ann and the now-napping Ida.

What was haphazardly presented to me was that after draining the fluid from Cecily's chest, the lung now had room to expand fully. But occasionally this re-expansion happens too fast, triggering a moistening of the lung tissue (don't ask me why). This moistening interferes with the lung's ability to transmit oxygen. Cec's blood/oxygen level had dropped precipitously. The danger was that in her anesthetized state, Cec's breathing apparatus might grow tired from exertion and oxygen depletion and give up. The remedy was to put her on a ventilator to do the breathing for her long enough for the problem to be corrected—a fairly easy fix which is scheduled for tomorrow (Monday) morning. Once fixed, her oxygen levels should be maintained by her own breathing and she could be removed from the ventilator.

Of course, I heard they wanted to put Cec on a ventilator and I catastrophized immediately. Laypersons usually only know about ventilators as some sort of last resort. This was not the kind of usage of a ventilator that Cec needed. She really just needed something else to take over her breathing for a while so she could rest and get her lung back into shape.

I called Dr. Orr, who explained that her condition was a serious one, but one he expected would be quickly resolved.

At the hospital, seeing Cec was something out of a loved one's worst nightmares. She was unconscious, strapped down, writhing, with tubes and hoses extending either out of her or into her from every direction. She's gotten swollen from anemia and malnutrition. She has enormous ugly sores on her tongue from breathing open-mouthed for several days. About a liter and a half of fluid had been drained from her chest (those big plastic soda bottles are two liters). Her eyes were slightly open and dull. She looked like someone on the absolute verge of death, and I was staggered. The knowledge that she was not actually on the verge of death did only a little to assuage my feelings. It was the unhappiest sight of my life, and I've seen some stuff.

Mark told me that he had been alone in the room with Cec when he noticed she was gasping for each breath. He saw that her oxygen level was abnormally low. He called for a nurse and when one didn't arrive in timely fashion, he began squeezing the inflating bag connected to Cec's oxygen mask, in an effort to get her more air. A nurse saw him doing so and came in and took over, using a hand-held pump. Only then did a team assemble to see what was going on. I still don't quite understand the details of what happened next, but there was apparently an argument over whether Mark had the authority to request that resuscitation efforts (the ventilator) be made. Technically, Mark, not a family member, has no say over Cec's treatment. Legally, with Cec unconscious, he can't force or prevent any action by the medical team, even if I, as next of kin, cannot be located. But aside from the authority issue, the regulations mandate that *all* resuscitation efforts be made when proper, *unless* there's an order from either Cec or me stating that such efforts should *not* be made. There never should have been a question or a moment's delay in regard to taking all proper steps to keep Cec breathing. With there being no instructions to the contrary, the staff should have ventilated Cec immediately, rather than arguing with Mark and spending time tracking me down by phone to authorize the procedure. I was told later that the problem lay with a nurse who was not a regular in that department and who got things backward. I was also told that the particular nurse and that particular problem had been "dealt with." It turned out not to be a disaster, but it certainly could have been.

Dr. Orr arrived and assessed the situation. X-rays taken after the ventilator was applied showed that the lung situation was beginning to clear up, and by morning they should be able to take her off it. But Cec's blood count is abnormally low, just days after her transfusion, and Dr. Orr's convinced that her ulcer has rebloomed and is bleeding. So tonight she got several more units of blood as well as a platelet transfusion. That, combined with tripling the dosage on her ulcer medication, should, Dr. Orr believes, alleviate the problem.

We talked together for some time and he made two things clear: one, that the current situation is quite serious and could pose an immediate danger to Cec's life, even though it's all only peripherally related to her cancer; and two, that all of these peripheral and serious problems are reversible. He said that if no new problems crop up, then the ulcer, the breathing problem, and the pneumonia will all be eliminated. The real danger for Cec's condition is that a new peripheral problem will arise while she's in a weakened state, and then another. A cascade of peripheral problems could prevent any of them being sufficiently treated to eliminate the threat to her overall health. So we have to pray that nothing new rears its head. If nothing does, then in a couple of days, Dr. Orr can go back to treating the cancer and not the mess it's making all around itself.

There were a couple of times today when I thought this was the day Cec would die. The phone calls I got relating to the ventilator sounded so much like utter catastrophe that I feared she would be gone before I could get there. And seeing her trussed up, bloated, thrashing, gurgling, with at least six tubes plugged into her body, I couldn't avoid the feeling that she might be taking her last breaths. But oftentimes the appearance of a patient at such a time is misleading to the untrained family member who can only recoil at the sight of their loved one in such distress. Cec was actually doing well when I saw her. What I saw was not truly indicative of her state. The writhing and the half-dead look in her eyes was mainly a result of her anesthesia starting to wear off. The tubes in her mouth and nose were giving her nourishment and oxygen, and indeed her blood/ oxygen level was perfect after the ventilator was put into operation. Just because something's painful and/or ugly does not mean it's disastrous. Dr. Orr assured me Cec was stable for the night, otherwise I wouldn't be here writing this.

He also assured me that Cec was not conscious of our presence or of any pain, and that her straining and struggling in the bed was related to her anesthesia. With that assurance, I was able to reluctantly let go of Cec's hand. Driving to the hospital, I had felt guilty about not having been there all day and equally guilty about leaving Maddie just when she needed her bedtime routine. Then, driving home from the hospital, I felt guilty about leaving Cec. What do I do about these guilt feelings? Well, as a great therapist once told me, "You get to feel guilty, and then you get to keep doing what you have to do." Ah, but knowing what you have to do—there's the trick.

At my lowest moment today, it occurred to me that if today were Cec's last, there would at least be the minor blessing of not having the anniversary of today's date come around but once every four years.

Then it occurred to me that I was pretty stupid if I thought I would
need the actual date to turn up for me to relive the pain of such an
event. And then it occurred to me that I'd prefer to put it off until several February 29ths from now.

No slacking, you prayers and hummers.

1:53 a.m.

Jim

March 1, 2004

Almost no change from yesterday.

I spent about eleven hours at the hospital today. Cec is being
given more blood and more platelets tonight, and that will make possible the implantation of a pain-relieving epidural catheter tomorrow
morning (Tuesday).

I got a job today, on an episode of *Crossing Jordan*. I told my agent
to make sure the producers have a backup, since the way things have
been happening, it wouldn't be surprising to find myself suddenly
unavailable to do the gig. Auditions tomorrow for other jobs I don't
know if I can do. I'll just cast my bread upon the water and if things
work out, then great. If not, then some other guy will have a job.

There's much to say about today, but it's so late and I'm so tired.
Maybe tomorrow.

1:11 a.m.

Jim

March 2, 2004

(No message)

March 3, 2004

My beloved Cecily died this morning, March 3, at 8:05 a.m. She was a brilliant actress and acting coach, a highly respected and beloved casting director, and she was, with our two-and-a-half-year-old daughter, the light of my life. She died peacefully, quietly. I was by her side, where I have been for nineteen years.

2:12 p.m.

Bye-bye.

Jim

Part Two

NEWS FROM

MADDIE AND JIM

SEVEN

March 6, 2004

For three days I've wanted to write about Cecily's last day, and to affirm that I'll continue this journal for as long as it takes to bring closure to the tale. The message on March 3 may have been short and, if not sweet, at least gentle. But it was also abrupt, and a life, like a good play, must have not only denouement but falling action. Cec's story did not end with her last breath. Neither will my telling of it. You may come along or not, but as I've been asked by a number of you to continue, I shall, at least for a while. That said, I am dragged by fate over the roughest road of all, one embedded with shards and shells and daggerlike stones. I simply have not the strength to write and have not for several nights. Perhaps tomorrow. The things I have to write initially have been spoken many times in the past few days, but writing them will be torment. Life is smashed into fragments, and retrieving and gluing the slivers back together will take time. Right now, I only have time for survival and the manifold duties incumbent upon me in preparation for the public last good-bye.

My thanks to all of you who have buoyed my spirits during this journey and who bolstered and comforted Cec in her travail. I'll never forget these kindnesses, nor the sorrowful ones that have been delivered since Cec's departure. I only wish that before she left, she had known the full extent of the love held for her and the place she held in so many hearts.

There will be more to come. In the meantime, Cecily April Adams lives in my heart, in the hearts of her family, and in the hearts of all those friends and fond admirers who struggled so hard to hold her up. And so, since she does still live, I feel I can once again say . . .

No bye-bye.

12:43 a.m.

Jim

March 7, 2004

Tonight as I lay in bed with Maddie waiting for her to drift off to sleep, she began singing "Old MacDonald." She got virtually every word right (of the ones she chose to sing), and I found myself talking to Cec. "Can you hear her, baby? Can you hear our little girl?" Maddie sang so confidently, so happily, I knew that if Cec could hear her, she would be overjoyed at the transformation that has overcome our daughter in the seven months since the first roof fell on us. That roof, it seems, is almost repaired. Maddie, we've been told, may well someday lose her diagnosis and have the normal, social, well-rounded life that Cec and I dreamed of during those long months and years of trying to bring her to being. I've only spoken aloud to Cec a few times since she died, usually in sobs and pleading. It brought a smile to my face and heart to talk to her tonight and to share with her how well the child of her dreams is doing. God grant that she sees and hears and knows.

12:58 a.m.

Jim

March 8, 2004

Today was spent doing a most arduous and painful task—calling a large number of people who needed to know, but did not know, of Cecily's death.

Theatre West held a small good-bye ceremony for Cec tonight. It's tradition that when one of our members dies, we send that member off with a standing ovation at the next Monday night workshop. I've participated in many of these ovations, but never dreamed I would still be around when one was given for Cec. I figured to be a dim memory by that time. Instead, I stood there with friends, many who had been long away but returned just for this ceremony, and applauded an extraordinary actress and woman who happened to be my girl.

Despite this, today was the first twenty-four-hour period in which I have not collapsed in sobs at some point. Naturally I feel guilty about that. I know, I know, it's natural, it's human, it's blah, blah, blah. Despite my awareness of the waves that emotions ride at such a time, it feels like betrayal to not fall apart a minimum of once a day, at least for the first week or two or ten. My excuse today is that zombies don't cry.

12:54 a.m.

Jim

March 9, 2004

I made up for yesterday's lack of tears. I walked around most of the first half of the day with my arms clenched around my guts as though holding them in. I drove to a meeting about the memorial service screaming so loud I hurt my voice. My car seems the safest place for that sort of thing, in terms of being audible, but it's probably not so safe for people crossing my path. I bought some clothes and ended up telling the salesperson about Cecily's death. I'm sure the woman could have had a nicer day without my dropping my load of anguish on her, though she was kind. It's simply that it becomes difficult to walk about, seeing people carrying on their normal lives, without giving in to the urge to yell, "What's wrong with you people? Can't you see what's happened to me?" I feel like I am being hit by an extremely slow-moving truck, the impact stretching into days (weeks? months? years?). The fact that so many millions of people have experienced something like this means nothing. Pain spread is pain multiplied, not pain divided.

My Maddie is my salvation. Once upon a time one of my friends told me that there would be no happiness like that I would experience when my child first ran to the front door and yelled, "Daddy!" It happened just like that today. It thrilled me and revived me, though it was of course diluted by the melancholy state I live in these days. My little girl talks more every day and explores more and listens more and responds more, and in one short week she's soared above where she was when her mother went away. And I want to share those new heights with Cec, to hold her hand as we exult in Maddie's growing personhood. More than anything, I want to hear Cec say how happy she is. I think that's all I ever really wanted.

It's time to revisit last week. It's been unfair yet unavoidable for me to leave you with the abrupt and comparatively unexpected news that Cecily had gone from us, without elaboration or explanation. Everyone who cares about Cecily should know how her last day transpired.

Tuesday, March 2, I had a late-morning audition in Santa Monica and planned to go to the hospital after lunch. Before I left for the audition, I called Cec's nurse, who told me Cec's vital signs were still good. She put me on the phone with Dr. Andrew Fishmann, the pulmonary specialist. He asked me to have a conversation with him when I got to the hospital.

I went to my audition. This world I live in is a pretty weird one. The weird thing was that here I was, pretending to be a cop, reading opposite the casting director, also pretending to be a cop, when in reality she was not only the casting director, but a woman who has been my friend for twenty years and the person who introduced me to Cec. Her name's Cathy Sandrich Gelfond, and the oddness of the situation was too great to ignore. As I left, Cathy stopped me and offered to give blood for Cec. Nothing in twenty years has leavened my belief that she's one of the best people I know, but she iced the cake that morning.

When I got to the hospital, I checked in with Cec. She was still unconscious, still breathing harshly, but regularly, with the ventilator. But something was different. She was relaxed. Her body looked comfortable. She had lost the slightly clenched look her body and face had had for days (and, in fact, had had most of the years I'd known her). The nurse told me that they had, in fact, implanted the epidural morphine catheter that morning and that it had been successfully done. I met with Dr. Fishmann immediately, at about 4:00 p.m., and he told me that the implant team was certain that the epidural had eliminated virtually 100 percent of Cecily's pain. And this fact, therefore, was behind her relaxed and comfortable attitude on the bed. In all my years with Cec, I had never seen her look so comfortable, so physically at ease.

Dr. Fishmann had more to say. He told me that Cecily's X-rays on Tuesday morning were dramatically different from the ones of the previous day. He said that Monday's X-rays showed her lungs almost completely clear, the pneumonia almost eliminated. He said Monday's pictures showed lungs so clear that the tumor at the bottom of her left lung was visible for the first time in weeks. She seemed well on her way to dispensing with the ventilator and, if they could stop the mysteriously excessive fluid drainage from her chest, she could probably have resumed both consciousness and regular cancer treatment within a day or so. But Tuesday's X-rays spelled the end of that hope. In fact, as it turned out, they spelled the end of everything.

In an extraordinarily brief time, fewer than twenty-four hours, cancer had invaded and breached Cec's lymphatic system. The airways and air sacs in the lungs are enclosed within the lung membrane. Therein they are normally bathed in lymphatic fluid, which fills the membrane and all spaces between and around the airways, much the way the fingers of a hand are bathed when the hand is placed into a container of water. Normally an X-ray of such a normal lung will read clear, as Cecily's did on Monday. By Tuesday, however, the lymphatic fluid had been invaded and utterly contaminated with free-floating cancer cells. Just as milk poured into a water bottle will thoroughly cloud the water, so the cancer cells had clouded the lymph bathing Cec's airways. While no new tumors had formed in Cec's lungs, both lungs now were filled with cancer cells. These cells were responsible for the irritation causing the fluid drainage from Cec's chest, and the massive influx of cancer cells was why the drainage would not ease up. More important, though, the cancer cells interfered with Cec's ability to make use of oxygen. The oxygen she breathed was being taken into the lungs well, but the cancer cells provided an obstacle to the oxygen passing from the lungs into the bloodstream, where it could be carried to where it was needed. As the cancer cells multiplied, less and less oxygen was being transferred from her lungs to her blood.

By Tuesday morning, the ventilator was pumping oxygen to her lungs at 100 percent of its capacity. And 100 percent capacity is all there is. Dr. Fishmann told me that her declining ability to make use of the oxygen she received meant that ultimately, even with pure oxygen being delivered to her lungs, she would reach oxygen starvation and die. He said that there was no mistaking the indications of the X-rays and the oxygen measurements. He said that, under the best-case scenario, Cecily could not last more than another week.

I staggered away from the meeting and ran to call Dr. Orr. He told me that he had not yet seen the X-rays and that he had a conference with Dr. Fishmann scheduled for 6:30 p.m. He sounded shaken by what I revealed of Dr. Fishmann's conclusions.

Dr. Fishmann, by my experience and Dr. Orr's description, is a relatively pessimistic man. I think he's a terrific doctor, but I was not prepared to take his word that Cec was going to die. Nonetheless, I felt in my gut that his description of the evidence supporting that notion was so clear and well-grounded in science that only a miracle would prove him wrong. I went out to my car and called my brother-of-choice, Tom Allard, and then my sister Denise and told them the news. And I sobbed pathetically, maniacally into the phone with each of them.

After a bit, I went back inside and waited. I spent time with Cec, who slept so peacefully, so pleasantly, in comparison to the tormented condition she'd been in. Friends and family drifted in and out. Mark Sobel was there, but I dared not tell him what Dr. Fishmann had said. First, I knew how utterly distraught it would make Mark, and second, I knew he had no great faith in Dr. Fishmann. I thought it best to wait until after Dr. Orr's meeting with Dr. Fishmann and to let Dr. Orr tell us, together, what he thought was true. There was, after all, a chance that Dr. Orr's optimism about the case would carry the day. Also, whatever Dr. Orr said, Mark was more likely, in my opinion, to believe him over Dr. Fishmann.

So we waited.

Dr. Orr arrived and Mark and I joined him in a private room. There he said, "The X-rays look very bad. Very bad." My demolishment was complete, and Mark's began precipitously. Dr. Orr revealed his concurrence with Dr. Fishmann's conclusion in almost every detail. The only difference—a mighty one—was that he felt Cec could last no more than seventy-two hours. I sat stunned but resigned. Mark crumbled, begging Dr. Orr to do something, even something drastic and unconventional, to save Cec. Dr. Orr could say almost nothing. Mark asked if he would try a last-ditch dose of the Chinese herb Mark had obtained, the one that several studies had shown to have amazing potential for cancer patients. Dr. Orr said that he couldn't legally do so, nor could the nursing staff. I asked if Mark and I could give it to her ourselves, and Dr. Orr finally agreed. But he warned us that he could have no official participation and that the nursing staff would attempt to interfere if they caught us. In tears, Mark flew toward home to prepare the mixture.

I had no confidence in this last resort. Everything Dr. Fishmann and Dr. Orr had said made it utterly clear that such efforts were futile and too late. But I couldn't let things go without Mark believing that he had done everything in his power to save Cec, and if it meant we gave her some herbs, then that's what we were going to do. And, remember, someone once said, "I don't believe in miracles, but I depend on them." I didn't want God ever to ask me, "Why didn't you use that Chinese herb I sent you?"

Thinking far too literally, I felt I should go home and get some sleep in preparation for the latter part of that seventy-two hours Dr. Orr had mentioned, when I might need whatever rest I could accumulate now. I planned to go home right after Mark and I dosed Cec with the herb mixture. But it took Mark far longer to mix and dissolve the herb into the food than we reckoned on, and it was 2:00 or 3:00 a.m. before he returned. In a scene that would have been quite funny if it weren't so horribly situated, I blocked the door and the nurses' view by pretending to weep quietly (not much acting required there). Mark similarly pretended to cry at Cec's bedside while actually filling a large syringe with the mixture. He expertly injected the mixture into Cec's feeding tube, then refilled the syringe. The proper dosage required repeating this process five times. It was an excruciating ten minutes, capped by one of the syringes squirting all over Mark, his clothes, the floor, and Cec's bed. He finished and got most of the mess cleaned up just as a nurse came in to see what was going on. Mark apologized for spilling his coffee everywhere, though I think the nurse was suspicious, because the spill looked more like Malt-O-Meal than coffee. Mark grabbed his gear and headed home for the night.

My plan was to go home, get a little rest, and be there when Maddie awoke. But I dawdled, sitting with Cec, or talking with Drew Katzman in the waiting room. (Drew spent almost as much of Cec's last days at the hospital as I did. Considering that the largest place to sit or lie was a bench about four feet long, he deserves high praise for his tenacity as well as his devotion.)

I talked with the night nurse and asked if there was any kind of warning that a decline was heading imminently toward demise. She said that the patient's decline would be gradual, normally, but that a sudden drop in blood pressure and/or heart rate would indicate that the end was near. I asked if Studio City was too far away for me to get back to the hospital in time, if I received word of such a turn at home. She said I would probably make it.

Still thinking I had a couple of days to contend with, I kept thinking I should go home and sleep. But still I dawdled. I sat with Cec and talked for a long time. Both doctors had affirmed that they believed that patients in Cecily's precise condition were cognizant of the comforting voices of their loved ones around them, and both doctors vigorously recommended continual conversation with Cec, however one-sided.

After a bit, though, the night nurse suggested I get some rest. I said I was considering going home. For reasons unknown, she said, "Why don't you lie down in the waiting room?" Whether she meant it as an omen or not, I took it as one and went to lie down in the waiting room. Drew went to sit and talk with Cec and I slept on a bench from 4:00 a.m. till 7:00, when Drew woke me with word that Cec's vitals were still strong and normal, and that he was leaving for work.

I wandered back into Cec's room in ICU. It was 7:15 a.m. The moment I arrived, something clearly changed. The nurses sat up, taking notice of Cec's monitors. Her blood pressure diminished substantially and her heart rate dropped slightly. The nurses searched her body for a pulse, and found it strong and steady. But it was slowing, and her blood pressure continued to drop until it didn't show up on the monitor. Dr. Fishmann was called. He evaluated the situation, and told me that Cecily was fading quickly. I asked that a priest be called, because I knew Cec's mom would take comfort in it. But no priest ever arrived. As Cec's heartbeat slowed, Ida arrived in the room, along with our friend Mary Lou Belli, who had been spending every morning at Cec's side for days. I went to call Stacey and sent Mary Lou to call Cec's mom, Dell. It was 8:00 a.m. when we made those calls.

Clearly Cec was going. Her hands were icy cold, a result of the sharp drop in blood pressure. Her pulse was slower, but still strong; her brave, determined heart still pumping vigorously, but with rapidly diminishing fuel. Her breathing was still strong and regular, but that was because the ventilator controlled her breathing. Her eyes—her beautiful chocolate eyes—were half open, as they had been for a couple of days. Sitting at her bedside near her head, I saw her eyes as though they looked directly into mine, though there was no movement or apparent life in them, other than a gentle blink every few minutes. Cec's great fear from childhood, never diminished throughout her life, was of suffocating or drowning. She had pled many times with me, even before her illness, not to let her struggle for air, not to let her feel she was choking or gasping for breath. I swore to her I would never let that happen. On Tuesday night, I had asked Dr. Orr what would happen if we removed the ventilator and let Cec go, in my terms, "peacefully." He said that rather than peacefully, she would feel, even unconscious, that she was suffocating and strangling for air. I told him that I would never let that happen, and so we left her on the ventilator, despite the fact that it prolonged her life several more hours. But she was, as I said, at peace, free of pain entirely, comfortable in a way I had never seen her, and, thanks to medication, completely devoid of anxiety. So prolonging her life those few hours was no disservice, I believe, and not remotely the cruel disservice removing her from the ventilator would have been. I could not save my dearest love, but I could save her from dying in fear.

As the sounds accompanying Cec's heartbeat on the monitors

slowed, as quiet alarms whined to inform, as though we did not already know, that life could not long be supported at these levels, I stroked her forehead and talked to her of how much I loved her, how much her Maddie loved her, and her mother, and father, and sisters and brother, how many friends she had who adored her, and how wide the circle of love encompassing her was. I thanked her for my life, for taking this near-derelict and making a man of substance of him, for giving me a daughter to save me from the despair bound to come, and I thanked her for her great and generous spirit, her forbearance through a painful life, and for her miraculous development from an awful and excruciating beginning into a person whose light flooded many hundreds of people with joy. Only at the last did I allude to her departure. I didn't want anything to frighten her, but at the last I told her she would soon be with her beloved grandfather, whose love had never deserted her.

I was pained by the failure of the priest to show up. But just at the last, a lovely, lovely thing happened. As I sat at Cec's head, stroking her brow, with Ida beside me and Mary Lou beside her, a sudden noise made me look up. All work by the nurses had stopped and someone had pulled the curtain around the bed. I saw six or eight nurses standing around the bed, holding hands. One of them, behind me, began reading from a prayer book. As she finished reading in her soft Filipina accent, another Filipina accent took over as the nurse across from her began a beautiful and heartfelt prayer. These nurses, who must have seen this scene repeated in ICU a thousand times, nevertheless gave tender attention to this little girl breathing her last in their midst. Cec, who so loved the Filipino people after making a movie in Manila (with Mark) so many years ago, would, I believe, have been happy and deeply moved to know that so many of them would gather around her to make her taking off a gentle, tender, and holy one.

I watched Cec's eyes, which stared, apparently sightless, into mine. The sounds of her monitors dropped away. Only the one calibrated to her heart rate continued. The quiet prayer never abated, until, at last, the electronic echo of her lovely, strong heart beat one last time and paused forever. Until that moment, I felt there had been no life in Cecily's eyes. They seemed dull, unwitting, unresponsive. But I know now that life was there in those eyes, real and true, for in the moment her heart ceased to beat, I saw the light go out in Cec's eyes. It was as if a switch had been flipped, and in that instant, she left. One second she was there, despite my uncertainty, and the next moment she was gone, undeniably. In the sudden absence from her eyes of that spark of life, I realized how alive her eyes had been only an instant before. It was only with the darkening that I could see how much light had once been there.

And so it was with Cec herself.

The rest was a whirlpool of sorrow and numbness, and is so still. Friends were called and soon arrived. Stacey arrived, and Dell, and the awful truth revealed. Cathy was on a flight from Las Vegas, and arrived barely in time to see Cec before we had to leave. Of all the things I've ever done, perhaps none was more difficult than turning away from my beautiful girl and walking away, leaving her there, never to look back. But my friend Tom, my ever-faithful good true friend Tom said, pointing down the hall away from Cec's room, "Life's that way. Let's go home."

And so we did.

2:12 a.m.

Jim

EIGHT

March 10, 2004

Last night's e-mail took it out of me. This one will be brief.

Most of the day was spent at my new job on *Crossing Jordan*. I fought to keep my mind steady and unemotional and not to look like a rough, tough forest ranger who'd been crying for two hours.

The only thing that gave me pause during the day was in filling out my new W-4 for this job. I found myself faced with the choice of two boxes on the form: single or married. I turned the form over and over and couldn't find any boxes marked widowed or suicidal or dumbstruck or bereft or catatonic. So I picked one of the boxes that were provided.

I must look for words to say at Saturday's service that will encompass a life and nineteen years without taking a lifetime or nineteen years. I've scarcely a clue what I'll say, and am certain of one thing: that I am uncertain whether I'll be able to speak at all.

12:32 a.m.

Jim

March 11, 2004

I don't know what I'm going to do when Ida goes home Monday, but at some point I have to grapple with the fact that I have to raise this little girl myself.

I'm having a hard time of it. The tears aren't coming as often or as tumultuously, but my gut feels as though someone's standing on it. Probably that elephant. I thought we were rid of him; after all, he got what he came for.

1:14 a.m.

Jim

March 12, 2004

I worked for a long while on my remarks for tomorrow, then went to work on *Crossing Jordan*, where I worked some more on them while I waited for my scene. I know I owe it to the show to maintain my composure until after I film, but I couldn't do it today.

I broke down in my trailer and sobbed, long honking, wracking sobs that threatened to ruin both my makeup and the sound track of anything shooting nearby. I thought that work would be a distraction, but one of the primary activities on a film set is waiting—and waiting, these days, means staring at the ground and thinking. And thinking eventually means crying. The idea that one can be this sad, every minute of every day, and still maintain a life seems inconceivable. Yet having Maddie creates a responsibility that can't be shirked in order to collapse from anguish. And having the life that was denied Cec confers a great responsibility, too, to honor and cherish and make meaningful that life. So I soldier on. I've been to war. I know that soldiers sometimes cry and whimper and call for their sweethearts. And now I know that war can come in many guises.

I must close so I can get back to writing tomorrow's futile attempt to capture Cec in mere words. I'm sure I'll see many of you.

12:28 a.m.

Jim

March 14, 2004

The response to yesterday's memorial service has been amazing. I had such difficulty getting my part of it prepared in time that I thought it would be an adequate but clumsy attempt to celebrate Cec's life. In fact, due in great part to the work of Cec's sister Stacey and of videographer/friend Bill Anderson and the music coordinator, David Burke, and to the eloquence and graciousness of the fifteen or so speakers, it was the most wonderful event of its kind I could imagine. I think everyone came away with both a reaffirmation of their love and admiration for Cecily and a sense that there were many interesting sides of her they had never known. That's precisely what I wanted from the service.

I found it deeply moving—at times almost unbearably so—but also filled with warmth and humor and boundless love. In particular, I thank the many speakers. Between them, they managed to convey with great feeling the special multifaceted nature of Cec's character and the reasons so many people loved her. There were people standing at the back of the packed 600-seat theatre, and I can't imagine anyone escaped unstained by tears.

My thanks and love to all who showed up, to all who wanted to be there but couldn't, and to all who participated. Most especially, to my dear Stacey, without whom I could not have made it to, or through, the event.

12:21 a.m.

Jim

March 15, 2004

It was the best of times, it was the worst of times.

It was sad to see Ida off, back to Maryland more than a month since her arrival here. She's been a godsend, for me, for Maddie, and especially for Cec. I am so happy (happy?) that Ida was with me when Cec died. Ida really is, as Cec always said, "pure love," and that's what she gave Cec, even in those last hours and moments. She promises to come back in a few months, or any time I truly need her. It's hard to imagine how anyone gets through this life without an Ida, or why anyone would want to. Ida, who told me she hadn't cried since childhood, cried with me today.

The hospital bed and oxygen machine were taken away from our bedroom today. This was another reminder, as if I needed one, that Cec is gone, and gone for good. It seems impossible, it seems a dream. And it seems astonishing that I can get from one moment to the next without collapsing under the weight of this loss, yet I do. I seem to be thinking in an orderly fashion and attacking various problems in an effective way—in some ways more effectively than ever. Yet there's this drone in my ear, "She's gone, she's gone, she's gone. . . ."

The night before last, I walked with Maddie through the yard. We came to a porch post and Maddie walked around it on the opposite side of the post from me. Cec and I for years had a little personal "love quirk" that required us always to go around an obstacle on the same side of it. Coming to a fire hydrant or a mailbox on the sidewalk, we never, ever split to go around it. We always chose one side or the other to go around it together, always unspoken, never forgotten. When my Maddie walked around the "wrong" side of the post from me, a little penknife slipped into my heart. Not for long, but just enough of a jab to remind me of something else I would never have or treasure again in the present tense. I'm told, and I already see, that the new normal is full of those things.

There's a peacefulness in the house tonight. I feel watched over.
12:16 a.m.

Jim

March 17, 2004

Today I went through Cec's vanity, collecting her cosmetics and assorted scents, shampoos, oils, sachets, makeup, paints, and powders, saving what was still of use for anyone who might want it, and tossing the rest. This made the morning at Social Security seem absolutely rapturous.

I'm taking it easy, not trying to get too much done at once in this matter of cleaning out dressers and closets and cabinets. If I do just enough to feel melancholy, then go watch some television or read the paper, I seem to be able to get things done. If I try to tackle too much, I end up on the floor.

Someone ignored the "Do Not Swivel" sign on the drinking-water faucet, and it's broken. The plumber came to fix it, didn't have the right piece of equipment, and left. And now—coincidentally?—the dishwasher's dumping water out all over the floor. In case you're considering having a tragedy in your life, just keep in mind that all the day-to-day problems keep right on happening, just as though your mind could concentrate on mundanities instead of the crack in your heart.
11:59 p.m.

Jim

March 18, 2004

I went grocery shopping today. Another twinge of loss, as I found myself reaching for things I normally would have picked up for

Cec: coffee, honey, tea bags, cream, all stuff I don't really use. One gets in a habit shopping at the same store over a course of years, and I suspect it will be a while before my hand stops reaching for the unbleached coffee filters.

11:31 p.m.

Jim

March 19, 2004

Yesterday I told a friend it felt strange that I seemed to be doing so well, actually functioning and occasionally having fun. It seemed odd that a mere two and a half weeks after Cec's death I could already be coming out of my despair.

Then today I cried all day. Wracking, heaving, pounding on the floor, rolling on the bed, screaming at the ceiling. There were occasional breaks in the action, and then I'd start over again. Tonight my eyes feel as though someone had used them for paddleballs.

I had no idea a heart could hold this much feeling. I am, today, inconsolable. The one who could always best console me is the one I mourn. I try to imagine her arms around me, comforting and supporting. The feel of that image is delicious and magical, but it's an image, not a reality.

And yet—my heart soared to see my little girl riding a pony around the neighborhood this afternoon, a special delivery pony ride provided by a woman I know only slightly, yet whose grace and generosity know no apparent bounds, Jackie Filgo, Cecily's boss at *That '70s Show*. A truck and trailer showed up at our front door, a beautiful bay pony named Champion was unloaded, and Maddie came out the front door in astonishment and glee. I haven't been able to make my little girl happy very well lately. Thanks to

Jackie and Champion, Maddie had a grin from ear to ear all day long.

11:35 p.m.

Jim

March 20, 2004

Today held nearly as much emotion, if not quite the amount of sobbing, as yesterday. I spent the day walking around aimlessly, unable to do much except mutter to myself questions without answers. I'm surprised to find that, after a couple of weeks beyond Cec's death, I am only now being confronted violently with something that I thought should have come and gone some time ago: disbelief. But I find myself stunned, as though I'd only just heard the news. How could this be real? And what can I do to make it not real?

Tears come, usually when I'm alone. I'm fairly competent at keeping my composure in company.

I'm never far from thoughts of my father and how close he lies to his own departure. I can scarcely think of Cec's illness without contemplating the horrific confluence of events that leaves Cec's father and her brother, Sean, and Maribel's husband, Mario, in harm's way from this same disease. To recount all the suffering active within arm's reach of just those reading these words would be an all-day task, and a fearful and unrewarding one.

Yet happiness exists and grows and thrives. And I think it does so by our pushing aside the horrors and the fears and the pain and insisting on having a world with happiness in it. Perhaps happiness is merely a construct we've created to help us to survive in a difficult and often horrific world. I don't know. I only know that when my friend Tom points away from Cec's deathbed and says, "Life's that way, let's go,"

I feel my soul pulled in that direction, toward not just mere survival, but toward happiness, despite the wretched ache in my heart.

11:16 p.m.

Jim

March 21, 2004

Maddie had a full day. She had an exciting time at a birthday party; then she got to go swimming for the first time since last summer. I had a painful moment—I think several people did—when Maddie, who had never been swimming before without Cec, suddenly started shouting, "Mommy, where are you? Mommy, where are you?" She didn't seem distressed, particularly, and "So-and-so, where are you?" is a game she plays often, sometimes with dolls or stuffed animals or even shoes. Nonetheless, it was disconcerting to hear her calling for Cec, and infinitely more disconcerting to hear the silence that followed her call.

Tonight I went off to a premiere party for *Deadwood* without Maddie and without the girl who so perfectly should have been on my arm. For her to live with me through the beginnings of this great artistic success—for her to be there for the beginning and not to be with me as it bears fruit—is hard for me to take. But the truth is, so many of Cec's struggles for achievement in various aspects of life were just beginning to bear fruit when she was taken that I can hardly stand to think of it. No one ever worked harder, in my estimation, to have a happy and meaningful life than Cec. That she made it so close to what she would have felt as happiness, but did not get to revel in it, is so painful to me.

That's all. Tomorrow, so I'm told, is another day.

12:54 a.m.

Jim

March 23, 2004

Sick today. Sore throat, aches. Figures. After a long, stressful period of activity, a period of relative calm is usually when it all falls in on you, healthwise. Not horribly so, but enough that once I got Maddie home from her therapy, I went to bed and stayed there all day and most of the evening.

I don't know how to take care of Maddie if I get really sick, since I scarcely know how to take care of her when I'm not. Kid needs a mommy a lot more than she needs a daddy. But, poor thing, a daddy's all she's got.

Maddie growing up without a mommy and, especially, growing up not *remembering* the amazing mommy she had, makes me want to scream. Can't. My throat hurts.

10:36 p.m.

Jim

March 24, 2004

On my desktop is a beautiful portrait of Maddie wearing beads and a feather boa and a wide, fluffy grown-up's hat, taken around her first birthday. It was one of Cec's most favorite pictures of Maddie. In front of the picture, inside a cardboard box inside a nondescript shopping bag, is the urn containing Cec's ashes. I brought it home today, in preparation for final disposition. I was afraid to see the box at first. I'd had such a wrenching experience on the day the cremation took place. The permanence of the action shattered whatever composure I retained, and I surpassed the most hysterical level of grief I'd ever known. It was almost as if, as long as the cremation hadn't yet occurred, maybe there was still a chance something could be done to save her.

I don't doubt that many people have shared thoughts like these, irrational as they may be. And so I met today with trepidation. I thought perhaps I'd have another breakdown—not that there's anything wrong with that, but it feels so awfully bad while it's happening. Instead, though, I found something steadying, almost comforting, and this surprised me. On my way to my car, I felt compelled to embrace this package that held all that was physically left of my girl. I'm not a huge believer in the metaphysics or symbology of this kind of contact, yet all I can say is that I was comforted.

I drove home with my hand resting on top of the box, and I felt closer to Cec than I have since the day she died. And when I got home, it was okay. It was okay to put the box on top of my desk and go about my tasks. Something had changed, and as strange as it may seem, the permanence of things as they now are, and the undeniability of that permanence, gave me some relief from the dreadful despair that has colored every one of the last twenty-one days. There's more despair to come, I know. Wise and experienced souls have told me so. But for this evening, I feel calm and in some way peaceful in the sense of presence I have with Cec. I know the girl I love is not in that boxed urn, nor anywhere else that I could go or find or see. She is, though, somewhere. And prime among those somewheres is my heart. There she lives forever.

10:11 p.m.

Jim

March 25, 2004

Sicker than ever today. It's a full-blown cold.

I spent the active part of the day at my attorney's office, working out Cec's estate and making sure my own is in order for Maddie's well-being. I scarcely saw Maddie today, except for putting her to bed.

She's so vital to me nowadays, and so encouraging and life-affirming, and she gives me strength she doesn't know I need. We will, I suppose, have plenty of time alone with each other in the days and years to come.

10:44 p.m.

Jim

March 26, 2004

I had trouble sleeping last night. I finally dozed off around 3:00 a.m. but Maddie awoke, ready to play, at 7:00 a.m. Maribel arrived at 8:30. I sped over to Warner's to work on Dan Bucatinsky's pilot, *Beck and Call*.

Two-thirds of the way through shooting, I began to flub lines I'd been saying perfectly well for hours. That and the incipient laryngitis that has been building kept me from being on my game. Exhaustion didn't help, either.

Afterward I picked up Maddie and we dropped by the studio where Cec had worked. Last week the director and actors on *That '70s Show* made an incredibly generous donation to Maddie's college fund, and I wanted to thank them and show them the little girl they were helping.

When Maddie and I left, Macaulay Culkin, whom I'd never met, was walking across the lot with Mila Kunis, one of the regulars on *That '70s Show*. We were introduced and he and Mila started talking about how they'd meant to call me about an autism resource he wanted to pass on to me. I was grateful but it's weird, though, when someone you've never met says he's been meaning to get in touch with you. It's considerably weirder when that someone is Macaulay Culkin.

When I got home, Maribel and her daughter, Krystal, took Maddie for a walk. Moments later, the floor dropped out from under me. My façade shattered like a sheet of ice. Cec's beautiful face smiled out at me from photos around the living room and kitchen and I could no longer stand. I crawled and clawed at the floor and reached toward the sky and howled and wailed and sniveled and keened. I was wrung empty by the time Maddie, Maribel, and Krystal returned. I played with Maddie a few moments and then went upstairs, where it started all over again. And eventually my tortured voice gave out and my sobs became near-silent rasping honks. And then, like most storms, it passed, leaving me afloat in a sea of numbness, my eyes raw from salt.

And the miracle is, a few moments later, I was checking the news and catching up on e-mails. The miracle is that there are rest breaks in the pain. It amazes me how a person could possibly feel this bad, and then it amazes me that in the midst of that pain, a person can actually feel good and enjoy life and laugh.

11:07 p.m.

Jim

March 28, 2004

I've heard from probably a thousand people how sorry they were to learn of Cec's death and how they'd like to know if there's anything they can do. So why is it the one that sticks in my mind (and my craw) is the one person who, being told that Cec had died, said, "Huh. I thought maybe that's what happened. I hadn't heard from her in a while. So what do you want to do about that dresser she ordered from me?"

10:38 p.m.

Jim

March 30, 2004

This evening, I called my mom. I haven't talked to her since the day Cec died. My mom is superb, but she's also occasionally unfathomable. She hasn't called since that day, but the fact is, she *may* not call when my *dad* dies. Oh, eventually she will, but it never quite occurs to her to pick up the phone. I'm not complaining, just describing. She's a wonderful woman with a heart the size of a tree house. Phoning her kids just isn't something she does. She's written to me, but today was the first time I've talked to her in four weeks. Obviously, I could have called her, but my whole family situation is difficult for me to confront, and I've been unwilling to reach out to my mom for fear of multiplying my conscious sorrows.

Of course, when I called tonight, I knew I should have done so many times in the past four weeks, because instead of feeling worse, I felt better. She's good and comforting and warm, and it helped.

My fears revolve around bringing my dad's condition too close to my surface awareness. I'm afraid to add that pain to what's going on here at home. But tonight, my mom asked if I wanted to talk to my dad. I wasn't aware that he was in a position to even listen to me talk, but she assured me he was, and that she felt certain he knew what was going on around him and would understand me. (I have mixed feelings about that, too.) But she placed the phone by his ear and I told him how much I missed him, and how hard it was to go through this without his counsel and guidance. I told him that nothing had ever been this hard in my life, and that many times I felt I could not get through it. But I also told him that I believed, with all my heart, that he had passed on to me the strength and courage to get through it, and that even though I couldn't lean on him in quite the same way anymore, the only reason I was still standing was because I was leaning on what he'd given me over the years. I told him how much Cec loved him, how deeply she cared for him and respected him, and how he was the closest thing she'd ever had to a real father, and how grateful she was and I am for that.

And I told him how much I needed him, but not to hang on longer than he wanted to on my account, because his strength would never desert me—he's already given it to me. And then—he said he loved me. His voice was thin and weak, but stronger than I'd expected. Anything would have been stronger than I'd expected. The words were seriously slurred, as slurred as they've ever been in these seven or eight years of his deterioration. But I heard them and knew them for what they were. That he could make a sound at all astonished me. That he could make at that moment the single sound I most needed to hear from him was transcendent. I cried into his ear for a long time.

I'm afraid to see him. The antitank gunner who fought the Japanese in the Pacific, the "giant" who balanced baby me sitting in the palm of his hand (I have pictures), the athlete, the amateur comedian, the Gospel minister are all still there, somewhere in his dwindling frame, but I dread seeing him stripped of his powers. The gestures are gone, the cock of the eyebrow, the quiet laugh, the muscled sinews of his hands and arms, and I fear my own fear. But though Cec's illness and death have been my excuse for not facing that fear, the time has come. I'm going to take Maddie to see her grandpa at least one last time, and I'm going to look upon my helpless father with all the strength I can muster from that which he gave me. And hearing his flimsy voice struggle to tell me he loves me tonight has given me the strength to make that decision.

At our old house in Van Nuys, we had a nice new shower put in right before Maddie was born. I used to give Cec a hard time about her insistence that we wipe down the glass after every shower to keep it from water-spotting. In my whole life, I'd never felt the need to do something as hoity-toity as wiping down the shower door after every shower.

Tonight I bought a squeegee.

10:15 p.m.

Jim

March 31, 2004

Lately Maddie's been making a distinction between her toy people and their real-life counterparts. There's a toy man in one of her play sets that she used to call "the daddy." But now she calls it "toy daddy," and I've become "real Daddy." She's been differentiating this way for about a week. Tonight she asked, "Where's real Mommy?" It's the first time she's asked, and I was unprepared. I just said, "She's not here." Maddie then asked, "Real Mommy be back in a minute?"

I held on to my composure with both hands—after all, Maddie wasn't upset or emotional, no need for me to make her so. I took her over to a picture on the wall of Cec holding Maddie and told her that Mommy loves her more than anything in the world and that Mommy didn't want to go away but had to. I didn't take it any further than that because Maddie is too young to comprehend the depth or nature of what's happened or my explanation. She seemed all right, though my emotions roiled. Maddie looked at the picture and said, "Mommy holding Maddie close." I told her she was indeed.

I used to write about how many, many people there were suffering from cancer at any given time and how astonished I was to learn the intensity of the family experience when the disease struck our home. How could so many people go through this thing every day and it still be an unfamiliar experience to the rest of us?

Well, now I wonder something similar. How can it be that there is such a colossal gap between what we think we know about grief and mourning and what we actually find out when it comes to us? People die every day, in such numbers that it would seem that on any given day I would personally know at least one person in deep mourning. Yet it doesn't actually seem that way, and nothing I've picked up from the grief of others in the course of my life has prepared me for what this feels like.

10:21 p.m.

Jim

April 1, 2004

I spent the day applying for permits to scatter Cec's ashes in Redwood National Forest. Cec and I spent our eleventh wedding anniversary hiking through Fern Canyon. Filled with new and ancient life, and a grandeur and beauty unmatched in my experience, the place was the living embodiment of everything Cecily cared about and loved. One day soon I'll take her back there.

At times I let go and give my grief voice. Other times I remind myself that my Cec would want my unhappiness to end, as hers has. Granting myself permission to be happy first causes me a reflexive guilt—how dare I be happy when Cec has lost her life. But then I think of how tenderly she treated me in sadness and sorrow and how intensely she wanted me to be happy. Then I know that moving away from anguish, however slowly, is what she wants for me. And I know that her daughter's happiness and welfare depend to a large extent on the happiness and welfare of Maddie's father.

I hope I'm right, that determination to move beyond pain will allow that move. I know there's pain ahead, and it's unavoidable. But the choice is either to sit in it like a missionary in a cannibal's pot or to climb out and move away as fast as I can. That choice is mine to make. I'm moving, slowly perhaps, but as fast as I can manage. I'm not ready to be soup yet.

11:26 p.m.

Jim

April 2, 2004

I got nothin' tonight. Except for the doorknob in my stomach and the awful quiet in the house after Maddie went to sleep, there's not much to differentiate this day from anyone else's normal day. Paid bills, showered, napped, going to watch a little TV. See? Life's completely back to normal.

Yeah.

11:35 p.m.

Jim

April 3, 2004

Today makes one month.

How can that be? How can I have made it a month without her?

4:53 a.m.

Jim

April 4, 2004

I feel so guilty these days. My intellect tells me that guilt is useless and an unnecessary burden that masks the truth of my relationship with Cec, that for all the pain we caused each other over the years, we always saw through it eventually to the true love and adoration we felt for each other. I hold to those thoughts with all my strength, yet I am assailed by the emotional response of guilt—guilt for every slight I inflicted on her; for every failure to provide for her or her needs or wants; guilt for every fantasy or speculation on some presumed happiness that would not involve her; guilt for the moments I wished she were dead or I'd never met her; guilt for all the moments when I made her wish I were dead or she'd never met me.

In my mind, anything that provided less than Cec's perfect happiness and joy with me is an occasion for at least momentary self-loathing. I always draw myself up with the rational understanding that at the bottom of it all, we loved each other desperately, with an undiminished passion after nearly twenty years. Yet there flits through my mind at least hourly a sorrowful pang for my failings and my spiteful hurts. She was difficult, but she was good, so good, and good-hearted, and in the fantasy perfection many of us create for ourselves, only a deservedly guilty, perhaps even evil, person could have returned pain for all that goodness.

I know that I could not ever expect to be a perfect husband to Cecily, nor did she expect me to be. And I know that outside of Maddie, there was no one she loved as deeply as me. I know that we saw clearly, most of the time, who we were and who we were to each other, and we treasured that. I know it. But even the most golden apple can have a tiny worm, and the worm inching around its curlicue way inside this apple is the worm of guilt and regret.

If I could have made Cec's life perfect, I would have. I never quite knew how. I don't really regret that or feel guilt for it. But losing her forever, it's difficult to bear the thought of ever having hurt her. Guilt may serve no purpose other than to cause pain, but knowing that scarcely makes it easier to banish.

11:58 p.m.

Jim

April 5, 2004

Last night, I put Maddie to bed and listened to her crying for an increasing set of minutes before going in to reassure her and to repeat again the process of teaching her to go to sleep on her own. Well, Maddie was eating breakfast this morning and out of the blue said, "Door was locked and Daddy said, 'I always come back to you.'" My jaw hit the floor. I hope it means she took what I told her to heart and she knows that she can always count on me to be back, even if I leave her to sleep on her own. Of course, these days, she couldn't be blamed for wondering if people might not occasionally just disappear forever.

I'm told most businesses give employees three days' grief leave when a spouse dies. Wow. That's two days for grieving and one for a round of golf, I guess.

I can't seem to get anything done these days. I look at my to-do list and can't find anything on it I can bear to do. So I do nothing.

Today I got a check for $255 from the Social Security Administration as full payment of my spousal death benefit. Looking at that figure, I almost wished they'd kept it. It's hard not to think, at least momentarily, that $255 seems awfully minuscule for a girl like mine.

1:11 a.m.

Jim

April 6, 2004

I've stayed up too late sorting papers. Birthday cards Cec never got to open. Get-well cards. Reams of research on cancer. Unfilled prescriptions. Pottery Barn catalogs and *Organic Cooking* magazines and ads for curtains, cosmetics, and comforter covers. The recycling bin is particularly full tonight.

There's a numbness that comes over one right after a death this close. It lasts a few days. It's not a complete numbness, just sufficient to dull the pain enough that you don't drive off the nearest bridge. If it were complete numbness, I'd almost wish I could have it back again.

I'm not a drinker. I don't do drugs. If I weren't all that stands between Maddie and an orphanage, I could see the appeal of such things at a time like this. Not gonna happen, though, no matter how much I'd like to take an eraser to my brain. And, truth be told, part of me feels like this is a good thing, getting to experience life in all its facets. I sure can't say I didn't go on the ride.

2:05 a.m.

Jim

April 7, 2004

Glenn Morshower and I went to see a gorgeous little park up in the Hollywood Hills off Mulholland. Glenn wanted to show me this ancient redwood that stands in the park. It was a beautiful, serene place in the midst of L.A., but isolated and quiet. If you've ever seen the opening to *The Andy Griffith Show*, with Andy and Opie carrying their fishing poles along the side of the lake, you've seen the spot where this tree stands. Glenn often goes there to relax and to clear his mind, and he thought I might have a good response to the place. I did. I wish I'd known about it when Cec was here. She'd have loved it. Cec was so drawn to nature and was particularly fond of redwoods. Well, this spot isn't exactly Longfellow's "forest primeval," but for something ten minutes from home, it would have pleased her greatly.

11:02 p.m.

Jim

April 8, 2004

I ran errands all day, then went to Tom Allard's house and watched a Western. Tom and I have been having cowboy nights like this for nearly fifteen years. We used to get together every three weeks or so, cook up a mess of something, shoot the breeze, and watch some old Randolph Scott movie. Then life got more complicated and the frequency (though not the enjoyment) dwindled. Tonight was the first time in maybe a year. Tom is my rock these days. He's been through this himself in large part, having lost his own mate a decade ago, and I heed his advice and value his counsel. His wardrobe's a whole 'nother thing.

12:28 a.m.

Jim

April 9, 2004

The story of "Pie."

About two months after Cec and I began dating, I went back to Texas for a family reunion. It was a campout at some lake, and two or three times a day I would walk a mile each way to a phone booth to call Cec. We were still a new couple and we couldn't go long without talking to each other. (Eighteen years later, I was on location in Mexico and we still had to talk to each other about five times a day. So much for losing interest.)

Anyway, I was driving back from the reunion in Texas and stopped at a truck stop outside Tucson, Arizona. Browsing around the gift stand, I saw a little doll, a cheap Hong Kong kind of item, dressed in cowgirl buckskins. The label on the package said "Miss Sweety Teeny of the West." I found this hysterical. One of those amusing foreign attempts to capture American vernacular, such as are often found on instruction sheets: "Please to be not using radio for watching in tub of bathing."

When I got home, I told Cec about this doll, and for a while, I used it as a term of endearment for her. I'd address birthday cards to "Miss Sweety Teeny of the West," or call her office and ask for

"Miss Sweety Teeny." Soon this turned into just plain "Sweety." And for a while, that's what we called each other. Then "Sweety" became "Sweety Pie." And finally, just plain "Pie." For some reason that stuck. For the next almost twenty years, each of us was "Pie" to the other. Seduced as I was by the notion of being a big tough man, I tried not to use it in front of other people, but Cec did.

As far as I know, neither of us was ever willing to disclose to other people why we called each other that. It was our little thing, a goofy, romantic, baby-talk kind of thing that signaled our affection for each other. At our wedding, I called her "Pie" during my vows, to show her how vulnerable I was willing to be at that moment. After that, a lot of people asked me what it meant. I wouldn't ever tell, not because there was any great secret, but because it was just mine and Cec's.

When I talk to Cec now, it's almost always as "Pie." Because that's the name that brings me closest to her; that's the name in our intimacy, in the depths of our love for each other. "Pie," as silly a word as it is, was not just a nickname. It was the name we gave to *us*. I share it now with you because I need to share who we were, who we still are. I need others to know of us, so that the collective knowledge will carry that "us" onward. I can't carry it on alone forever. And I'd hate to think someday it might be lost to time. I'd like someone, sometime, somewhere to hear the word "pie" and just for a moment remember that once a great love was encompassed in those three little letters.

Good night, Miss Sweety Teeny of the West, wherever you are. 3:00 a.m.

Jim

April 10, 2004

I lie in bed each night, thinking of the same things, over and over again. Cec used to do that. We'd hit the rack and I'd go right out, but she'd lie there hour after hour, thinking of horrible things that might happen. Now I lie there, thinking of horrible things that did happen.

All my life I've been able to get what I wanted, usually, by scrounging or manipulating or researching or just plain determination. I was an irresistible force. Well, the irresistible force has met the immovable object. Like it or not, the immovable object wins.

I cannot have what I want, no matter how ferociously determined I am, no matter how many mountains I'm willing and able to move, no matter how I wheedle or cajole or manipulate. I want her back. I miss her so. She had a deep-seated fear of physical suffocation, but the emotional suffocation I feel without her seems a thousandfold worse than any physical gasping for breath. At times today I felt like a man caught in a boa constrictor's coils, trying with every sinew to reach out for something I couldn't reach, all the while having the life squeezed out of me.

And yet yesterday seemed like a pretty good day. This whole thing's a mystery to me.

I'm going to go to bed and lie there an hour or two and think about it. Whether I want to or not.

12:34 a.m.

Jim

April 11, 2004

Does anyone know where I can find a copy of the rules of thought, feeling, and behavior in these circumstances? It seems like there should be a rule book somewhere that lays out everything exactly the way one should respond to a loss like this. I'd surely like to know if I'm doing it right. Am I whining enough or too much? Am I unseemly in my occasional moments of lightheartedness? At what date am I supposed to turn off the emotion and jump back on the treadmill of normalcy?

Is there a specific number of days or decades that must pass before I can do something I enjoy without feeling I've betrayed my dearest love? And when, oh when, am I ever really going to believe this has happened? Next time you're in a bookstore, ask if there's a rule book.

11:54 p.m.

Jim

April 14, 2004

Cec was so looking forward to a big tax refund this year. We owned both our old house and the new one for almost the entire year, so our mortgage interest deduction was huge. But despite being an amazing in-her-head calculator, Cecily didn't have much feel for the way taxes work. It turns out that we actually owe a couple of grand. She'd have been surprised and angry—not at owing taxes, but at being wrong.

It used to be frustrating, trying to get her to understand that just because she needed something didn't make it deductible. Now, of course, it's just quietly amusing to remember. I'd be happily frustrated, spending the rest of my life trying to get her to understand taxes, if she'd only stayed.

There's nothing certain in this life but death and—well, you know.

1:46 a.m.

Jim

April 15, 2004

I spent some time today at the mortuary that handled Cecily's cremation. They helped me prepare for this weekend's scattering in the Redwood National Park in northern California. Some division of the ashes was necessary, since a portion will be placed somewhere near here for easier visitation.

As with so many things in the past few months, my predictions of how I might feel in such a situation bear little resemblance to how I actually do. I never, ever had any feelings about cremation and scattering other than that it seemed a clean, civilized, and proper way of returning the body to the earth.

But now it feels strange. I get on a plane Saturday morning to take this parcel containing just a hint of who Cec was to a forest where once we hiked together. Cec's sister Stacey is going with me.

Touching the box gives me a strange, unexpected comfort. Yet I dread seeing what's in it. I'm already reluctant to leave what's in it behind when I head back south. I look forward to placing a portion in a beautiful spot near here, where Maddie and I and friends and family can go and pursue the thought of Cec in serenity. And all the while, I know that these ashes, this dust, now held in more than one container, this stuff isn't Cec any more than the hair left in her comb is her.

"Do I contradict myself? Very well, then, I contradict myself. (I am large. I contain multitudes.)"

And one question, of course, remains: Checked . . . or carry-on?

12:02 a.m.

Jim

April 19, 2004

On less than ninety minutes' sleep, I caught a 6:45 a.m. flight out of Burbank on Saturday morning. I changed planes in San Francisco and flew out on a turboprop commuter plane for Arcata, California, where I met Stacey. (The plane was so small that the passengers had to check even their carry-on bags. So much for the question at the end of the April 15 e-mail.)

The road north to Orick, our destination, is surrounded by deep green forests. Occasionally the road will swoop down to reveal open meadows on one side and driftwood-strewn beaches on the other. The farther north one goes, the thicker the forests and the trees become.

Just past Orick is Rolf's, a meaty Germanic restaurant that specializes in elk steaks, presumably made from the very elk that congregate in the meadow outside the restaurant's big windows. The turnoff to the restaurant is Davison Road, which leads west a few miles through foggy green forests of massive redwoods to Prairie Creek Redwoods State Park. Just past the gate to the state park, the road dead-ends. Stacey and I parked and walked about a tenth of a mile along a path until we came to a brook and the entrance to Fern Canyon. It had been raining off and on all day, and there were fewer people around than when Cec and I visited back in 2000.

Cec had called Fern Canyon the most beautiful place she'd ever seen in her life, and I know she would have been delighted for her sister to see it. It was never enough for Cec to have a good experience. She always wanted to share it. (Which is why I'm being so detailed in giving directions.)

We hiked up the canyon, which seems as though it has been cut with a knife. The walls are vertical, shimmering with dripping water, and covered fifty feet high on both sides with a rich, moist carpet of ferns. I use the term "carpet" deliberately. The walls feel like a cold, wet shag carpet. Their green is all the green you've ever seen, concentrated in a rich and vibrant texture. Far above, redwood giants of lighter green tower over the canyon.

Hiking the canyon is simple; the stony bottom is basically level. But fallen trees and shin-deep pools block the way here and there, and either a willingness to get wet or good balance and good scampering skills are necessary.

A quarter mile or less up the canyon, we came to a spot between two trees, each fallen and leaning against the canyon walls, creating between them a space which, while not exactly private, delineated a recognizable and discrete area. In the center of this space was a patch of ferns and flowers. Somehow Stacey and I both sensed that this was the spot. We opened the package, and there, in the center of the canyon, in the center of the gathering of ferns and flowers, we spread Cec's ashes. The white-gray dust coated the moist leaves of the flowering plants and sprinkled down among the roots of this island of life in the middle of a rocky streambed. Neither Stacey nor I felt compelled, or perhaps able, to say anything out loud, though I did reflexively quote Stevenson: *"Home is the sailor, home from the sea, and the hunter home from the hill."* I'm not sure why I felt this was apropos, other than the sense I had that we were bringing Cec back home—not to a home of family and friends, but to her deeper home, the place where she felt at one with the earth—the kind of place where her spirit most fearlessly and hopefully blossomed, the place where, she said, she most knew there was God.

A month or two before Cec and I visited Fern Canyon, she had had a miscarriage. She was tormented by the loss and wanted to go someplace where nature was at its ripest and most fertile. Her need to be in the midst of the deep green cauldron of life seemed to be met by visiting this lush gash in the hilly forest of redwoods. It seemed so fitting to bring her back here, where she asked to be, and where the body she left behind can become part of the tapestry of life at its richest.

I saved a small portion of the ashes to place at a redwood tree growing in a park near our home, where friends and family can easily visit. But anyone who visits Fern Canyon in Northern California will find themselves richly rewarded by the experience, even were it not for the fact that Cec herself is now part of the canyon.

We flew back Sunday night. When I got home, Maddie's face lit up and she said, "Daddy say, 'I always come back to you.'" Even in sorrow there are so many blessings.

Maddie went to bed, Maribel left, and the house was quiet, empty but for three souls—one writing, one sleeping, and one watching over.

2:42 a.m.

Jim

April 20, 2004

On our eighth wedding anniversary, in 1997, Cec and I went to Monument Valley, Utah, a place I had long dreamed of going. It's the filming site of most of those wonderful old John Ford Westerns, and has more geographical iconography of the Old West than any other place in America.

Cec hated the desert. She hated the dryness, the sand, the apparent total absence of life. She thought cactus, dirt, and rocks, no matter how thrillingly arranged, were just awful. But for our anniversary she took me to probably the most famous desert landscape in America. She set it up so we could stay at Goulding's Lodge in the heart of Monument Valley, where John Wayne, Henry Fonda, and Jimmy Stewart stayed while they were making movies there. She got a Navajo guide to take us on a horseback ride through the valley.

We spent an entire day riding through some of the most gorgeous scenery in the world. Cec rode well for someone who rarely got a chance to ride. I'd been riding all my adult life, and considering how feeble these little Indian ponies were, we got along well on the trail.

Around midday, Cec's saddlebag came loose and slipped down below her horse's belly and began to bump his hind legs. The horse, thinking something was grabbing at him from below, began to buck. Cec did a terrific job of staying in the saddle—for a few seconds. (Long enough to win her a prize at the Pendleton Rodeo, but not long enough to outlast the horse.)

I was scared, because falling from a bucking horse in rocky terrain is no joking matter. But Cec was fine and she laughed about it, even though she was a little mad at the horse.

Our guide took off after Cec's horse, which was trying to kick free of the tangling saddlebag. Finally the horse was caught and calmed. When our guide came back, Cec and I were sitting on a rock eating the "meal" provided by the stable, a mayonnaise sandwich with a slice of bologna waved over it to impart that real meat flavor.

We hoped our guide would tell us tales of all the movies shot in Monument Valley. Instead, he occasionally flipped his hand toward some rock formation and said, "That rock looks like a chicken," or "That rock looks like a cow." I was mightily disappointed, but there's a chance that was Cec's favorite part of the trip. For years afterward, she'd point at some sight—say Michelangelo's *David* in Florence or Boulder Dam or the Chrysler Building and say, "That rock looks like a chicken."

I loved that.

We covered twenty-seven miles on horseback that day. Cec never once complained or asked to go back early, which made this an undeniable and unforgettable gift for me. Little did I know.

We were getting ready to clean up after the long day, and that's when I found out what the day had done to Cec. Her rear end and inner thighs were blistered as if someone had laid a hot iron across them. Her hips had blisters the size of my hand. The inseam of her jeans had worn vertical slices into the insides of her legs. She had blood from her bum to her ankles yet she hadn't said a word all day. It wasn't in her to ruin a once-in-a-lifetime experience for me.

Oh, she made plenty of noise the next few days. But that's okay. She'd earned it. I can't say if it had been I who was getting flayed alive that I would have done twenty-seven miles in silence for anybody, even Cec. Cecily was as capable of complaining as anyone I've ever known, but that's what makes the gift of her fortitude that time so remarkable and so deeply touching.

I always said that when my time came, I wanted my ashes scattered in Monument Valley. Now, though, I think I'd prefer to have them in Fern Canyon, near the girl who gave me Monument Valley.

11:16 p.m.

Jim

April 21, 2004

I took Maddie to our first concert tonight. The Wiggles. She was thrilled.

I had a difficult time when I thought how much Cec would have loved to go with Maddie, and how much Cecily's already missed in only six weeks of being gone.

It's so hard not to think of Cec regretting, now, in death, the things she's missing. Or that she's consciously suffering somehow from the unfairness of her early departure. As much as pain fills me, I think this all would be infinitely more bearable if I could shake the notion that she's unhappy *now*. I know in my brain that it's not that way. But the brain is no match for the heart.

I was married before, briefly, in college, to a nice girl who rather quickly realized her mistake and found a girl she liked better than me. In hindsight, I have no regrets, either for not being a good enough woman or for being forced into a turn of path that led me to today. But I recall thinking then that the loneliest place on earth was an empty house from which someone had deliberately left you. Not true. The loneliest place on earth is an empty house from which someone was *taken* from you. There's nothing emptier than a bed that once held two that now holds one. Unless it's a closet full of dead girl's clothes.

But hope springs eternal, they say. As traitorous as it feels to say, I will feel better, I will feel happiness, I will feel less lonely, I will *be* less lonely. Even as Cec once awaited me a few months or years ahead, good things surely are poised just beyond the crest of this hill. It's steep, no denying. But my legs are good and my heart is determined. I'm sure it can't be too far. Since "life's that way →," that's where I'm headed.

11:41 p.m.

Jim

April 24–28, 2004

Well, it seemed like a good idea at the time.

Saturday, April 24: Maddie and I flew to Texas to see my family.

At my folks' house, it took me a while to get up the nerve to go in to see my dad. I hadn't seen him in nearly ten months, and he'd been ambulatory then. Since September, he hasn't been out of bed on his own. My sister Teddlie prepped me for what to expect, and it wasn't as bad as I'd anticipated, but it was no fun. My strong, athletic dad, always a more formidable physical specimen than I, now looked like a baby bird that had fallen out of its nest. His right hand, twisted from arthritis and disuse, clutches rigidly at his right collarbone. His left hand, slightly more usable, lies at his side, except when he occasionally lifts it to ask for something. Unfortunately, not once while I was there was I certain what he was asking for. His voice is weak, in terms of volume, and nonexistent in terms of intelligibility. The only thing that was communicated easily was the fact that his mind is still there.

I think his attention wanders at times, but he is absolutely as quick-witted, conscious, and clearheaded as ever. He simply cannot tell anyone anything. At all. I tried to establish a blink-once-for-yes, twice-for-no kind of communication, but he can't focus the conscious use of the muscles in his eyelids any more than he can for his speech. But his reactive responses were clear. If I told him a joke, he laughed.

When I talked about Cecily, he cried. When I brought Maddie in to see him, his face lit up. He's there.

I just can't decide whether that's a good thing. In prison camps, the mental isolation without communication drove many a POW over the edge. And *they* could move and walk and talk, if only to themselves. My dad can't scratch his leg.

The first day in Texas was a revelation and a portent. Maddie immediately bonded with the family she hadn't seen in two years. But the unfamiliar surroundings affected her in a way that colored the entire visit. She became distraught if I wandered away more than a few feet. This made it virtually impossible to be alone with my dad. A screaming child is the last thing he needs in the vicinity, so I did my best to keep her settled. Some well-chosen videos captured her attention for short spans and I was able to spend a few minutes here and there with my dad. But between the obstacles to communication and the brevity of the trips to his room, a true revisit of our bond and any hoped-for moments of true catharsis were denied.

Monday, April 26: Again, I got almost no time with my dad. I did sit with him for a few minutes in the evening. I felt so idiotic, not being able to talk to him. Here he lay, with thoughts and feelings begging to be released in speech, completely unable to make them understood. And here I sat, with all my powers of speech and communication intact, and I couldn't think of anything to say that didn't trivialize the moment. I never realized how hard a one-sided conversation is.

He was watching a basketball game when I came in. "How's the game?" A raised eyebrow, meaning—what? (And just what did I expect?) "I love you, Papa." A slightly raised hand. Okay, I can give that a meaning. "I'm sorry I'm so bad at this." A slight facial movement. "Are you comfortable?" Nothing. (This is excruciating.) "It's hard, isn't it, Papa?" A struggle to form his mouth and then a slight high-pitched croak. "We had a really good life until recently, didn't we?" His mouth tightens and a tear forms in each eye. Okay, well,

I understand that. And how lovely, I've said nothing of true conse-
quence and I've made him cry. Great.

So I sit and hold his hand and we watch basketball. Eventually
I get up to put Maddie to bed. I tell him good night, looking for a
sign that he's okay with my leaving or that he'd rather I stayed a little
longer. He tries to speak and gesture, but I have no idea what he's
trying to convey. And so, reluctantly, I leave.

I decide to rock Maddie to sleep, even though we're past that,
because I need to hold her close. I rock her and clench my jaw to keep
from crying over my old man. Then Maddie says, "Where Mommy?"
and out it all comes and I can't stop crying. All I can do is try to do
it silently, so as not to distress Maddie or keep her awake any longer.
She touches my face as I rock her and she says, "Daddy's mustass
all wet . . . Daddy cwying." Yeah. Daddy cwying. Is there no end to
Daddy's cwying?

Tuesday, April 27: Early rising to catch the flight home. I sat with
my dad for a few minutes, again almost completely stymied by my
own inability, but as I always do when pressed, I managed to say everything I needed to say. When I told him we had to leave, he looked
surprised and dismayed. Obviously, I can't know if that's what was in
his mind, but I felt traitorous. Traitorous for leaving him and traitorous for not having made more of the time this visit offered me to be
with him. I told him how amazing he was as a father, how impossible
it would have been for me to get through what I have to get through
without his guidance and example, and how every question I ever
had about how to be a father was answered if only I looked at the
father he had been. I told him how desperately I loved him and then I
lied to him. I said I'd see him again, and soon. A lie needn't be a false
statement. A lie can also be a true statement you believe to be false.
Never for a moment did I think I would ever see him alive again. It
seems so intensely unlikely. I cling to the prospect that I might be
wrong, that we will have more time together. But it was a lie when I
said it. And he knew it was. His lovely face crumpled and he wept,

hard, wrackingly, but almost without sound. His beleaguered body wouldn't even vouchsafe him a sob. His left arm lifted—in a wave? a beckon? a graspless reaching? There was no signal that he was ready to let me go, that everything was wrapped up. I just said, "I gotta go, Papa. I love you. I'll see you soon," over and over, like some kind of distraught robot, and I backed out of the room, leaving him there reaching toward me with his knobbed hand, his face a mess from tears he couldn't wipe.

And we got in the car and left.

I have more to say, more about this journey through grief and disbelief and long good-byes, but I meandered so through the recap that I haven't the spirit or the energy to go on.

12:49 a.m.

Jim

April 30, 2004

I've been pretty emotionally stable since getting home from Texas. But yesterday I had a moment that hit me strangely—a realization that I've started occasionally thinking of Cec in the past tense. That's a new sensation. It was a mixture of my awareness that my life contains nearly two months of subsequent existence without her, and of a sense that the vital, vibrant part of her, her life force, is, atom by atom, slipping out of my hands. There were moments, brief moments, when some thought of our life together flashed by and I experienced it in the same slightly removed way I remember aspects of my life with my granny, or with friends who died a decade or more ago. The automatic twinge of pain and loss was there, but it echoed slightly and felt as though there were a touch of reflex to the reaction. At this juncture, such a detachment (not exactly the right word) is only split seconds in duration. But to feel anything at all that wasn't completely here and now about this loss was a surprising feeling. And though any thought that maybe I was getting used to Cec being gone is instantly (and reflexively) greeted with shame and not a little disgust, at the same time some happier feelings were there too.

For a moment or two yesterday, I felt as though I might get through this. I felt that maybe, as horrible as it seems to believe, I might someday reach a point where I feel the loss in the same way I feel deep losses from long ago—still real, still sad and painful, but tucked away in that closet of previous times where they can't hurt so much.

And that made me think that maybe I can have a livable kind of life. It will mean confronting my own demons of insecurity and shame about moving on, but that's just what those feelings are—demons.

Cecily's mom, Dell, has been quite helpful to me lately in battling those demons, encouraging me to see and believe that Cec is not anguishing somewhere over the possibility that I might move on. Aside from the fact that, given a choice, Cec would certainly want me to have a happy and meaningful life, there's also a concept that Dell placed before me, that there's no sorrow in the soul, only in the body. The image of Cec being eternally happy and comfortable and at peace with herself and with my future is a blessed image, and though it's a fight to maintain that image in my fretful mind, it's one worth fighting for.

The worst guilt and shame following the loss of one's love is that which accompanies imaginings of future love. And my confession is that even before I lost my Cecily, I wondered if I would ever find love again if she died, and with whom. I wondered if I would ever be able to love anyone the way I loved Cec, and if that were so, would it be possible to do so without Cec looking over our shoulders? Would not Cec, from some mystic vantage point, feel betrayed? Would I not feel traitorous to her memory?

And yet I knew and I know now that nothing's so valuable in life as having the comfort of another mated soul. The worst, the absolute worst of all this passage, has been to make it alone. But the worst of a joyful passage, too, is to make it alone. To be unable to share each day's delights and troubles, to be unable to hold in tight embrace that one who knows and shares all, whether in torment or in grand happiness, is the curse of a loss like mine. And it's the hunger that first rears itself after the shock recedes. It does not care that another part of the heart is still wracked with loss, that part of that heart sees no future, or that duty to one's love does not die when she does. It simply wants what it had from that love: to be held, to be deemed vital to that person's existence, to be tender to and to receive tenderness from. And it wants, oh so desperately, not to be this lonely anymore.

And there's Maddie. Who would love her as much as her mother? Cec was terribly afraid of Maddie becoming a victim of the stepchild syndrome, and begged me to protect her from that. (So Cec *did* think I might find a life with someone else someday. Hmm. Hadn't remembered that.) I can't imagine that someone I felt close enough to share my daughter with would not be someone who would love her to the depths of her soul. But I don't have any idea how to guarantee that. Do I protect Maddie by denying her someone to mother her? Or do I protect Maddie by finding someone for just that job? I know, I know, life's that way →. But are love and joy that way, too? I think I hope so. If nobody minds.

1:20 a.m.

Jim

NINE

May 3, 2004

Today makes two months Cecily's been gone. There are other milestones arriving soon. Friday is our fifteenth wedding anniversary. Sunday is Mother's Day. . . .

I was so busy today that I scarcely had time to think about Cec. Only this evening when I walked a few blocks, past her office at the studio, to get my first meal of the day at 6:30 p.m., did I feel the melancholy bubble up to the surface. The milestone of two months is arbitrary, but it's a milestone. Still, aside from the actual missing her, which trumps all emotions, the overwhelming feeling I carry is one of unrelenting disbelief. Two months and I'm still asking, "How can this be?"

If I want to make meaning from Cec's life, I've got to get a lot braver than I've been. I don't mean bungee jumping from helicopters—I mean getting up and doing things for the sake of accomplishment. Exercising mind and body. Tackling hard jobs rather than planning to tackle them. If it weren't for Maddie, I fear I would read and sleep and surf the Web and watch movies till my muscles atrophied. I feel mentally half asleep, as though I just drifted off and someone's gently nudging me. Never an auspiciously sparky kind of guy, I've got less spark than usual. Before it wisps away into a thread of smoke, I need to fan that spark.

Oh, God, how can it be two months already? How can she not have been here for Maddie's pony ride around the neighborhood, and to tell me weeks ago that Maddie needed new pajamas 'cause her legs have gotten too long for the old ones, or to show me what window shades to buy, or to lie with her cheek just above my collarbone and say, "Oh, Pie, aren't we lucky?" just one more time?

How?

11:51 p.m.

Jim

May 4, 2004

Never, ever tell anyone you're feeling better. Sometime within the next day, you will certainly find out just how better you ain't.

Looking through some boxes in the bedroom closet today, I found the photo album from our wedding. There's a big picture of Cec and me from our wedding on the mantelpiece downstairs, and I've looked at it long and hard every day for two months. So I figured, "Wedding pictures? Piece of cake." (So to speak.)

At first I just reminisced warmly, smiling at how pretty she was, how happy she looked. But there were a lot of pictures. And before long I was sobbing. Hard. Harder than I have in weeks. Twenty, twenty-five minutes later, I was finally sobbed out. Or so I thought.

I put away the pictures and began cleaning up papers that had been lying around the bedroom since probably January. I hadn't been quite up to the task of going through the papers stacked on the little table that stood next to where Cec's hospital bed had been. But now, all sobbed out, I thought maybe it would be a good time to clean up.

The papers were mainly phone messages and numbers, and notes and questions for doctors. But at the bottom of it all was Cec's journal. It had a lot of get-well cards tucked inside, and truthfully they didn't bother me. I was touched by what many people had written, but like I said, I was all sobbed out. Then I saw what the journal itself contained.

Starting a couple of days after I started sending out these e-mails, in late October, just after her diagnosis, Cec had written letters to Maddie. At first they came every night, then less frequently, very much in tune with the ups and downs of her treatment. I began to read these messages and I realized that Cec was more convinced than I'd thought that she was going to die, even in the early period. Her letters to Maddie were so excruciatingly sorrowful and, most painfully, apologetic to Maddie for the possibility of leaving her here without a mother. Everything I knew she felt and everything I feared she felt was magnified a hundred times in these letters. But also there was the fire of her determination. She never promised Maddie that she'd make it, but she promised her every night that she'd give everything she had and take anything she had to take in order to make it.

Reading her words, in her handwriting, was so close to hearing her say these things in her own voice. It was exquisitely painful, the pain softened only by the immense love that arose anew within me. In my entire life, even as a child, I've never cried for more than an hour straight, and certainly not in the heaving, wracking manner I cried tonight at almost hearing her talk again, hearing her say how much she wanted to stay, how she feared going, and how much she loved us.

I know this: some day that journal will almost certainly be our daughter's most prized possession. No one could ever doubt the depth of love Maddie's mother had for this little girl, after reading her words. There is, of course, no cause to doubt that love, but here in Cec's journal is the greatest proof of mother love I've ever seen captured in ink.

It's five hours later, and I'm still wrung empty, a scrunched-up husk with all the tears squeezed out. Tears heal, they say, and I feel a little better. Oops. I wasn't going to say that anymore.

12:07 a.m.

Jim

May 6, 2004

My sister Denise called to tell me that in church recently, she was suddenly conscious of Cecily speaking to her, asking her to tell me that she watched and knew and loved, and that she was far happier than she'd ever been in life. I don't know what I ought to believe. But I believe I'll try to believe that.

The feelings come and go, without ever going entirely. At best these days, there's always the whisper from the other room, the voice that never lets me forget what's gone. Or as that smarty-pants Kahlil Gibran put it, *"Joy and sorrow are inseparable . . . together they come and when one sits alone with you . . . remember that the other is asleep upon your bed."*

I'm glad somebody's getting some sleep.

11:39 p.m.

Jim

May 7, 2004

Our fifteenth wedding anniversary.

Around 3:00, I put my little girl in the car and drove up Coldwater Canyon to Mulholland Drive and then down into Franklin Canyon Park. We parked and walked down a little path to a huge redwood tree, near the lakeside. It's the tallest tree in the park, with branches spread out and down like the spokes of an umbrella.

Maddie said, "We go under a tree like a tent." There, at the base of this huge sheltering tree, with Maddie at my side, I scattered the portion of Cecily's ashes I had saved from the trip to Redwood National Park. I poured them in such a way, I hope, that they will be taken up by the roots of the tree, and that Cec, therefore, will always be at one with this monument to life.

For all her fears and her ultimate frailty, she was herself a monument to life. The fraction of herself that she left behind is now mixed inseparably with the forest life she loved, both in the beauteous spot up north and in a nearby glade where we who loved her can walk and visit and know she is near.

I talked to Maddie about her mommy, for the first time breaking my own rule about always letting Maddie bring up the subject. I told her how much her mommy loved her, how much she wanted to stay, and why she had to go away. I told her that Mommy loved the trees and we could always come back here and visit and know that we were as close to Mommy as we could be. Maddie listened, then said, "No like bugs," as she brushed away a fly. Then she said, "Maddie climb tree." I think my speech was lost on her. Probably as it should be.

I had said good-bye to Cec one more time, believing that the last of my symbolic tasks was done. I couldn't help crying as I carried Maddie back up the path to our car, and on the drive home I alternated between sobbing and explaining to Maddie in the mirror that Daddy was crying because he was sad, but that everything was okay.

"Daddy cwying," she says, but then says, "Maddie want juice."

I think I've got a pretty healthy kid here.

At home, I realized that the symbolic tasks weren't quite over. They give you the ashes in a plastic bag inside an urn. When the ashes are poured out of the bag, there's a residue of ash dust left inside the bag. For reasons far outside my normally resolute sense of practicality, I couldn't bring myself to just toss the bag into the waste bin and I couldn't leave it on the ground in the park. And although I considered rinsing it in the lake to send the last dusting of Cec's remains back to a natural kind of nature, I couldn't get near enough the water with Maddie in tow. So I brought the bag back home. And on the trip home, I decided what to do.

When we bought this house from Ellen DeGeneres, it was a little cottage surrounded by a gorgeous garden of roses planted by Ellen's mother, Betty, who lived here. The garden, unfortunately, had to be ripped out, because it lay in the path of the additions we had planned. But Cec, in her wisdom, had the dozens of rosebushes potted rather than thrown out, and they've been waiting in a corner of the yard for the house to be finished and the garden replanted. Our dear friend Dorothy Apple has been caring for the roses, at Cec's behest. (Cec had no confidence that I could preserve the roses myself.)

Today, upon returning from Franklin Canyon, I filled the dusty plastic bag with water and poured the water on her beloved roses. Call me a sentimentalist. All I know is that had I not found a meaningful way to remove the last of the ashes from that plastic bag, I'd never have been able to throw it away.

So now nature and its blossoms feed on her, just as her soul fed on them. I'd rather she were here, telling me what a great idea this would be in fifty years when she died of old age. But as it is and must be, I suppose feeding redwoods and roses isn't too bad for a girl who felt as she felt. After all, she named her daughter Madeline Rose.

2:06 a.m.

Jim

May 8, 2004

Nanci Christopher brought her son Joshua over for a playdate with Maddie, but it fell apart like a Kleenex hat in a rainstorm. We took the kids for lunch, but Maddie wet her pants, and mine, rather severely and wouldn't stop crying, so we turned around and went back home. (I can't blame Maddie for the soaking. This morning, she asked for pull-ups, and when I couldn't find regular ones, I put swimming pull-ups on her. Apparently vast leakage isn't a problem when the child is in a swimming pool.)

We went shopping later, and I got everything—except diapers and pull-ups. I expect the county to show up soon, take Maddie, and put a sign on the front door: "Too stupid to have kids."

12:30 a.m.

Jim

May 9, 2004. Mother's Day.

A couple of simple days. No great turmoil. Then, playing with Maddie tonight, helping her "cook" something on her little toy oven, I remembered the effort Cecily went to finding just the right toy oven, searching store after store, wanting it to be perfect. Cec was so excited to present it to Maddie on Christmas, fearing this might be her last Christmas. Watching Maddie turn knobs and stir "food" tonight, that thing I don't believe in, the unfairness of the universe, jumped up and punched me in the nose. Sometimes recollections and reminders of our life and love together come and go without a sniffle. Other times a strand of hair on the nightstand will throw me into a whirlpool.

Tonight, after I got Maddie to bed, I checked my phone messages. There was a message from Anna Maria Alvarez, who was our housekeeper for many years over at the old house in Van Nuys. She hadn't worked for us since just after Maddie was born and I haven't seen her or talked to her since. She called today to wish Cec a happy Mother's Day and to say she hoped Cec was happy and having a wonderful time with Maddie.

There's a call I wish I could avoid returning. Maybe I'll wait till Monday. No sense two people's Mother's Day being ruined.

In honor of this day, I'm going to include something I found in Cecily's journal, a letter she wrote to Maddie a mere five days after the discovery of Cec's illness. It's hard, painful, to read, but it contains such love and much of the essence of a mother's hopes and dreams, that I felt I should share it.

October 30, 2003

To my dearest, darling baby girl, Madeline,

Oh, my sweet baby, how sorry I am for this terrible turn of events. I can't bear the idea that I have brought you into this world to leave you here to navigate it without me. I have so much that I want to share with you, show you, teach you, love, love, love you. You are the greatest gift from God anyone could ever receive. How lucky I was that of all the people in the world, you came to me.

I had some sad and rough times in my childhood that I was SO determined to protect you against. I so want you to grow up feeling SURE of YOURSELF and LOVED to the core of your being.

One of the reasons we named you Madeline was because of the little girl in the Madeline *books. When I was a little girl— four or so—I was in a Catholic boarding school. I was the youngest and smallest by far. And I was, during my childhood, pretty sick from time to time. So I related to the little girl in the Madeline story very much. Naming you Madeline was symbolic to me: starting over with a new little Madeline who would have a clean slate—who had no scars or heartache to handicap her through her journey. And I was going to protect you from it all.*

Oh, my darling baby, how sorry I am!

What big plans I had for our mad love affair together! I am so grateful, for you are, along with your father, the greatest thing that has ever happened to me.

My greatest fear right now is that I may not live long enough for you to remember me. That would be heartbreaking and tragic for me. And yet, on the other hand, your tender little heart may not need the horrible memory of losing your mother.

My darling angel, how I wanted to protect you from such wounds!

I promise you the all-out fight for my life. I will take whatever drugs they have available to beat this back—knock it out—kill it. I will take them gladly—I will be sick, I will fight my way toward you.

You are so special and such a miracle. You're everything I ever wanted. You.

Your father and I wanted a baby, and I so desperately wanted a little girl—but YOU—YOU are so far and away above any of the expectations we had! You are so magnificent a child—so happy, loving, SMART!, eager to learn, try new things, find joy, and you break my heart with the willingness you have to face your fears and deal with them creatively!

I adore you, need you, love you with all the force of the universe—my precious angel I am fighting for you—fighting my way toward you. I love you more than you can imagine.

—Your mother

First Corinthians 13:13 says, "*And now abideth faith, hope, and love, these three; but the greatest of these is love.*" Cec's love abideth, I know, even now.

11:30 p.m.

Jim

May 10, 2004

I sure miss Cec tonight. I need so badly to talk to her—and to have her talk to me. First my dad, then Cec. If one is lucky in life, there are people who serve as pillars to hold one up when one is weary or confused or lonely. I've had a few, most still abiding nearby. But no longer to have these two to talk to, at the time when I most desperately need to talk to no one so much as them—it is difficult, so hard. Sometimes, I think, too difficult. But, no, *"kites rise highest against the wind."* The choice now is to fly or to fall. The wind I must run into is gentler than what they faced. So with a manufactured smile, I face that wind and force myself to run. What else can I do?

11:18 p.m.

Jim

May 11, 2004

Maddie's speech therapist said that Maddie's speech progress is phenomenal. I'm so proud. She can almost say, "Hey, I never asked to be born!" I can't wait.

I got an e-mail recently from Susan Rudd, someone who gets this nightly e-mail forwarded to her, someone in a second or third circle of the ripple. She wrote:

I attended a Relay for Life ceremony two weekends ago here in Wilmington, N.C. There were approximately 4,000 people there, and we raised over $500,000. Luminaries were purchased for cancer victims by friends and families. There were hundreds surrounding the track. As I walked to the track to watch the first survivor lap, the first luminary I saw had Cecily Adams's name on it. Obviously, she was loved around the country! Just thought you might like to know about this.

10:10 p.m.

Jim

May 12, 2004

Therapy, errands, shopping, nothing out of the ordinary. Except I started yelling, "I want her back, I want her back!" at the top of my lungs driving down Ventura Boulevard this afternoon. A number of people, myself included, found it disconcerting.

10:19 p.m.

Jim

May 14, 2004

My little middle sister Renée wrote me from Florida this morning with her notion of why I can't easily get past the feeling that Cecily got a "raw deal," and the unfairness of it all. Renée wrote: *"Maybe the sadness you feel is your loss of sharing Cec's joy over the house. When we love someone, one of the greatest joys we have is watching them be happy. So maybe the real cause of the pain is your loss of sharing the house with Cec and watching her enjoy it."*

I think Renée's onto something.

I found this concept moving. It hasn't yet allowed me to feel free of the anguish I've described, but it has given me some breathing space, a slight comfort that I feel might easily grow into a happier response. If it's *my* loss I'm really grieving over, then I can handle that. It's hard, but I can and will handle it.

What has been so hard has been the way I reinforce within myself the idea that Cec is still suffering from her own loss. Renée's insight has helped me bridge the gap between the emotional and the intellectual. I hope I can start reinforcing that bridge.

I went to Cec's redwood tree today. I looked up at the tree from its base and said, "It's really beautiful from this angle, isn't it, Pie?"

Then I realized something and added, "But I guess you've got the aerial view, haven't you?"

12:18 a.m.

Jim

May 15, 2004

Today was the wedding of our friends Renée Ryan and Collin Seals. It was a beautiful affair at a mansion in the lower Hollywood Hills, with sumptuous gardens, an expansive rolling lawn, and a grand and enticing view of the city below. I told Renée that she was one of the two most beautiful brides I had ever seen, and indeed she was.

It was a touching ceremony, but to hear two people deeply in love pledge themselves to each other "in sickness and in health" slammed home to me how lightly such phrases are often uttered, and how terribly difficult they can be to live up to. To hear the hope-filled vows to grow old together, from young people in love, tore at me, because not all couples get to grow old together, no matter how desperately they want to. I thought of how for nineteen years, I had a complete image in my mind of what Cec and I would be like with each other as we passed into our seventies and eighties. It was so hard to remain composed, wishing that we could have had that time together as I hoped with all my heart that these two marrying today would have theirs.

10:49 p.m.

Jim

May 16, 2004

My father died tonight.

I'm told by my sister Teddlie that he was comfortable, watching television, and simply, quietly, went. My mother was with him.

He was a North Texas farm boy who fought the Japanese as an antitank gunner in World War II, served in the Japan Occupational Forces (and moonlighted as a minister) for one year after the war, and spent the next several decades as a minister for the Church of Christ in various locations in the Dallas–Fort Worth area. He supplemented his meager ministerial income with work as a certified public accountant. He believed in tolerance and love of mankind, and he believed in law. He was ashamed of having once gotten a speeding ticket, for he believed that adherence to the law was the glue that held the social contract together, and if he disagreed with a law, he had avenues to pursue to change it. He would not knowingly break one.

He was the funniest man I have ever known, in a corny way. And he was the kindest, most guileless, and most loving person I have ever met. A few days ago, I mentioned my dad in an e-mail to my boyhood friend Lon Smith. He wrote in return: *"It brought back old memories of a jillion different things. Especially your father and how he was. How he always talked to you calmly when you were in 'trouble.' You've no idea how many times I sat on the steps of my porch and looked across the street at your house, and wished that I could live there. That I was in your family."* I've heard the same sentiment from several friends during our childhood and after. I've never expressed similar thoughts about anyone else's family. I knew what I had.

It's impossible to convey what a man my father was. I've spent my entire life dreading this night, and now, in light of recent circumstances and his depleted strength, I find myself unable to grieve in the way I had imagined I would. He is free from pain. He was clear and resolved in all his relationships. He was deeply, deeply loved, and he knew it. And he was completely ready. He knew there is a Heaven. He is there now. I've not met anyone who deserved it more.

11:24 p.m.

James Norman Beaver Jr.

May 17, 2004

I've spent the evening writing my dad's obituary for the Dallas paper, so I'm pretty well spent. I have nothing to say that others have not said better. Two from Shakespeare, and one from Harper Lee:

From *Romeo and Juliet:* "*And, when he shall die, take him and cut him out in little stars, and he will make the face of heaven so fine that all the world will be in love with night and pay no worship to the garish sun.*"

From *To Kill a Mockingbird:* "*He would be there all night, and he would be there when Jem waked up in the morning.*"

From *Hamlet:* "*Now cracks a noble heart. Good night, sweet prince, and flights of angels sing thee to thy rest!*"

2:00 a.m.

Jim

May 19, 2004

Agonizing over my dad's eulogy. Not over what to say, but what to leave out. It's the same as writing Cec's. Words are a dust speck on the river of what they were, and using words to try doing justice to them is folly. But I've got nothing else, and people expect words. Maybe if I weren't so numb.

I'm afraid if I haven't had a big emotional collapse prior to the memorial service, then that's where I'll have it. Oh, well. I've seen my dad cry, standing up there in church in front of everyone. It usually happened when he had reason to mention his father.

My dad's father died when my dad was twenty-six. I wasn't quite one year old yet. All I remember of my granddad, besides pictures, is how my own dad felt when he talked about him. I'm lucky. I got my dad more than twice as long as he got his. On the other hand, I figure he gets to see his again now, so that's pretty lucky, too.

12:33 a.m.

Jim

May 20, 2004

The afternoon was spent signing wills, trusts, guardianships, affidavits, powers of attorney, advance directives for medical care, and all the other stuff that makes sure Maddie doesn't have to live in a cardboard box if I get hit by a pie wagon. It's finally all taken care of.

Visualize me not coming unglued in front of 500 people Saturday morning. I know I pulled it off once, but twice in two months? My confidence wavers.

11:10 p.m.

Jim

May 21–26, 2004

I flew to Dallas on Friday, May 21. The rest of my immediate family (except Maddie, whom I left at home with her Aunt Cathy) was already there. After brief greetings, I girded my loins and did what needed to be done: I marched into my dad's room and forced myself to confront the empty space where his hospital bed had stood. Then I went into his closet for the extremely mixed experience of his clothes. My dad's closet had always had a nice smell that was uniquely him: the soft tang of leather shoes and wallets and belts, the light bouquet of his suits and sports coats. I know how powerfully redolent smells can be, and I fully expected to be bowled over with a Pavlovian emotional response. But it didn't come; I could no longer detect my father's aroma in the confines of his closet, where it had lingered for many, many years.

I had had the same disquieting experience in Cecily's closet. In both, I hugged items of clothing close to my face, hoping for a hint of the lost one, but not finding it. In my dad's case, there was a reason for the absence. It turns out that most of his clothes had been given to charity quite some time ago, long before his death. There was scarcely anything left to conjure with.

Saturday morning, I got up and put on the same charcoal suit, shirt, and tie I'd bought for Cecily's memorial. I picked up my mom and we went to the church. We placed the many flowers that had been delivered to our house, along with a large portrait of my dad, in front of the pulpit. A slow trickle of family arrived—aunts and uncles I hadn't seen in decades, all looking surprisingly spry, considering that several were older than my dad. By the time the service began, the auditorium was well populated, perhaps two or three hundred people. Since a man nearing eighty has likely already lost a good proportion of his friends, it seemed a fine turnout.

There were some of my dad's favorite hymns. His current minister gave a précis of the milestones in my father's life, and then I spoke. I got through it with only a fraction of the aplomb that attended my remarks at Cecily's memorial. Several times I had to stop and gather my breath and my wits and my strength before continuing. It was a longer presentation than I gave at Cec's, but that seemed appropriate, as I was the only non-minister speaking at this funeral. I was proud to say the things I said, and proud to have gotten through it without blubbering like an idiot. A little more composure would have been helpful, but there was no harm done. And I was given encouragement afterward to believe that my dad would have been proud of me. Perhaps. I like to think so.

And then it was over.

I flew home. Maddie threw open the door to greet me with a bubbly joyousness that I will never forget.

I lay with Maddie tonight, putting her to bed, saying our prayers, and readjusting the ritual prayer to address the missing elements. It used to be, "Please bless Mommy and Daddy, and Grandma and Grandpa, and my other grandma and my other grandpa." Now, it's— something different. And at that moment, I feel bound so tightly to my daughter yet otherwise quite alone, quite bereft and forlorn.

1:35 a.m.

Jim

May 27, 2004

I don't know what depression is. Perhaps I am depressed. I don't feel depressed. I feel sad. I feel lonely. I feel sorrowful. But I don't feel weighed down, unable to smile or laugh, unable to find moments of joy and lightheartedness. I don't feel like pulling the covers over my head. I don't wish for happy oblivion. I look forward to each day. I feel that good things are around the corner. I believe the blessings Maddie and I have now are just the beginning. None of that keeps me from being sad. I spend half my waking hours tight-throated, holding down the urge to cry. But I still have fun and carefree periods. I don't know if that's healthy or just plain weird.

I wouldn't want to feel less good, and I don't know if it's possible to feel better just yet. So the balancing act goes on. Every day is a learning experience, a new lesson in how to grieve and still reach out for life. I've made some big mistakes, reaching too fast for a new life, and hard lessons have come of it. But I will not wallow.

At my father's funeral, I saw Bonnie Ewing, a family friend. Her son Mort, once my sister Renée's boyfriend, had been killed in an automobile accident nearly twenty years ago. My first reaction upon seeing her was to feel sorry for her and her loss. Yet she's had two decades of full life since then. Is that really how she'd hope people would initially react to her? In twenty years, will pity be the first reaction people have when running into me? Pity mixed with love is what I sense everywhere I go these days, and it's fitting and comforting, generally. But do I want that to be how people see me for years to come? I think not. But for now, I'm not sure how well I would survive without it.

Does it strike anyone else as funny that I had to cancel my attendance at a grief recovery seminar this past weekend in order to attend my father's funeral?

I sure loved my old man. And I sure loved my sweet wife. And nothing can adequately describe how I miss them. Hold tight to those you love. Hold tight.

12:55 a.m.

Jim

May 29, 2004

Not one to remember his dreams, I have no previous recollection of dreaming about Cecily since her death. But I remember the one from last night. I dreamed that in the throes of loneliness and desire, I made advances to a woman. This woman is a real person, someone close to Cec and to me in our real lives. In my dream, I was afraid of her reaction to my advances, afraid of angering her or losing her respect, for despite my longings for some surcease from sorrow and loneliness, it had been in the dream only three months since Cec's death, just as in real life. But the woman in the dream never got a chance to reveal anger or disrespect or even acceptance, because at the instant I reached for her, I broke down in tears, begging the forgiveness of both Cecily and the woman. I believe I felt I had betrayed Cec herself, as well as the love and respect this woman had for Cec and me. The funny thing was that I'm hard-pressed to imagine a real-life scenario in which I would make advances to this woman, even without the issue of Cec's demise.

But what's clear from the dream is that I am quite caught on the barrier between letting go of any of my past life and taking hold of a new life. I don't even think it's about romantic life. My sense is that I have intense feelings of guilt about doing anything that acts to relinquish Cec's hold on me, that moves me away from where we were headed together. And at the same time, for survival's sake and for the sake of honoring life, I have new inclinations to move ahead and away from the old life. It's a massive wrestling, grappling, tug-of-war between conflicting emotions, and I feel torn to shreds by it.

It's not merely *Will there ever be another woman in my life?* or *Will I raise Maddie according to different precepts than Cec might have?* but *How dare I buy blue curtains when I know Cec wanted tan ones?*

How does surviving Cec give me the right to make decisions differently than she would have? There's something silly about worrying over this kind of thing, yet anyone who has ever found themselves deprived by death of a life partner must know what I'm saying. It may be silly in the long run, but I guarantee you it doesn't feel silly. Sometimes I make a decision about paint or curtains or flooring and my heart pounds as though the secret police were marching up the walk. They aren't, of course, and I go ahead and make my decisions, and sometimes actually feel good about this autonomy. But in the moment, there's always a sense of "How can I do this when Cec would do it differently?" Somewhere down the line, I suspect, there will be a dinner date or a walk in the park with someone. What flood of guilt must be withstood then, I can only guess.

12:25 a.m.

Jim

May 31, 2004

Crac!

It's the sound that a rocking chair makes when one of the rockers breaks off.

It's also the title of a short animated film made in 1980, which won the Academy Award for Best Animated Short Film in 1981. Cecily and I stumbled across the fifteen-minute film years ago when it was used as filler on the late, lamented Z Channel in L.A.

Crac! tells the story of a French-Canadian family from pioneer days through the modern industrial era, all through the "eyes" of a rocking chair made by hand by the patriarch of the family.

The father has carved a face in the crest rail, and with smiles or frowns, the chair watches all that goes on around it. Children are born, and they are rocked in their mother's arms in the chair. As they grow, they use it as a plaything, their imaginations metamorphosing the chair into a sleigh, a fort, a locomotive, whatever their little minds can conjure. At night the family sits around the fire, lost in individual reverie, huddled near the father as he rocks and smokes his pipe. Seasons pass. Children grow and wed. At a wedding dance, the old ladies rock in the chair and watch the young folks celebrate.

And when the chair is old and rickety, just like the man who made it, finally one of its rockers breaks. *Crac!* Yet there's life in and for the old chair, and though the world around the rocking chair transforms with the passing years into something not so pretty or bucolic or likely to render tender memories, eventually the life that the chair has seen, the glories and warmth and security of family and love and community, find their revival, and the resonance of the brief story lingers long, long afterward.

Something about this little movie touched me and Cecily deeply. The joys of family love and tradition that she longed so for in her life were beautifully presented in *Crac!* The music, French-Canadian folk-type music, was redolent of a quieter, more peaceful, and communal time. The detail of the animation, the quirks in the chair's little face, the subtle shifts of mood, made this one of the most treasured experiences Cec and I had together. We saw it many times on the grainy videotape I'd made of it, accidentally captured at the tail end of some movie in the mid-eighties. Eventually, I found it on DVD and we saw it again, this time with new appreciation for the artistry and color. I am certain that in all the many times we saw this little film, there was not one time that Cec didn't turn to me afterward and slowly dissolve into tears. Everything she ever wanted in her life was somehow literally or figuratively captured in this little strip of animation. The continuum of love and family, the resonance of happy times that she always believed lingered inside inanimate objects, the traditions of shared affectionate life that she so hoped to create in her own world, all of it was there. She cried with happiness and longing and with sadness, too, every single time she saw it.

We discovered this little film a few months before we got married. When we came home from our wedding, sitting in the middle of our living room was a richly dark cherrywood rocking chair with spindle stiles and a crest rail broad enough to carve a face in. In our nineteen years together, Cecily gave me many, many gifts that took my breath away and left me in tears. I think in all our nearly two decades, this rocking chair was the only time I ever really returned the favor. She knew instantly what it was, what it represented. I don't think I ever saw her cry harder for joy.

Tonight, as I lay with Maddie, listening to her drift snufflingly off to sleep, I began thinking of videos that Maddie might enjoy, now

that she's near to outgrowing some of her favorites. I remembered
the DVD with *Crac!* on it. And I wondered how long it would be
before Maddie could appreciate that film in something like the way
her mother had. And, of course, then I began thinking about the film
itself and its depiction of a young husband and wife, starting their
lives together, having their family and building their home, and growing old together with such love and tenderness for each other and
such interdependence, such shared support as their hair grew white
and their paces slowed. And I thought of how much Cec wanted that,
and how much I wanted it with her, and how difficult it is to imagine
growing old without her, how unutterably sad it is to walk that road
alone, without the one who made my soul sing.

Crac!

It's the sound a heart makes.

10:29 p.m.

Jim

June 1, 2004

Perhaps you recall my February 23 entry. It involved what, but
for the grace of God, was almost my last conversation with Cec—
one that ended with an argument and me smashing my phone on my
desk. I didn't elaborate, but maybe you remember that my, um, poorly
resolved tensions ended up sending me and my damaged finger to
the emergency room? Well, it's taken me three and a half months to
finally get in to see a doctor about the damaged knuckles. Turns out
it's scar tissue in the knuckle joints and I'll have to do some physical
therapy for a few weeks. None of this is important.

What's important is how bad I feel that in the midst of cata-
strophic illness, the volatility of my relationship with Cecily came so
close to ending our relationship in screaming and anger. *Missed it by*

that much. I'll be grateful the rest of my life that we had that next day in resolution and happiness together before she fell asleep for that last long final week.

I've lived my life trying to live by the command of Ephesians 4:26—*"Let not the sun go down upon your wrath."* But like so many useful and good things, it's not always easy. Had that relatively meaningless flare-up been the last conversation I ever had with Cecily, I can assure you that whatever I'm feeling now would be but a spit in the ocean of the sadness I would be living under.

"Let not the sun go down upon your wrath." Words to live by.

And then there are those other words to live by. *"No one is completely useless. You can always serve as a bad example."*

10:23 p.m.

Jim

June 2, 2004

This morning Maddie woke up and for the first time said, "I want Mommy!" I hesitated a second, then said, lamely, "Yeah, I want her, too."

This evening, River Jordan, Maddie's most frequent playmate, came over. The two of them were on the sofa watching *Elmo* videos. River said, "Where's Maddie's mommy?" Another hesitation, then I said, "She went away." And River responded, "Yeah, she dieded." I said, "Yes, she did." I watched Maddie carefully during this. She seemed interested and a little concerned, but as the moment passed, both kids turned back to *Elmo* and began laughing at Mr. Noodle.

I sure wish I knew what I was doing.

11:21 p.m.

Jim

June 3, 2004

Today makes three months. How can that be?

Tonight was opening night for a play I'm doing at the Blank Theatre's Young Playwrights Festival. I actually had a moment, getting into my car after the show, when I thought, "I hope Cec is still up so I can tell her how the show went." The things you shared, the things you wanted to share, the things you didn't share—they all rise up and kick you in the head a few times a day, usually when you're not paying attention.

Three months. Un-stinkin'-believable.

1:16 a.m.

Jim

June 4, 2004

I ran into an old friend of ours, a man who'd directed Cec and me in a play a few years ago. This was the first time we'd crossed paths since I lost Cec. Sometimes I get weary of talking about her illness and death, having to go over it again with someone who wasn't around to know about it as it was going on. But I suppose, especially with someone as widely loved as Cecily, there will always be these encounters, and there's no way to avoid the conversation topic. But sometimes I grow weary.

Lots of little business things, acting things, show stuff, that I would normally be going over and over with Cec right now. We had great conversations, we two. I know I repeat myself here so much, but I miss her. Not just the wife and lover, but the friend. Guy who gets a wife who's also a pal is an awful lucky guy. That's me.

1:12 a.m.

Jim

June 6, 2004

Having a hard night tonight. I don't think I can do this.
God, I miss her so.
1:17 a.m.

Jim

June 7, 2004

Before anyone else gets the wrong idea, when I wrote last night that "I don't think I can do this," I was referring to last night's e-mail; I just didn't have the wherewithal to write anything meaningful.

I did *not* mean "I can't take this anymore." Some folks apparently got that idea, and I got e-mails from people telling me not to give up. What I said back to those people is: "Give up? That'll be the day."

Maddie and I spent half the day together at her therapy sessions. She was so happy and delightful and delighted through most of it, and I was so proud of her. Her advancement is astonishing, far beyond what Cec and I feared would be her lot forever.

The only bad part of the day arose later, alone on the drive home from an errand downtown. It was late, I was worn out, and I'm not sure what triggered it, but I got to thinking about Cec and I got that little whimpery feeling in my throat and I said, "Oh, little Pie, I miss you so," and then it was as though the dam at Johnstown had broken right there in the car. I cried for thirteen miles, all the way home, and then had to sit in the driveway and pull myself together before going in to let our wonderful new weekend nanny, Fabi, go home.

Waves, they say this stuff comes in, and waves it does, indeed. Good days followed by bad ones, good hours followed by bad ones, and always the fool's gold of contentment which seems to say, "You're getting past it, now," and then crumbles away into new shards of pain.

I always used to crab at Cec because I never got enough time to myself. Yeah, well. Careful what you ask for.

10:53 p.m.

No bye-bye.

Jim

June 8, 2004

Today, one of Maddie's therapists put her hand on my arm while talking to me and it was a shocking sensation. For some reason it gave me almost a flashback. I get the occasional hug whenever I run into anyone I know these days, but just having someone reach out and touch my arm was warming in some different kind of way. It was personal without being formalized, I suppose, and it caused feelings to well up in me, a sense of echo and remembrance of Cec touching my hand or arm as we talked. I had no idea a person was so many things, that her abduction from my life would leave such voids. It's not hearing her voice, it's not smelling her hair, it's not seeing her things in new arrangements in her closet or on her nightstand, it's not seeing her car move for months, it's not seeing her favorite foods diminish in the refrigerator or pantry, it's not being called on my various omissions or commissions. It's realizing that it doesn't matter anymore if the sheets are tight and wrinkle-free on the bed, that no one leaves the cap off the toothpaste, that no one says, "What's wrong?" if I don't speak for half an hour, that no one's reading all those catalogs that keep coming in the mail. It's realizing that this is forever and still not believing it. It's knowing I could pour a bucket of purple paint over the stair rail into the hallway below and nobody would be upset. It's knowing I could bring home ten dozen red roses and a string quartet and nobody would be happy. It's hard and it's relentless and it's got more facets than a crateful of engagement rings. And every time I know, I just *know*, that I've plumbed the final depths of it, I find some new trench.

All I can say is if you have someone you can share with, someone who cares about your life and wants to be involved in it in some way, any way, then share. Share, share, share. If a day comes when you've got no one to share that day with, nor the next nor the next, that's when you will know what you don't want to know. That even the best life can be hollowed out in a moment or in a week or in four months.

One may be the loneliest number, but there's an equation that's lonelier still: $2 - 1 = 1$.

Somebody ought to come up with a new way of doing math.

2:38 a.m.

Jim

TEN

June 10, 2004

Tom Allard came over. We played with Maddie, then went on a grocery run. A lot of talk, much needed in my case, a good dinner, and a pleasant evening. We played with Maddie some more, and she charmed Tom, I think. I don't think he's got Idea One what to do with a little kid, but he's got a huge heart and she read that right away. She talked a lot about Uncle Tom after he left. I know, everybody talks about him after he leaves. But this was nice.

Tomorrow I start Russell Friedman's grief recovery seminar. I'm looking forward to it with hope and trepidation. I can't imagine it will be easy, but I think it will help. I'm all up for help. It's all day, for three straight days. He said to bring a pen and a notepad. I guess that means he's supplying the Kleenex.

10:24 p.m.

Jim

June 12, 2004

Grief recovery seminar. Too early to comment.

Maddie and I played together and both of us had such fun, I

thought we would throw up from laughing. She's currently the first-prize winner in the Make Jim's Life Worth Living Contest.

11:43 p.m.

Jim

June 14, 2004

Today was the first day I've felt lighthearted and even happy for anything resembling a whole day, since Cecily died. I attribute it to the work I did this weekend at the Grief Recovery Institute. Today I was able to think about Cec and look at pictures of her without feeling pain and despair as the predominant responses.

There are a number of pictures that have captured Cec's laugh visually. I loved the way she threw her head back and roared when something nailed her funny bone. She was so free with her good feelings. Of course I miss her, and will miss her all the days of my life. But as I looked at pictures, I simply felt happy to have had her in my life, grateful for the experience of her, and appreciative of the wonderful contribution she made to my existence. And I am grateful now and forever to Russell Friedman for helping me find the freedom to enjoy her more than sorrow over her. It was a transcendent experience which gave me tools to transform anguish into something akin to happiness.

10:46 p.m.

Jim

June 15, 2004

As an upcoming publicity trip to Deadwood, South Dakota, draws nigh, I am nervous about being away from Maddie for a week. Not for her sake so much; she'll have a great time with Stacey and Cathy. It just seems such a long time for me to be away from my little girl, who is my greatest source of emotional support these days.

Maddie's still working on some issues such as eye contact and concentration on tasks, but her therapists think that otherwise she's pretty typical for her age. Her persona has developed immensely in the past couple of weeks. So have her self-confidence and her independence. She makes me so happy I could dance. Pretty little girl, too, if I do say so.

My spirits continue buoyant. Twinges of pain exist, surely, but I've lost much of my melancholy. It will perhaps never go away entirely, and may indeed come back to visit me soon. But for now, I feel a corner has been turned, and that Cec's spirit travels with me, sustaining me. I think less in terms of missing her than in terms of loving her. That seems a good shift. I daresay she would approve.

1:16 a.m.

Jim

June 18–19, 2004

I didn't get an e-mail off last night because my hosts here in Deadwood kept me, um, entertained until zero-dark-thirty in the morning. It was 5:00 a.m. before I got to bed.

Friday was an interesting day. People here are either cowboys or bikers. But what I've found is that they are all extremely nice. Of course, I'm on TV, so that probably skews their opinion of me.

I did some press interviews with local newspapers and a TV station, then signed autographs. Clearly a quarter of the people standing in line (yes, there was a line) didn't quite know who I was, but, hey, it was free. This was the first time I've ever done an autograph session, but it's not the first time I've sat behind that table. I used to go with

Cecily to her *Star Trek* convention appearances and sit with her for hours while she signed and chatted with her fans. (Now *there* was a line of fans.) Cec was so friendly, so eager to make everyone she spoke with feel as though they'd connected with her, it was a joy to watch.

There were moments of sadness as I signed things for people, remembering all the times Cec and I had been together while she signed. I wished she could have been by my side, because I think she would have been so happy that I got to experience a little of the kind of attention and treatment that had been hers in such a situation. And I'd have been so proud to have her by my side. One woman got my autograph and flirted so sweetly yet definitely that I got the impression she might have liked to get to know me better after the formalities. Later, one of the chamber of commerce staff informed me that the lady in question was a hooker. Of course she was.

After the autograph session, I was delivered to a parking lot and ensconced in a hundred-year-old, horse-drawn buggy, beautifully restored. After a few minutes, the parade started up the main street of Deadwood—probably about a mile long. The town was packed with people, and they waved and I waved, and I got a kick out of people reading the sign on the side of the buggy telling them just who the guy in the buggy was. It was a little embarrassing. But then some got excited and started yelling some of my lines from the show back at me. That was cool.

2:35 a.m.

Jim

June 20, 2004. Father's Day.

This morning I talked to Maddie on the telephone. She said, "Happy Father's Day." I melted into a formless lump of protoplasm. This was my first Father's Day as a single father and my first Father's

Day without a father. One might presume that the day was melancholic and tainted with sad memories. But no. First, I got to talk to
my daughter and she made me so happy to be a father. Second, I've
come to the conclusion that the work I did at the grief recovery seminar is having a lasting result and isn't merely the case of mistaking a
brief uplifting of spirits for real change.

I have my sad moments, of course, but so far they've been manageable and transmutable into happy moments. The overwhelming
feeling I have now when I think of Cecily or my dad is one of wistful
happiness. Yes, there's an undercurrent of sadness, because I miss
them both so. But I am so happy to have had them in my life, so
grateful for all they gave me, and so complete with my feelings for
them that I can now enjoy them when I think of them. I have tools to
use when sadness comes, and thus far the tools work.

1:33 a.m.

Jim

June 22, 2004

Tonight, staying at a motel a few miles from Little Bighorn, I
walked to a restaurant. Along the way I began talking to Cec, and
I came closer to crying than I have in a couple of weeks. I began, as
I talked to her, falling back into my anguish over the possibility that
she's suffering in some way from the loss of her daughter. I caught
myself, but it was hard to pull back. It's so easy to lean into worry and
anxiety over things that cannot be known, and I am convinced that
those leanings derive more from doubt of myself and failure to complete the relationship than from a real fear that Cec's spirit suffers in
some way. And the work I've done on that self-doubt and completion
is what allows me to pull back from the edge of the pit of painful
regret. It's amazing to me, and not at all a mark of disloyalty to Cec,

that I've had such a transformation from the man I was a few weeks ago, incapable of going more than a day or so without a debilitating crying collapse. Miracles happen. Especially if you do the work.

12:32 a.m.

Jim

June 24, 2004

I'm home.

When I got home, Maribel was driving up with Maddie in the backseat. I opened the door and Maddie burst into excited laughter—laughing harder even than when I tickle her. I don't recall ever before being the subject of joy that could only express itself in laughter. When she stopped laughing, she yelled "Daddy!" and she grabbed my face and just stared into it, like she was memorizing it. And then she started laughing again.

In the week I've been gone Maddie's language has exploded! Full, complex sentences—and jokes! Plays on words, puns, real jokes! Tonight was one of the happiest moments of my life.

10:39 p.m.

Jim

June 25, 2004

The saddest thing in my life is not having anyone to share with. Oh, Maddie and I have a great deal to share, but I mean something other than those father-and-child things. I've been able to overcome most of the regret that caused so much pain with this loss, but I doubt I'll ever overcome the feelings of lost sharing. We had such fun together, Cec and I. Perhaps something similar will arise again in my life, but for now, it's an addiction without a fix. It is withdrawal of an intensity to put alcohol or nicotine to shame, for those things are physical addictions and don't come with an attachment of emotional loss when one decides or is forced to give them up.

I miss her, with all my heart.

Some surprise, that, I bet.

11:02 p.m.

Jim

June 26, 2004

I had trouble going to sleep last night. I could not clear my head of images of Cecily's death. For the first few weeks this was a common event. But I haven't been troubled by it in a long time. Last night, though, reliving her last moments and the aftermath played as a continuous loop in my head. I'm thankful I was so sleepy, or I might be lying there still, trying to clear my head.

I think it's natural to have such experiences, and I don't completely reject them. But they are accompanied by such heartache that it's difficult to concentrate on the things that make me happy with Cec and her memory. Concentrating on those things is now a wonderful remedy to feelings of sadness and loss, and that action has saved me from many a relapse into deep pain. But it doesn't function so well in regard to recollections of that specific morning, March 3. It's inevitable that I'll occasionally relive it, but I truly hate doing so. It focuses my mind on the part of this experience that's most clearly painful, and I think it inhibits the transition from paralyzing grief to a livable grief in which happiness can still thrive.

10:40 p.m.

Jim

June 27, 2004

I took Maddie to a swimming party today. We had a fine and happy time.

There were many there who were part of Cecily's circle, so there was heartache and a great void amongst us. Nonetheless, a good time was had by all, especially Maddie, who swam and laughed and just seemed utterly thrilled to be alive. From where she was a few months ago to now is a miraculous path. A child who cried and melted down (remember that term?) almost without ceasing has transmogrified into one who virtually *never* seems unhappy.

Allah akbar!

12:08 a.m.

Jim

June 29, 2004

Lessons from the world of grieving.

What a grieving person does *not* want to hear:

1. "I know how you feel."
2. "At least she's not in pain anymore."
3. "He's in a better place."
4. "He had a good life."
5. "At least you've got your daughter."
6. "It just takes time."
7. "At least you had him a long time."
8. "You'll find someone else."
9. "God doesn't give us more than we can handle."
10. "You need to be strong."

Every one of these things may, indeed, be true. But I guarantee you, every one of these things makes a griever feel worse, either consciously or unconsciously. They're all variations on either the "Don't feel bad" or the "Don't make *me* feel bad" school of thought. A lesson gleaned from my own experience, from some training I've had, or from the statements of other grievers: almost any attempt to make a griever "feel better" will make the griever feel worse. Anything that suggests to the griever that he or she (1) should not feel bad, (2) can and ought to replace the loss, (3) should grieve in private, (4) should just wait it out, (5) should be strong for others, or (6) should "distract" him- or herself by activity and busywork is counterproductive and, frankly, alienating and distressing.

It goes against the human grain not to try to "fix" things. Yet these fixes I've listed are the most commonly noted sources of anger in grieving people, and I can attest to that myself. Every grief is unique; no one knows how anyone feels. Though Cecily's sisters and I all lost her, none of us knows how the others feel, for we all had our own personal relationships with her, and it would be presumptuous of any of us to tell the others we know their experience. And many of the fixes I've listed actually consist of telling the griever that the person who has died is doing fine, but do nothing to help the person left behind. I believe that Cecily's in a better place, but I am *not* in a better place, and it's my loss, not hers, that causes me pain. And the presence of good in one's life does nothing to erase pain, so "at least you've got your daughter" does nothing for the pain of my loss. If the presence of good in one's life erased pain, then people with large loving families who have all they desire and need in life would grieve little or none compared to people with few blessings. Yet we know that's not true. And, frankly, many attempts to comfort a griever seem born of an unconscious desire to minimize the impact of this grief on others. It's not comfortable to be around someone grieving, so people tend to try to fix things by comforting.

On the other hand, comfort of a sort is providable. It consists in large part of copping to the inability to be comforting. As contradictory as this seems, I (and, I'm told, many other people) have found it immeasurably more helpful for someone to say, "I have no idea how you must feel," or "I can't imagine your pain." Just saying this and making clear that you hear and acknowledge the pain, though you have no answers, goes light-years beyond any attempt to repair a griever's spirits. The knowledge of a loving soul's presence and willingness to be present and to hear and absorb one's grief is a powerful resource for the griever. I've had more comfort from people saying, "I don't know what to say," than from a hundred people telling me good reasons I shouldn't feel as bad as I do.

I know that whatever is said to a griever by concerned friends, whether ultimately helpful or distressing, comes from the very best of intentions. But if you happen on a broken heart, stand nearby, whisper, "I'm here," and never, ever, tell it you know how it feels.

1:58 a.m.

Jim

June 30, 2004

Several people have written to me today asking if I could share what I learned at the grief recovery seminar. I would, if I thought I could do it justice. But I can't, partly because this is a well-honed idea that I could never adequately encapsulate, but primarily because it's a process, a procedure that involves and requires more than a recapitulation of the teaching. I'm no proselytizer, nor am I inclined to do sales pitches, even for my beloved Russell. But what I learned through this procedure, and the ability I've gained to free myself from a notable portion of the pain associated with the loss of Cecily and my father, have made me an enthusiastic supporter of the work Russell and his business partner, John, do. Rather than try poorly to do in their stead what they do so masterfully, I would recommend to anyone who's suffering the pangs of loss, from death, divorce, abandonment, or any other cause of deep sorrow, that you do one or both of the following: pick up a copy of *The Grief Recovery Handbook* by John W. James and Russell Friedman and/or visit their website at www.grief.net.

11:42 p.m.

Jim

July 1, 2004

Today Maddie asked some questions about Mommy and about Granddaddy, and then announced, "They went away." I've read and heard a lot about how to handle this stuff, but when she surprises me with moments like this, I am not certain I handle it well.

Maddie's entering that "What's that?" "Who's that?" stage, which means I'm entering the "I don't know" stage. How can a kid not yet three think up so many questions I can't answer?

10:28 p.m.

Jim

July 2, 2004

I saw Karen Kondazian in Terrence McNally's *Master Class* tonight and had one of the transcendent theatrical experiences of my life.

I love talking about my profession, about technique and style, and I loved talking about it with Cecily more than with anyone. She was so expert at it, and her analysis of other people's work was precise and insightful. It's what made her a respected and beloved teacher and coach. It was powerfully attractive, being linked to one so respected in her field.

Oh, how I'd like to be in bed, talking over tonight's play with her. Or just listening to her breathe. It hurts so much to miss her, and I hope I always do.

1:05 a.m.

Jim

ELEVEN

July 4, 2004

In a year that has already cost me dearly, I'm sad to report the death yesterday of my grandmother, Pansy Adell Crawford. She never did anything of note, never made a remark that anyone would have written down, tended to disappear in even small crowds. But she got her nursing degree as a widow in her fifties (she tended to country singer Johnny Horton after his fatal car wreck—I guess that's something of minor note) and was a sweet, sweet woman. She told me she hated the name Pansy, but her middle name Adell has been passed down through four generations.

She lived exactly the same years as Ronald Reagan, 1911–2004, and though no fame ever attached itself to her, she was special. Quite wonderfully, quietly special. She had four children, my mother the eldest. I think she had fifteen grandchildren, of whom I am the eldest. I couldn't begin to count the great-grandchildren. She seemed hardly to age for most of her ninety-three years, then spent her final year or so in serious decline. One is grateful at my age to have a living grandparent. One is not grateful to see her suffer. And so though it saddens me to my soul to lose her, it's my loss, my family's loss, and not hers. It is my prayer and my belief that she is embraced and welcomed into bliss by my dad and by Cec and by all those she loved who lived not so long as she.

My favorite, favorite story about my grandmother:

About four years ago, when she was eighty-nine or ninety, I called her on her birthday. She sounded down, and I asked her if everything was okay. She said she was just a little depressed, she hadn't been able to get any exercise lately. See, the wind had blown down her basketball hoop.

Sleep in peace, Grandmother.

11:03 p.m.

Jim

July 5, 2004

This morning, I had a difficult time. I had not been able to get through to my mom on Sunday after learning of my grandmother's death, and as I prepared to try again this morning, the sadness of everything that has transpired these recent months fell on my heart like an anvil. Some of it, a great deal of it, was missing Cec and missing my dad. Most of it, though, was just this blanketing sadness, the feeling that it was all such a shame, such an unhappy and unfortunate set of events. And despite everything I've learned about the myth of being strong for other people, I felt like I needed to help my mom in this new loss when I talked to her.

So of course I cried and she comforted me.

It seems increasingly unlikely that I'll go to my grandmother's funeral, for a number of reasons, both logistical and emotional. Because my grandmother was from Cameron, a small Texas town, many miles from a useful airport, there's no way I could make the trip there, attend the funeral, and come back home in fewer than three days. And after all that's gone on, I am spent, and the idea of being gone from home and from Maddie for that long is almost unbearable right now. I'm not sure yet. But given my wildly fluctuating emotions these days, I am going to try to listen to my heart and act accordingly.

12:12 a.m.

Jim

July 8, 2004

My grandmother's funeral was today. I think my choice not to attend was a wise one. My mom and my grandmother both know how I feel, how deep my love was for my little grandmother. I think I made the right decision. My sister Teddlie brought a surprise from my grandmother's house. She's bringing me my grandmother's basketball hoop.

12:33 a.m.

Jim

July 9, 2004

I got things done today. I felt good today. Maddie let me sleep till 9:30 a.m. today. I went to a play today. I had dinner with a friend today. Someone asked me out on a date today. I played with Maddie today. I went for a walk today. I missed Cecily an awful lot today.

1:28 a.m.

Jim

July 10, 2004

Maddie was at a birthday party all day. She returned home around 8:00 p.m., exuberant and excited. It took me what seemed like hours to get her to sleep. I tried to teach her how to count sheep. I thought she was out when I (doing the counting) got to sixty-something. Then she suddenly asked if we could count ceiling fans instead. We counted ceiling fans jumping over a fence until we got to twenty or so, and then she wanted to count *turning* ceiling fans. I told her she should do the counting, so I lay there next to her, listening as she counted, "One turning ceiling fan, two turning ceiling fans, three turning ceiling fans . . ." It was cute, but it didn't work. We went through The Three Little Pigs, The Three Bears, The Three Kitties, The Three Dogs, The Three Monkeys, everything but the Three Stooges and *The Three Sisters.* It took forever, but I didn't care. She's delicious to lie next to and to whisper to and to feel her breath on me and to have her take my hand. Finally she began to yawn—I'd been faking yawning for ten minutes, trying to make her "catch it"—and she got stiller and quieter. And then just when I thought she was gone, she turned on her side, put her hand on my cheek, and said, "You're very nice, Daddy. You're very nice." Then she flopped over and was out.

12:19 a.m.

Jim

July 11, 2004

She loved Gene Wilder.
And Gilda Radner.
Coffee.
Cats.
The *Lord of the Rings* books.
Nanci Griffith.
The Indigo Girls.
Acting.
Actors as people.

Decorating her home.

Decorating magazines.

Bill Clinton and Al Gore.

Spencer Tracy.

Katharine Hepburn.

Wildflowers.

The mockingbird that lived outside our house in Van Nuys.

Our giant bed.

Long baths.

Harry Potter.

Travel.

Travel magazines.

Paul Theroux's books.

Law and Order.

Writing songs.

Archie comics.

Rollerblading.

The beach.

Time-travel stories.

Prison movies.

Documentaries, especially on serial killers or prisons.

The letter from Sullivan Ballou in the documentary *The Civil War.*

Air fries with ranch dressing.

Gardening.

The redwoods.

Mel Brooks.

Survivor.

American Idol.

Pottery Barn.

The Gap.

Historical fiction.

Spanakopita and dolmades and keftedes and kalamatas.

Designer combat boots.

Candles.

Back rubs.

An Affair to Remember.

Angels.

Carved wooden saints.

Poker.

James Taylor.

Autumn in New England.

Animals.

The scene in *Frankenstein* where the monster clutches at the sounds of music.

Fake Rolexes.

Real Rolexes.

Initiative.

Whales.

Sierra Club calendars.

Myths and fairy tales.

Yoga.

The Womphopper Stomp.

Honesty.

Scrapbooks and photo albums.

Hats.

Italy.

Light.

Taking pictures of windows.

Taking pictures of herself and me with our backs to the camera.

Pinocchio.

Her friends.

Her family.

Me.

Life.

Maddie.

Maddie.

Maddie.

Maddie.

9:49 p.m.

Jim

July 12, 2004

Lots of twinges and groans from the heart today. No special reason, no identifiable triggers. Highs in the upper nineties, clear skies, with occasional melancholy.

This afternoon, Maddie looked up through a window and saw an airplane. She said, "Maddie and Daddy go on a airplane. To Dallas." We went to Dallas in April, and I haven't mentioned it to her since.

This morning, Maddie and I came downstairs to greet Maribel. Maddie said, "Good morning, Maribel." Then she turned to me and said, "Very nice to meet you, Daddy."

Very nice indeed.

12:15 a.m.

Jim

July 13, 2004

I wrote last night about Maddie seeing the airplane and mentioning how we'd gone on an airplane to Dallas—three months ago. Well, today on the way home from her therapy, she said, "Where's London?" I blew some Dr Pepper out my nose and said, "What?" She repeated,

"Where's London?" I said, "London's a place. It's a town, far away." And Maddie said, "Maddie wanna go on a airplane to London."

If I find out she's bought a ticket . . .

Nothing in my life has prepared me for the blessing of having this child. I was always afraid of the burden, of the responsibility, and of the impact on my career having a child might present. I was a go-along daddy-to-be, not the instigator. As much trepidation as I felt, I could not deny Cec what she wanted so badly. And now there's this burden, this responsibility, this career-impacter of a little girl who's so bless-edly angelic that she removes all the weight and substance of those once-presumed-important obstacles. I still worry about the impact on my career. Someday someone's going to hire me to go shoot a movie someplace and I'll need to have a plan of action in place. And when I go back to work on *Deadwood* in a couple of weeks, I'll need to have arranged something for those mornings when my work call is 5:00 a.m. But good golly, Miss Molly, I am so euphoric over this little girl! God could not have blessed me with anything finer, and to have her as my life preserver at a time when sorrow often drips in my heart with the sound of water falling in a deep well—how splendidly I am blessed!

11:22 p.m.

Jim

July 16, 2004

Listening to the musical *Les Misérables* in the car today shoved me completely over the edge for a few minutes. Cec loved that show, as did I. I remember when she was casting a Disney Channel show called *Adventures in Wonderland* and she was seeing young girls about ten or so for the part of Alice. So many of the girls came in to audition with Fantine's song from *Les Miz*, and Cec thought it was so strange that these little girls were singing their hearts out about how the dreams of their lives had been smashed, leaving them in a hellish reality. We thought it was amusing but at the same time kind of weird for the girls (or their parents) to consider such a song appropriate.

But the real power that exists in that song hit me so hard today. I know that for all the troubles in her life, Cec had great happiness and great joys, and that she would never have considered her own life to be as miserable as Fantine's.

Yet to hear this heartbreaking song about despair, the loss of hope, the destruction of dreams, all in connection with a show that Cec loved immensely, brought me as low as I've been in weeks. Coincidentally, I was on my way to Russell's office at the Grief Recovery Institute when this musical sledgehammer hit me. I'd talked to Russell on my cell phone, told him I'd be there in a couple of minutes, hung up, turned on the CD, and three minutes later walked into Russell's office with tears and snot running down my face. I guess I'd come to the right place, though. We had a quick talk and I left a few minutes later feeling better, as I always do when I've talked to Russell.

Note to self: lay off *Les Miz*.

12:31 a.m.

Jim

July 19, 2004

I walked over to CBS Studios where Cec's office used to be and visited with G. Charles Wright, formerly Cec's associate and now the casting director on *That '70s Show*. I needed to go over and be done with the mini-trauma of seeing Cec's office without her or her presence in it. Fortunately, G. had transformed it completely from its former setup, and it was not all that painful a visual reminder of what had been.

He was invaluable to Cec, as she said over and over to me, and I found him an absolute barrel of fun from the beginning. It was good to see him. We hugged (with back-burping, the manly way) and had a good time talking and, for the most part, avoiding the obvious. Then I went upstairs and had a visit with Deb Barylski, who gave me my first TV series and who gave Cec such comfort and aid during her illness. It's only now beginning to sink in that (1) I am not the only one shattered and changed forever by this experience, and (2) the kindness and support we got during the hardest days were often from people who had enormous difficulties and sorrows and troubles of their own at that time.

1:11 p.m.

Jim

July 24, 2004

Tonight I went to a birthday party for Carolyn Nelson, whom Cec and I had met in a program for first-time parents called Baby's First Class. There were a lot of women in the class, all mothers of new first children. Apparently none of the other women were married to out-of-work actors, for I was the only man in the class. It was a terrific experience, being around all these new kids with a couple dozen mothers who were just as bewildered and dumbstruck as Cec and I were. Cec and I were both drawn to Carolyn and her adorable daughter, Willow, and Carolyn and her husband, Peter, became our good friends.

Tonight's party was to celebrate Carolyn's fortieth birthday. She sent out invitations to her many friends, including me. Inside the invitation was a card in which she talked about Cecily and her friendship and her feeling of loss. She asked all her friends if, in lieu of gifts for her, they would contribute to Maddie's college fund. When I read this, I was so touched. You people, you good people out there in the world, you keep finding new ways to buttress my belief in mankind, to help me shake off what few doubts I have about the ability of people to open their hearts and let goodness flow out. I am touched in new ways every day, still. And tonight, at Carolyn's party, I was able to thank her for her incredible act of generosity and thank those who had opened themselves up for someone they didn't know for the sake of someone they loved.

1:04 a.m.

Jim

July 25, 2004

Tonight I was telling Maddie *The Three Bears*, and though she usually listens attentively, this time she started extemporizing her own version of the story, throwing in new plotlines in the middle of my narrative, until I finally stopped telling and just asked her, "Then what happened?" And she told me. There seems to be a fairly strong Winnie-the-Pooh influence, as the interwoven plotlines of the four main characters all exhibited a strong penchant for climbing trees in search of honey. Even Goldilocks climbed trees in search of honey. And she *spilled* it. And got it all over her *face*. And made a *mess*.

Then she said, "Oh, I love you, Daddy," and conked out.

1:36 a.m.

Jim

July 27, 2004

Today, at work, I took my wedding ring off for the first time since Cec died. I took it off because it isn't proper for the character I play.

It was always a "thing" with me that I never took off my ring unless it was wrong for a part. It was just a piece of personal expression for me, a way of saying to myself and to Cec that we were always happily bound by that little gold circle. She was not so sentimental in that particular way, and often took her ring off, for comfort or other reasons. But she always seemed quite pleased that it meant so much to me to keep mine on. It was an emotional moment taking it off today, for an old reason, but in a new light. I've been encouraged by some to stop wearing it, as part of my pathway toward new life. But I'm not sure I'm that evolved yet, that ready to let go of that symbolic bond. I don't know what's right. I just know that "right" is subjective and fluid and I'll do whatever I do as "rightly" as I know how.

11:08 p.m.

Jim

July 28, 2004

I was away filming all day, and only saw Maddie when I put her to bed tonight. There was one lovely moment. For no particular reason, she said "Gracias, Daddy." I said, "You're welcome, angel." And she said, "No, Daddy, you are the angel." I liked that. Then she said, "Daddy, are you a king?" After a moment, I said, "No, but I feel like one."

I had a long conversation with Cec tonight. I told her that lots of times, I don't feel like going forward. I just want to go back. I don't want something new. I want what I had. I walked to the grocery store and talked to her all the way. Out loud. Maybe I'm going nuts. I don't think so, but I don't really care. I had a good talk with her. I felt sad, but it was okay. It's funny, I don't think she's up in the sky, but that's always where I end up looking when I'm talking to her. I really do want her back. I really do want to talk to her again, and have her talk to me. I really do want her next to me. I know I really can't have any of those things. But just in case anyone's wondering, I really do want them.

12:13 a.m.

Jim

July 31, 2004

Today, I watched Maddie playing, and the beauty and growth of our little girl sent me headlong into a sudden crying jag I couldn't stop. I hid in the garage. I'm not afraid to show emotion to Maddie, but I don't like to let her see me in great distress. She needs to know that I have deep feelings, but she also needs to know that I am upright and in control of our situation. So I've cried in her presence on many occasions, but I try not to lose control in front of her.

I was done with it, I thought, by the time I put her to bed. I was lying next to her, getting ready to tell her the one about the housebreaker and the trio of bears. Before I commenced, she started telling me a story. It went like this: "One day, we going to Mommy's house. And we knock on the door and Mommy say, 'Come in, Maddie.' And then Mommy say, 'Come in, Daddy.' " That's all there was to it. Succinct. But it was enough.

The tears flowed once more.

I wish I had a clear notion of what Maddie knows and what she feels. It seems obvious she knows things are different and that she's lost something, yet she does not seem sad or in any way traumatized. Yet how would I know what such things look like in a three-year-old?

It's hard to keep my head in *today*, in here, in now, though I know madness lies in "futurizing." I think of Maddie without a mother, without that love and care that no father is truly competent to provide in a mother's way. And I feel so sad for her, which often leads me to feel sad for Cecily, and then for me. Of course, it's all for me, ultimately.

It's work, this losing/grieving/recovering/regrouping stuff. Hard work. It makes my heart sweat.

1:41 a.m.

Jim

August 1, 2004

I accomplish a task of Herculean proportions today, transporting a gold shipment across endless miles, almost single-handedly. By which I mean I moved my wedding ring from my left hand to my right hand today. When I mentioned my hesitance to remove my ring a few nights ago, I received a number of touching and useful suggestions. Tom Allard, of course, offered to buy the ring for ten bucks. But the suggestion I chose to follow was one that made great sense to me. With the ring on my right hand, I can cling to its meaning and the connection I have to Cec in this little band, without feeling separated from it or forgetful of its symbology. At the same time, I mislead no one and I take a pace forward toward new life, which is, as Tom said, "That way →." It was a substantial change to make, but I feel awfully good about it. I forget who suggested it, but thank you.

Cec's brother, Sean, continues his fight. Those of you so inclined, please continue to join me in prayer. The rest of you, hum along.

11:02 p.m.

Jim

TWELVE

August 2, 2004

This morning Maddie had a three-hour assessment by the school district. All through it I missed Cec dreadfully, partly because she would have loved to have seen Maddie's progress and the fine impression our daughter made on the assessors. But partly I missed her because no fact of Maddie's life escaped Cec, and the assessors asked all kinds of questions I couldn't answer. They wanted to know when Maddie first sat up, first walked, first spoke. I could provide little more than "Oh, a couple of years ago sometime." Cec would have said, "She first sat up at 2:30 p.m. on Tuesday, February 16, 2002." She might have had to look it up in one of the journals she kept on Maddie's development, but she'd have had the information. If I knew where those journals were, I could go in and tell you what Maddie had for lunch on that date. Today didn't allow me to feel like a good mother, at least as Cec would have defined it.

And in so many ways, Cec did define it. Yes, she was neurotic and obsessive, but with Maddie those were just extreme forms of determination and devotion.

The assessors today were trying to determine Maddie's vocabulary and enunciation. They showed her some toys and asked her to name them. She did well with a cow and a ball and even a yo-yo. Then they put a little yellow toy vehicle with big knobby tires in front of her.

Maddie stared at it and said nothing. They asked again. Still nothing. With slightly raised eyebrows, one of the assessors said to the other one in a whisper, "I guess it's just too much for her, to say 'truck.'" Maddie looked at her and said, "It's not a truck, it's a bulldozer."

You know, even if she were a tantrum-throwing, snotty little brat, I'd love her. But this? This is a piece of cake. Angel food.

10:00 p.m.

Jim

August 4, 2004

Maddie had her psychiatric evaluation today, and it turned out about the way I expected. She still has some social issues, such as avoiding eye contact and inconsistent focus, but her progress otherwise has been extraordinary. The doctor said she was functioning like a normal four-year-old. Except that she doesn't turn three for two more weeks.

12:27 a.m.

Jim

August 5, 2004

My little Maddie asked tonight if I ever see Mommy. I said no, I didn't. She said, "Yes, Mommy had to go away. She was cwying." I don't see signs of emotional trauma in Maddie, certainly none of the signs I see in me. She appears to take it all in a matter-of-fact manner, in a wistful rather than desolate way. As I said her prayers with her tonight, I added my silent one that she never experience the heartache and loneliness I'm going through. I found myself hoping that she have a life free from this kind of pain, even if it means a shorter life, rather than to live long and unhappily.

I don't know if that's a good thing for me to wish for her. (As though what I wish for her will have anything to do with how her life turns out.) I've said often, even recently, that I'd rather feel bad than feel nothing, but is that something I would wish on my daughter?

There are many days I feel life with this much sorrow would be pointless if not for Maddie. That doesn't mean I would want life to end if not for her, but that so many of the things that gave me focus on the future have lost intensity for me. I still believe in being the best that I can be, and that there is good that can arise from me and my actions. But lately I find less importance in what I can bring to the world than I used to feel. Without Cec, much that seemed worth doing and being seems less so now. Maddie inspires me, guides and goads me onward. If she'd never been born, I would be completely unencumbered now, free as a bird. But I'd have no wings. Thankfully, Cec and God provided me with a lanky little angel who turns three in two weeks.

12:29 a.m.

Jim

August 7, 2004

I went to the Golden Boot Awards ceremony tonight with my *Deadwood* castmate Paula Malcomson. She was presenting an award. The Golden Boots are a celebration of Western movies, presented every year as a fund-raiser for the Motion Picture & Television Fund, which runs the Motion Picture and Television Country House and Hospital. It's perhaps the single-biggest Hollywood fund-raiser of the year. I was interested in going because it's fun to see so many stars and familiar faces from Western movies all in one place. Also one of the recipients of the award Paula was giving out was a friend of mine, Noel Neill, a one-time Western leading lady and also Lois Lane from the 1950s *Adventures of Superman* TV show. But as it turned out, there was a more important reason to be there. The final award of the evening went to *Deadwood*, and I and four other cast members were called upon to accept the award. It was a big surprise to me, since I didn't even think they knew I was going to be there and thus didn't expect to have a part in the evening. And the truth is, our producer was supposed to accept the award, but they called the actors to stage instead, by mistake. So Brad Dourif ad-libbed an acceptance speech and we all got our pictures taken with the trophy.

It was quite a fun but lengthy evening. Sidney Poitier and Tom Selleck made presentations, and Paula and I sat within four feet of Mickey Rooney. That kind of stuff probably shouldn't impress me after all these years in the business, but it does.

12:38 a.m.

Jim

August 8, 2004

The only meaningful thing I did today was fill the new medicine cabinet with all the medicine that's been sitting around in boxes. It involved going through a hitherto unseen box of Cec's stuff—most of it old drugs from years ago, some of it cosmetics, hairbrushes and bands, and bath stuff. I threw it almost all away. I pulled hairs from a brush and held them, but decided not to jump into that pit. I don't need to save a loofah she might have used or her eye makeup remover.

Just before I left her for the last time, the morning she died, I cut a lock of her hair for me and for Maddie. That will suffice. What I want is to have all of her back, not just a lock of hair. But as a very wise group of men once said, *"You can't always get what you want. . . ."*

Whether they're also right about being able to *"get what you need"* is, as far as I'm concerned, still up in the air.

9:01 p.m.

Jim

August 9, 2004

I was sick last week and didn't note here the passing of the fifth-month marker. On one hand, it seems impossible that my girl could be gone that long. On the other hand, I miss her so badly that the quantity of missing makes it seem much longer.

It occurred to me that if the statistics are true and 85 percent of all widowed men are remarried within a year, then it's likely that by this point a large percentage of them are already in new relationships. How can that be? Not that I'm not willing and interested in exploring that part of this new life, but how do those men do it without feeling either incredibly guilty or incredibly incompetent to the job? I don't feel guilty. I've brought Cec in as an adviser. I talk to her about people I meet who might be, uh, interesting. Shoot, all during our life together, she had definite ideas about who or what sort of person would make a good mate for me if something ever happened to her. She had suggestions. But this doesn't mean the concept is now easy for me.

How would I adjust to someone else? Would another woman forgive me for all the times I accidentally called her by Cec's name or endearment? Would I have the patience to build a relationship all over again? Would another woman forgive me for breaking down in tears at a sudden memory of Cec? Would I want to risk the possibility of losing someone else, going through this again? Or causing them to have to go through it?

There are times I think I'd do better just to spend the rest of my life alone, with Maddie. But then I think of Maddie without a mother, without the gentle heart and tender sensibilities of a woman to help her become a woman, a task I feel cosmically unqualified for. And how long dare I wait before bringing someone into Maddie's life—until she's five or seven or ten, or sooner, so she'd never remember not having a mothering love in her life?

I have no plans, no schemes. I'm merely ruminating.

Thanks for listening. This is cheaper than a therapist.

11:25 p.m.

Jim

August 10, 2004

I love my work so much, I'm usually—no, always—in great spirits on the set. But today there was a moment during one of those rare chances to sit down that I closed my eyes and began to think about Cec. I tried to remember details of the shape of her mouth, her nose and eyes, her ears, the feel of the muscles in her shoulders I massaged so many times. I tried to take inventory of her, just as sort of an exercise. But after a few moments, the tears were running down my face and I couldn't quite stop them. I managed, in full view of the company, to keep what was going on a secret, but I found it difficult to pull myself together when it became time to do the next take. Every time I would regroup a little bit, some image of Cec would come to mind and the tears would begin again, streaking my "dirt"-covered face.

11:15 p.m.

Jim

August 12, 2004

My daughter sang "Happy Birthday" to me tonight. It bore no relation to the familiar tune, and the words were fewer and more repetitive, but it did the trick.

For the first time in nineteen years, my champion, my heroine, is not here to make me believe she thinks August 12 is the most important date on the calendar and that I'm the reason.

I often have treated myself to something special on my birthday, but the one thing I truly wanted today was to share it with a girl who had chocolate eyes and a bewildering sense that I was it for her.

I didn't get that. But I did get "Happy Birthday" sung to me by her chocolate-eyed daughter. And that, my friends, was a birthday.

1:22 a.m.

Jim

August 13, 2004

I was just getting into bed when I realized I hadn't written tonight's e-mail. The only thing notable about the day was running into my old *3rd Rock from the Sun* colleague Wayne Knight at the grocery store. We stood and talked for nearly an hour, our first conversation since long before Cecily's illness. He's been going through his own hard time lately, and we—I guess there's no better term for it—compared notes. Wayne's a sweet man, far different from his Newman character on *Seinfeld*. He spoke of how he enjoyed the relationship Cec and I had, and that when we showed up on the *3rd Rock* set (Cec was the casting director, I had a recurring role), he always sensed there was something special about us. It was heartwarming to hear that. I don't think Cec and I ever gave much thought to what people thought of us as a couple. But it was special, and I find delight in the idea that someone else saw it as such.

2:01 a.m.

Jim

August 15, 2004

Well, I turned a year older last Thursday and today I turned about fifty years older. Maddie's birthday is in four days, but the weekend is now, so today I threw a birthday party for Maddie and all the three-year-old people I could think of, and I feel like I been rode hard and put up wet.

I got a lot of credit for a good party, but the truth is I simply repeated what Cec did last year. Same venue, same routine, mostly the same kids. The big differences this year were the fact that Maddie was not so subdued and nonsocial as last year, and, of course, the Big Difference.

11:55 p.m.

Jim

August 17, 2004

Right after Maddie was born, someone said, "Welcome to never not being scared again." I knew then exactly what they meant. But lately, my fear for Maddie's welfare has become intense. The responsibility for bringing her up safely, let alone well, rises up before me like a tidal wave in the night when I want to sleep. And I fear for myself if something should ever happen to her. I know, I'm worrying too much. But that's what I used to tell Cec, and now look at us. The difference between my worry and Cec's worry is that my response to worry is generally to go ahead and live as normally as possible and try to let the worry roll off me. I don't make huge shifts in direction or action due to worrying. But with a child and with a recent history like ours, worry has proven a new and persistent entity in my own life. Before, I let Cec worry for both of us. She was the pro. But this little girl is, unfortunately, improving my game.

Some of you may have wondered why the word "cancer" shows up so rarely now in these missives. I know some people go through a procession of events and disaster like this of mine and they re-dedicate their lives to eradicating the disease or circumstance that has otherwise wrecked their lives. So many powerful advances in research or activism have been made because of the work done by those who've lost loved ones. I admire those people beyond calculation. But I don't have the crusader gene. Perhaps one day I shall, but for now, I would dearly love never to hear the word "cancer" again. The word sickens me. I've heard tell of members of murder victims' families being unwilling or unable to pronounce the name of the killer who stole their loved one away. That's how I feel about "cancer."

Even as we approach the six-month mark, less than two and a half weeks away, I sometimes find myself in something that I tend to describe as denial, but which is really just a recurrent astonishment. Like a vicious version of that movie *Groundhog Day*, I have a repetitive experience of realizing, almost anew, how permanent this thing is. I realized tonight that at a subdural level, I've been thinking, "If I can just bear this till she gets back, I'll be okay." And twenty times a day that *Groundhog Day* alarm clock clicks over and I sit up and realize, freshly, that she isn't coming back.

11:56 p.m.

Jim

August 19, 2004

The scent of ash and sulfur in the air today. Not hell, but the wind was blowing from that direction.

Looking for the receipt for the now-defunct battery in Cec's car, I went through the glove compartment. I didn't find the receipt. What I found were parking stubs from the hospital, copies of medical treatment authorization, a half dozen expired car registration certificates, a sheet of paper with the names of various home decorators on it alongside several doodles of Cec's, and several miscellaneous receipts of importance only because they each contained several examples of Cec's blotted lipstick. There, along the edges of the receipts, were Cec's lip prints, one lip on each side of each edge. Like fingerprints, but much more evocative. It had been some time now since I'd cried. I suppose it was time.

I finally got Cec's car started, after it had sat unused for nearly five months. Driving it simply exacerbated the feeling of sadness. The car still smelled of her, too. It was full of her belongings: her sweater, the James Taylor CD I bought her for her last Christmas, her hairbrush, and her sunglasses. And not having been in it for a while, I suddenly got an intense reminder of just how bumpy a ride that car is, and thus a reminder of how painfully it had jounced Cec those last few months. I hate that car. I'd like to kill it.

I'm refinancing. Going through the trust and deed papers had its own share of pain. Page after page of references to me as "an unmarried man," to affidavits of the co-owner's decedence, to death certificates, all of which left me dullish and downcast.

I went to the mall to buy a bathroom mirror at Restoration Hardware, a place I'd been in a thousand times, but always with Cec. I'm making little attempt to decorate this house to my own tastes. I'm trying, as much as I know how, to do what Cecily would have done. It may not make her happy, wherever she is, but at least I know the place won't look like a college dorm.

The last thing this house needs is my taste.

Today was another of those days when I wonder, why would I want to go on here without her? And today was also the third birthday of what I'm doing here, why I would want to go on. Her name is Madeline Rose Beaver and she has a dimple in only one cheek, the same single dimple in the same cheek her mother had. And she held my hand and pulled me into the living room where she showed me her Barbie and her Beanie Baby bear riding together on the back of a horse named Champion—a bronze horse that is part of a lamp. An antique lamp that lit my grandmother's living room. And that's what I'm doing here, and why I want to go on.

11:17 p.m.

Jim

August 20, 2004

I spoke with Cecily's brother, Sean, today. He's undergoing chemotherapy, but says he's not suffering many ill effects. He believes he's losing his tendency toward seizures. We talked about how much we miss Cec and I am proud that he thinks Cec and I were helpful to him in his life.

Sean lived with me and Cec for a while, when he was about twenty. He once nearly set our kitchen on fire making coffee. Now he's a master professional chef. (I still don't let him too close to the stove!) Of course, with his illness he's been unable to work or even drive for a while. But between prayers and humming and medicine and determination, I see a day where he's back in the kitchen, whipping up a gratinée de Coquilles St. Jacques and setting the coffeemaker on fire.

Me, I'm gonna have some Doritos and go to bed.

12:23 a.m.

Jim

August 21, 2004

I got a massage this evening, as I'd thrown a real kink into my neck and shoulder. Massage is a Heaven-engendered thing. Cec and I used to get them frequently, even when it was hard to afford, because life just seemed much more worth living after one. I haven't had one in nearly a year. And what I realized tonight was that I was starving for the tender, helpful touch of another human. A full massage was a blessing and a luxury, but to tell the truth, just having someone run their fingers through my hair nearly made me weep.

9:52 p.m.

Jim

August 22, 2004

Today was the first time I experienced the kind of overt grieving for my dad that I've gone through almost daily for Cec. I talked to my sister Denise yesterday and we both expressed similar feelings that my dad's death was, for want of a better word, timely. And so it didn't carry with it the kind of trauma to the soul that Cec's death has for me and for so many. But today I got hit with a wave of loss and sadness about my dad that was unlike anything I've felt since his funeral. He was such an ally, such a friend, such a Dad with the biggest capital D. And sometimes I feel as though he's unjustly been lost in the emotional shuffle surrounding the loss of Cec. Not today, though.

Big argument this morning about Cec's dying wish(es). I'm calling a moratorium on people telling me that whatever favor it is they want from me was Cec's dying wish. That stuff doesn't work on me. Not to mention the inclination to spit fire it engenders in me.

11:36 p.m.

Jim

August 23, 2004

Today I spent the bulk of the day playing catch-up with the bills. The majority were medical bills. And in order to make certain that I wasn't paying a bill that insurance had already paid, I took each medical bill and compared it to the record of payment on the insurance company website. What that allowed me to do was to relive individual days of Cec's illness, purely in terms of what they charged us for those days. *October 17, CT scan, $758. December 14, oncological hemoglobin labs, $138. February 29, emergency airway inserted, $429.* Dollars and pain and fear. Nothing in these papers reflected love or generosity or bravery or any of the myriad wonderments we found in the midst of those times of suffering. No, just the suffering. And the cost. The little cost. The big cost isn't on anyone's insurance form or doctor bill. There isn't paper big enough to write the big cost on.

11:39 p.m.

Jim

August 24, 2004

I decided to tough my way through *Les Miz* again. As I reported, last time I tried to listen to the musical cast album, I couldn't get past Fantine's song.

Today I forced myself through the song. I won't let it simply be a trigger for pain. I listened and forced myself to think how happy Cec was every time we saw the show, how she loved to listen to it. I made myself think of it as a positive experience, what it would have always been for us had Cec never gotten ill. And it worked. I got through the song without anything more than a couple of winces.

And then, a couple of songs later: on her deathbed Fantine sings

"Come to Me" to her little daughter, Cosette, then delivers the child into Jean Valjean's hands for safekeeping as she dies.

Why on earth do I insist on listening to *Les Misérables* when I could be listening to the Wiggles? Then Maddie and I both would be happy.

But I will make it through this album and then I'll listen to it again, and again, until the whole miserable thing is happy again—or as happy as *Les Miz* gets. It's one of the tasks that must be tackled in order to go on. I'll not move forward and leave these icebergs behind me to sink me when next I pass this way.

10:26 p.m.

Jim

THIRTEEN

August 26, 2004

One night long ago, I was attending the acting workshop at Theatre West. At the end of the workshop, an announcement was made of the results of the recent board of directors election. I was one of the ones elected. A few minutes later, we were all standing around in front of the theatre, talking about the workshop and the election results. A girl in a pink-and-gray sweater-vest and a perfectly coifed head of Dorothy Hamill hair came up to me. I knew who she was but didn't really know her. I knew her well enough to say hello whenever we crossed paths, and I liked to say her name with a faux English accent, à la Oscar Wilde's *The Importance of Being Earnest*, which had a character of that same name. I think I knew that her aunt, Alice Borden, and her uncle, Dick Yarmy,[5] were members of the company, and possibly I knew that her father was the famous comedian Don Adams. Other than that, she was a cipher to me, barely a passing acquaintance.

I was in conversation with someone else when she walked up. She waited for a pause in the talk and then she said, "Congratulations

---

5. Dick Yarmy was Cecily's father's brother. He died in 1992. In recent years, Cecily's Aunt Alice has shared life with Russell Friedman, who plays a prominent role in this narrative.

on the election." And then she kissed me on the cheek. I was a little taken aback, since I didn't know her well enough to expect such a thing. But that was nothing. Then she pulled back from the kiss, said, "Oh, that was nice," and kissed me again on the other cheek. Then she said good night and walked across the street to her car.

I was dumbstruck. Now you have to understand what my life was like back then. I was a shy guy throughout my twenties and early thirties. I didn't exude or even possess much confidence. During those early adult years, my shyness and timidity caused me many lonesome times. I was uncomfortable pursuing romance, scared to call a girl, scared to talk to her even if I did call, and in retrospect I recall my few dates as intensely painful and humiliating.

But joining Theatre West in 1984 had an unexpected positive effect on me. I found a community, a family of players who became my closest circle. I found immense encouragement for my work, my creative endeavors, and every other aspect of my life. In the spring of 1985, a play I had written was produced at Theatre West, a semiautobiographical piece called *Verdigris*. The production was a hit, a success in virtually all of the ways that were important to me. As a side effect, I began to feel more respected than I had ever felt, and my self-respect grew accordingly, as did my confidence. Everything in my life changed that year. One of the things that changed was I lost much of my fear of the pursuit of the opposite sex. That was a *great* year. I dated more often in the first half of 1985 than I had probably done in the entire rest of my life. It got to the point where I was kidded a lot by my friends about what a "player" I had turned into. Well, I don't know about that. But I had fun and enjoyed the company of a large number of wonderful girls during that time.

And then a girl I had never gone out with or even spoken to for more than a word or two came up and congratulated me and kissed me on both cheeks and walked away to her car.

I watched her get in her car, abandoned all the other congratulations, and sprinted to my own car. I got in it, threw it into gear, pulled a quick U-turn, and sped off in pursuit of the little reddish Datsun the girl in the pink-and-gray sweater-vest had driven off in. I caught up to her a few blocks down the street and pulled up alongside her. I honked. She glanced over then decided to ignore whoever it was harassing her. I honked again and she looked more clearly at me. I made a gesture like drinking and put a big question mark on my face. She got the picture and nodded. I indicated for her to follow me and we drove to a nearby restaurant called L'Express, the regular hangout for Theatre West members after Monday night workshop. We went inside and were soon joined by our regular crew, though this girl was not a regular in our after-workshop group.

We talked together and with all the gang for an hour or two. Finally the girl said she needed to go, so I walked her to her car and asked her if I could call her sometime. She said yes. Three years, eight months, and eleven days later, we were married.

Eighteen years, six months, and six days after that first night, it came to pass that we were parted, for the first time and forever.

That first night was nineteen years ago tonight. August 26, 1985.

Cec, tonight I went to the theatre and stood on the spot where you boldly took our future in your hands. I felt your presence there—not in a spiritual way, but in a sense-memory manner. I could hear your voice as you spoke to me that night; I could feel your closeness and your gentle but vivacious self. I've gone back to the theatre to stand on that spot every year on this date. Tonight was the first time I went there without you. And yet, there you were. In front of me, making me start with surprise, making an unexpected thrill run through me.

The only thing that keeps me now from chasing after you again is that I let you get too far ahead and I can't see where to follow. Keep watching in your mirror, though. I'll be along eventually.

Good night, my Pie. Thanks for the kisses.

11:22 p.m.

Jim

August 29, 2004

Maddie called me "Mom" two or three times today. I'm not sure what that's about.

12:49 a.m.

Jim

August 30, 2004

I'm going to cheat a little tonight. Much of this e-mail will be what I wrote this afternoon to a dear friend. Nancylee Myatt wrote to me about an annual event that Cecily's wide circle of girlfriends have been undertaking for a number of years—a girls' weekend at a beach house in Malibu, where they relax, shed stress, and enjoy one another's company. Cec was not so good at shedding stress, and despite the fact that this was a circle of women who to a large extent knew one another due to her, she rarely if ever made it to this annual beach weekend, always having some pressing engagement or piece of work that needed attending to. This year's gathering was held last week, and Nancylee wrote to me of how Cec's concurrent absence and presence affected the experience for her and the others.

She wrote about last year's retreat and how the girls had awakened on Sunday to a newspaper story about the house purchase Cec and I had made. The article mentioned my age and misrepresented Cec's by several years in a youthful direction. So the girls at the beach called Cec and used a rewritten version of the song "Sixteen Going on Seventeen" to tease her, and they all—including Cec—had a great laugh at her expense.

Here's what Nancylee wrote about this year's weekend:

At the end of the day, we stood on the deck and joined hands—this beautiful, powerful, nurturing, loyal circle of women—and

sent up a message to Cecily. I looked at this group who had taken
some tragic hits of their own this year, who had spent most of the
year caring for their own families while circling around Cecily
and [another friend fighting a similar battle], and felt truly
blessed. The message to Cecily was bittersweet—mad she was
gone, happy she was at peace, mad she had missed this party in
the past, happy she was finally there today, proud of Maddie's
growth and your care for her, and grateful for this tragic reminder
of how precious this family of friends is.

Trust me when I tell you, this didn't stop my tears, but it
helped put them in the right place. You'd have been proud of this
group that your beautiful wife was so much a part of. Know that
she'll always be there as long as we are.

I had a hard time typing a reply to Nancylee, because I couldn't
see through my flooded eyes. But here's what I managed to peck out:

Thank you for sharing this experience with me. I haven't stopped
sobbing since I read it, but that's okay. It's so hard to think about
all our lives going on as if they were normal but without her. The
picture is so skewed, so terribly "what's wrong with this picture?"
We're days away from six months, yet I still have the feeling she'll
walk in the door in a minute and ask why all those empty boxes
are cluttering up the hall. And then she'll hold me and I'll not be
empty inside anymore.

The image of all you girls on the beach thinking about my
girl—our girl—and communing with her and enjoying her and
sorrowing for her is a treasured image. I will hold it in my heart
forever. Thank you for sharing it with me. You, who were her so
beloved friend, thank you for sharing her with me, too.

This evening, I attended the annual membership meeting of Theatre West. At one point, the chairman of the board read off the names

of those members who had died since last year's meeting. Almost all those named were dear friends, and one of them was Cec. We held a standing ovation for these departed colleagues, and I struggled without success to maintain my composure. By the end of the evening, I was wrung out, exhausted, sandy-eyed, and spent.

1:11 a.m.

Jim

August 31, 2004

Maddie suddenly, unexpectedly, started asking questions about her mom. She asked, "Where's Mommy?" I told her Mommy had to go away, even though she didn't want to. Maddie then asked, "But *where* did she go?" I told her I didn't know. (There are clear psychological guidelines against telling a child this age that "Mommy's gone to Heaven.")

I told her Mommy got sick with cancer and she died. She doesn't know what it means now, but when she does learn what it means, it will not require changing my story later. And since she doesn't know what it means, it means it has no trauma quotient for her.

We just talk about the fact that Mommy loved her very much and wanted to stay with her, but couldn't. We've gone through this before, but today, she asked a lot more questions. Nothing about it seemed troubling to her. She just seemed curious about it, and seemed to miss her mommy. After her questions, she said, "Let's go in the living room and see her." There are two framed photos of Cec on the mantel and a large poster-size photo on the wall, still there where I left it after the memorial service. Maddie asked questions about Cec, looking at the pictures. I told her Mommy was beautiful, just like Maddie, and that she looked like her mommy. She pointed to a picture taken around Maddie's first birthday, with Cec holding a bald

Maddie, both of them grinning so delightedly. Maddie said, "Tha's when I was little. I didn't talk then. I didn't hab no hair."

11:12 p.m.

Jim

September 2, 2004

One day short of six months after Cec's death, I took down her clothes from where they hung in her closet and packed them in wardrobe boxes. Perhaps I've mentioned that, by fluke, the clothes hanging in her closet were not the clothes she wore in the months leading up to her illness. Because we had the help of so many volunteers in moving us into our new house and because Cec was unable to participate, our belongings were unpacked and put away to a large extent by people who didn't know what went where. Several boxes of Cecily's clothes were unpacked and hung up, but almost without exception, they were boxes of clothes from the eighties and nineties that Cec had packed up to be put in storage or given away. The clothes she wore recently are presumably still in boxes in the garage. What was hanging in her closet were the clothes she wore in the early days of our courtship and marriage.

That meant several things. Try as I might, I could find no whiff of her scent among these dresses and blouses and sweaters. I really, really wanted to, have always wanted to, but have not. Perhaps that's a blessing. Another blessing was that many of these items of clothing were unfamiliar to me, faded in memory.

But there were surprises every so many hangers. On one hanger was the pink-and-gray sweater-vest she wore the night we found each other. On another was the oversize necktie and baggy pants of Houli the Clown, whom I met the night of our first real date. Some of you know about Houli. Cec worked as a clown, doing children's birthday parties, when I met her. She'd gotten her start entertaining at Houli-han's restaurant, where she worked during college, becoming their resident clown, Houli. Later, it was a good way for a struggling young actress to make ends meet.

Cec had a Houli appointment on the day of our first date. And she was late arriving home from it. So when I arrived to pick her up, she still had white makeup and blue hair. I sat for half an hour while she cleaned it off and got dressed. She always spoke of it as a humiliating experience, but I found it cosmically endearing. She never did Houli again.

I was able to get through the process of emptying her closet today because I felt somewhat numb. Not numb as in shock, but rather just tired and weary of deep grief.

I'm giving whatever clothing that isn't otherwise asked for to the drama department of Valley College, where my friend Stephanie Shayne-Parkin's husband, Pete, is the department head. Maybe I'll go see a play there someday and see one of Cec's outfits onstage. I think she'd like that.

11:07 p.m.

Jim

September 3, 2004

At times past, I've occasionally wondered what it would be like to be in prison, incarcerated for life. How would it be, knowing that the terrible circumstance you found yourself in was never, ever going to go back to what it was before you came there? The ability to tolerate any individual minute or hour or day of your harrowing imprison-ment would be, I think, undermined by the knowledge that many, many more days just like it were ahead, without surcease. It seems to me that many things can be suffered under the knowledge that the suffering will end. In many ways, I think the worst punishment is that with no ending allowed.

Tonight as I lay in bed with Maddie, as we said our prayers and asked God to let her mommy know how much we love and miss her, I was suddenly struck by the similarity of situation. I realize that I get by, to a greater or lesser extent, every minute and hour and day that comes along. Some of them are prodigiously difficult to tolerate, but each passes and the hard ones are separated by relatively kind moments, periods where forgetfulness is allowed and anguish is kept at bay. But the realization I had tonight was that there's an aspect about this of the life sentence, the trammeling without parole or hope of escape.

Just as the notion frequently arises in me that if I can just go on long enough for Cec to get back from wherever she's gone, I'll be all right, so too does the idea that there's a finite and discernible end to this loss and the feelings that chaperone it. These notions and ideas are subliminal mostly. Tonight was the first time they rose high enough into my consciousness for me to realize how false they are and the implications of that falsity.

I will bear this grief, I will endure it, I will reach a point where it doesn't kick me down an abyss whenever I turn my back on it. But tonight was the first time it hit me squarely between the head-handles that it will never go away.

I will always mourn her.

I will always miss her.

And getting on with life does not mean finding the hidden passage into a Shangri-la where sorrow stops and a new and idyllic life begins. Rather, getting on with life means learning to walk and even run with this new weight on my shoulders.

Today makes six months.

11:08 p.m.

Jim

September 4, 2004

A notary came to the house to witness my signature on a couple of follow-up documents relating to the refinance. These documents included an affidavit regarding Cecily's death, moving the house from our joint ownership into my sole ownership, a necessity when creating a new mortgage. The notary was a pleasant, sweet woman. She asked if I minded if she asked who had died, thus making this transfer necessary. I told her my wife. She asked how old Cec was. I told her. She asked what she'd died from. I told her. And then she told me that she worked part-time for a company that sells products that are free from the many chemical carcinogens in our environment, and that it was such a shame that people didn't know about these products, because there was no reason for anyone to die of cancer, and it was too bad my wife hadn't known, because there was no reason she had to die.

Once or twice in my life I've had what some might call out-of-body experiences—a sensation of leaving one's body and watching it as an observer from some slight remove. I quite nearly had one of those at this moment. I managed to rein myself in. I swallowed hard, clenched my teeth, and explained that no one on earth ever paid more attention to dangerous factors in the environment than Cecily. I restrained myself from telling her that Cecily probably could have recited the brochure the woman had handed me. And I restrained myself from asking her why, if Cec had already focused her energies on environmental safety to such an extreme for her entire adult life, why she had died anyway. People occasionally tell me I'm a nice guy. I suppose I must be, because I did not strangle this woman on my living room sofa. However, if wanting to do so precludes me from being a nice guy, so be it.

2:16 a.m.

Jim

September 6, 2004

Perhaps people are tired of hearing me say that I cried again, one more time. It wouldn't surprise me. But what's so notable is how surprising the crying is. It's easy to understand when I'm cleaning out Cec's closet or, when, like the other day, Cec's driver's license suddenly turns up in the pocket of Maddie's diaper bag. It's more difficult to know why I'll be feeling terrific and doing something I really enjoy and suddenly burst into tears. I have no doubt that this is a common phenomenon. But I doubt that anyone has ever adequately explained it.

11:47 p.m.

Jim

September 9, 2004

A little over a year ago, on my birthday, as I recall, I was on the set of a show called *Lyon's Den*, produced by my friend and former groomsman Remi Aubuchon. Alone in my trailer, I got a call from Cecily on my cell phone. She was in tears and desperate distress. An assessor from the county agency in charge of health and development issues for children had come to the house to evaluate Maddie regarding her lateness in speaking. Maddie had once, by eighteen months, had about four or five words, but by age two, she'd lost half of them and was having trouble with the remaining two. Cec, at home alone with Maddie after the assessor's departure, sobbingly told me the woman from the county said that she believed that Maddie was, most likely, autistic. Cec's devastation became my devastation. Visions of the collapse of the castle of dreams and hopes we'd built for our little girl filled my mind, and I know Cec felt the despair far more powerfully than I did. That was the day the world cracked open. It would not break completely apart for another two months, but a gaping chasm suddenly ran through it.

Today, I was on the set of *Deadwood* when I got a call from our caseworker from the county agency. She told me that the team of psychiatrists and psychologists she worked with had done a thorough evaluation of Maddie's condition. They'd read the initial diagnosis and all the subsequent medical and therapeutic reports. They'd gone over her progress reports from her speech therapists and occupational therapists and behavior intervention therapists. They'd examined her pediatric evaluations and her neurological exam reports. She said they had conferred and reconferred, until they were confident in their analysis of the situation, despite their initial skepticism.

She said they had come to the conclusion that Maddie is no longer autistic.

She said that in her twenty-seven years in the field, she had never seen a child progress so far, so fast, and had never seen a child lose a diagnosis of autism. She said that other doctors were coming in to look at Maddie's reports and evaluations, not to consult but to gaze in wonder.

She said the doctors were tossing around—and not tossing around lightly—the word "miracle."

I hung up after our conversation, and once again I was alone in my trailer, carrying an emotional load that I needed so badly to share with Cec. Although I know she knows, what I needed then, at that moment, was to hold her and squeeze her little torso until she gasped and to cry into her hair and her neck and to feel her crying into mine. And in that form she wasn't there. I began to weep. Staring at myself in the mirror, covered in faux filth, dressed as an Old West prospector, I watched my eyes brim up and overflow, tears running down into the faked dark brown of my beard, leaving streaks in the makeup. I never felt more alone in my life.

And then they called me to the set to shoot the morning's scene. I ambled about while the crew finished setting camera positions, responding with false casualness to the various greetings from grips and techies and camera operators, all the while trying to maintain my composure for the upcoming scene. Yet what I wanted to do was grab someone, anyone, and well forth upon them my joy and sorrow and hold on to them as if they were the one I needed.

Finally it came time to get in place for the scene, and I fell in beside the lovely, sweet actress Molly Parker. There was a moment's delay for technical reasons, and in that moment, I told her what had occurred. She took my face in her hand and kissed me and when she drew back, I saw her eyes flooded and I saw her lip tremble, and she embraced me and gave me strength and love and pity and kindness. And when she broke the embrace, I was refreshed and reinvigorated, and the despair had flown and I was left with such joy at this blessing that had come so miraculously upon my child and me, and at the ability of a gracious soul to impart strength and well-being to one such as me, who so mightily needed it.

My strength was reinforced again and again during the day by other true friends with whom I was pleased to share, in person, this wondrous news. Never underestimate the power of an embrace from a kindred heart.

And that, my comrades, was my day. Oh, there were other things, but the day and, likely, the rest of my life, was colored a most gorgeous hue by a phone call in an actor's lonely trailer early in the morning. I thank my God, and my friends and family, none of whom ever ceased in their entreaties, be they prayers or humming or shaking their fists at the sky, on my little Madeline's behalf.

And I thank the girl who was the messenger of these blessings, whose tenacity in the face of despair is the single human reason I have this news to report tonight. My Cecily never stopped, never gave up in her quest to find whatever could be done for Maddie's condition. She was tireless and irresistible. She was pugnacious and painstaking in her quest to locate not merely treatment, but the best treatment possible.

I shudder to think of Maddie's life now had it been up to me alone. I kept my head in the sand far too long, hoping to convince myself that the experts were wrong, that Maddie would be fine if we were only patient. But in retrospect I know that her situation a year ago was a grave one, that she was backsliding on the developmental road, and that without immediate and intense intervention, her fate would have been grim. It was Maddie's mother alone who saw to it that my complacency had no part in determining our daughter's future. And as if I had no other reasons, I will be grateful to her, my beautiful, ferociously dedicated, and loving wife, forever. And I will tell her daughter of the great gift her mother gave her—a gift approximated only by the gift Maddie gave to us.

12:37 a.m.

Jim

September 12, 2004

Long before Cec became ill, I could get weepy over some song that reminded me of some moment of loneliness, or of the feeling of loneliness even if the event was lost in the haze of ancient memory. There was a song that used to do that to me, every single time I heard it. Mel Carter's record "Hold Me, Thrill Me, Kiss Me" used to send my emotions careening downhill whenever I heard it. I can't say why, exactly, except that something about it reminded me of every Saturday night I ever stayed home while my buddies went out on dates, every night I longed to be with some teen angel or other but didn't have the social or emotional wherewithal to make it happen. I spent more than twenty years, at least, getting that tightness in my throat whenever I heard that song. And then I met Cec. In the course of our courtship, she learned an awful lot about me, and I presume she learned that little tidbit, of how that song, which I deeply loved, nevertheless provoked a sweet sorrow because of old, sad memories.

After our wedding, there was a big reception/party in the ballroom of the Riviera Country Club. The various couples in the wedding party were paired off and announced by name as they entered the ballroom together. Following them, the bride and groom were announced and Cec and I swept majestically (it seems to me) into the ballroom as the band began to play the music for our first dance. As we swung onto the dance floor, what I heard was one of the best wedding bands ever assembled playing "Hold Me, Thrill Me, Kiss Me." Cec looked up at me, reveled in my surprise with tears in her eyes, and held me and thrilled me and kissed me. As the song peaked—I absolutely guarantee this—I was never, ever in my life so happy as at that moment. And the "curse" was lifted from the song. From that point on, it has never been anything but a reflection of one of the most blessedly ecstatic moments in my entire life, and I thrill with happiness whenever I hear it.

You don't have to *"make me tell you I'm in love with you,"* girl. I always will be.

10:26 p.m.

No adieu.

Jim

September 24, 2004

It's so sublime to watch Maddie playing with other kids, enjoying them and their company, and inventing games and stories with them. A year ago, she scarcely looked at another child, or even an adult, for that matter. A year ago, she had lost 50 percent of her vocabulary. A year ago, she would stand at the bookcase and tilt one book at a time out and then back in, one after the other, all the way down the shelf, and then start over again when she reached the end, over and over and over again. A year ago, she would stare into the distance and not react at all if you called her name or took her hand or shook her arm. And now she jokes. She laughs. She makes up stories. She pretends one doll is another doll and the other doll is the first doll and that they've switched identities to fool another doll. She asks to see other kids when they're not here, and she runs to greet them when they arrive. She sings. She sings songs she's heard once or twice. She sings songs she makes up as she goes. She sings while she plays the piano. (Okay, for some reason she still can't actually play the piano, but she bangs on it while she sings, and she bangs on it in time with the music.) She's everything a mother would dream of a three-year-old being, everything her own beloved lost mother dreamed she might be at this age.

There was an intriguing confluence of feeling today, paradoxical, contradictory. I felt the same as every day, missing Cec and aching for her with present intensity. Yet for the first time, I also had fragments of feeling that were closer to those I have for others I've lost in my life, those I lost long ago.

Today was the first time I had that feeling, fleetingly but palpable, that losing Cec was something that happened quite some time ago and that I had come some distance since. I suspect there will be more and more of that sensation. It will likely be outnumbered for a long while by the feelings of still-present pain, because those feelings have not diminished much. But I sense that a transition is in fact slowly occurring. It may take many more months or years, or maybe less. From what I hear, from those who know best, and from my old friend Hamlet, *"If it be not now, yet it will come; the readiness is all."*

1:42 a.m.

Jim   •

September 26, 2004

Cecily's cousin Dino e-mailed me this morning, telling me he'd finally screwed up the courage to delete Cec's number from his cell phone's caller list. I had a similar experience with my cell phone. I didn't delete the number, but I finally had to change the name of the listing. Cec had her own phone line, which we still use. My caller ID looks through my phone list whenever an incoming call arrives and displays the name instead of the phone number if it's one from the list. I kept getting these little jolts when Maribel or someone else at the house would call and I would look at my phone to see who it was and the little screen would read "Cecily." That split second of hope before it crashed was finally too much to take, so I relabeled my caller list. It was hard to do, but harder not to.

11:38 p.m.

Jim

September 27, 2004

I had only my second flash of Cecily in a dream night before last. She smiled and waved at me as she was walking past a window. That's all. That's massive, compared to the only other time she's appeared to me in a dream. Two quick cameos in seven months of dreaming. Not much to curl up with, is it?

This morning, Maddie pursued the question of where Mommy is further than she's ever done in my presence.

"Where's Mommy?"

"She had to go away."

"Can I go away?"

Yipes.

"No, we have to stay here."

"Can I go ride the merry-go-round?"

Safe at last.

She seemed completely untroubled—just wanted to know what we could do and couldn't do. I suppose all is well, as well as can be.

1:22 a.m.

Jim

September 28, 2004

I watched the opening scenes of the movie *Washington Square*, from the Henry James novel, during lunch. The scenes where the wife dies in childbirth, leaving her lonely, old, embittered husband to raise their daughter on his own. And I thought, well, at least I'm not embittered.

12:00 noon

Jim

September 29, 2004

I went to the theatre tonight to see a show directed by Jim Newman, Cecily's scene partner in lots of sketches at the Acme Comedy Theatre. She put such energy and time into writing and performing sketch comedy with that company, and she loved it. It was strange going back to that theatre, where I'd been scores of times to see Cec perform but had never been without her. Several of her friends from the old days were there, and it was great fun, in a bittersweet kind of way. I suppose it was simply the fact of being in a place so deeply associated with her that brought about a strange phenomenon. Probably five times in the course of the evening, in the audience and in the lobby before and afterward, I thought for a split second I had caught a glimpse of Cec. It was unsettling, yet clearly understandable. In one

case, the person I actually saw bore a strong resemblance to Cec. I
suppose the eye sees what it wants.

11:32 p.m.

Jim

September 30, 2004

Maddie started school today.

Yes, it was "merely" preschool. But a year ago doubt rose like a
gape-mawed dragon threatening to devour any hope that we would
ever see this day. The graces of Providence have instead fulfilled that
hope, and no happier or prouder papa ever walked his child through
school gates than did Maddie's today.

She showed some slight tremulousness when Maribel and I
announced we were leaving her to the kind attentions of her teachers,
but spinning between timidity and a roomful of new and unexam-
ined toys, she'll opt for Mattel every time, five will get you ten.

When I returned a few hours later to retrieve her, she was jubilant
and glowing. I think she's going to like it. Next week, we will transit
from being delivered in Daddy's car to pickup and delivery by school
bus. She's excited about that, asking of every big vehicle we passed
on the way home, "Is *that* the school bus?" I worked hard at imagining Cec watching from some lofty perch, thrilling more happily than
even I at the miracle she and God wrought.

Last night, I watched the A&E *Biography* show on Cecily's dad.
It seemed well done, without too many egregious errors. It was
interesting seeing how strangers interpreted aspects of this family's
life and history. Near the end, the program dealt with Cec's death.
Dick Van Patten spoke sweetly about her, and there were lovely pictures of her with her dad, Cecily looking radiant and classy and lumi-
nous. They didn't dwell on her, but what they did was stylish and

touching. I played that section over and over again. And still it plays, in my mind.

11:06 p.m.

Jim

October 2, 2004

Tonight, one of my friends from the show mentioned a play he had been in with Cecily a few years ago, then apologized for bringing up the subject of Cec. I reassured him, as I reassure all of you and anyone else: *Do not fear bringing up the topic of Cecily.*

First off, I think about her all the time, whether anyone brings her up or not.

Second, I enjoy sharing thoughts about her. I love when people talk about her to me. One of the major topics discussed last night with my friend Hilary Roberts is how unhelpful it is having people "spare" us from having to talk about the person we lost. Certainly, no one feels particularly comfortable bringing up the topic of someone's dead spouse, but that's mainly because few people feel they know what to say. And as I've always said to people who seemed to struggle with talking to me about Cec, I don't know what to say, either. It's okay. The last thing I want is to go henceforth through life having conversations that excluded any mention of Cec, out of someone's fear that it would make me sad: (1) there's not a good-hearted soul among you who could possibly *make* me sad, and (2) whatever sadness I have and whatever intensity it has at any given moment is present whether or not someone brings Cec into the arena of conversation. Sometimes keeping a lost loved one out of conversation gives the impression that people don't want to have to deal with the griever's unhappiness. *That* is saddening.

1:20 a.m.

Jim

FOURTEEN

October 3, 2004

A year ago, Cecily and I were approaching the watershed of our lives. We were still in our old house, Ida was here helping us pack it up, Cec's back and chest were in a lot of pain we couldn't figure out, Maddie was less than a month into her therapy, and we were terribly afraid for her.

Within a few days, we would be leaving our home of fifteen years to stay briefly in Debi Derryberry's rental house until we could move into the home of our dreams, the one Cec had designed from the studs out. We would be a mere 300 steps from Cecily's office and she would be able to come home on a moment's notice to spend time with Maddie. I was in the middle of shooting the first season of what seemed to be a promising TV series. We had some apprehensions, mainly about Maddie, but most of the bumps ahead seemed small.

Tonight, I thought that for the next few days here it would be interesting to go back to my calendar for this month in 2003 and revisit what we were doing during those days leading up to the discovery that the world as we knew it was about to end. But my calendar reveals nothing. There are occasional references to picking up a refill for the Diaper Genie, or to taking our cat, Sigourney Beaver, to the vet, or a service call from the cable guy. Nothing to dramatize what simmered beneath the surface of our lives, no coincidental or ironic predictors, nothing.

I remember those days. It was tense, with the subtext of Maddie's diagnosis rubbing us raw from the inside out, and with the house being torn apart for packing. Cec was in bed much of the time, in pain and unable to manage the packing the way she wanted to. She was irritable and so was I. When Cec was irritable, she could nitpick you to death. And when I'm irritable and being nitpicked, I can get awfully resentful.

I remember seething on the side porch one morning after Cec picked some bone or another with me, and telling Tom that "if it weren't for that kid, I would be out of here!"

It was never easy being with Cec when she was unhappy or hurting or angry. But most of the time there was a transparency to it that allowed me to see through to the essence of the girl I loved, and grin (infinitesimally) and bear it. Even when the hard times were translucent or even opaque and impervious to revelation of the bright side, I was saved many times by a sense that we were inevitable together and that considering anything else was futile. But ultimately, there was such love binding us together that even our own childish thrashings couldn't pull us apart. We lived a breathtakingly passionate life together, but the passion supporting our difficulties was trifling measured against the furious devotion we felt for each other.

And that, in the end, was what saved us.

I look back now on that calendar and see no sign of these things, only the mundane.

Yet when I look back through the pages of the calendar that is in my mind, there is an opera of Wagnerian proportions and passions reeling back through that October and the one before and the one before, incessantly alive and trumpeting, echoing back nearly nineteen years, the sounds and glories of which I will carry with me until the day I find out where she's gone.

Watching the TV series *Six Feet Under* this season has been a strange experience. The lead character lost his wife at the end of last season, leaving him alone to raise their toddler. This season's story line has been the impact of this loss on him, the second-guessing and the mourning and the coping and the anguish. He's passed through regrets and anger and irrationality, struggled with the concept of ever being with anyone else (and the feelings of disloyalty and betrayal and self-loathing that that concept creates in him), and ached from loneliness and loss of meaning. And he's forced himself to go on, less for his own sake than for his little girl's. All of this has not been lost on me, either as information or a source of ironic amusement and bemusement. He went through all these passages without help or real support, and he refused what help was offered.

We differ in that.

Tonight I watched the season finale and was taken by the closing lines, lines in a scene featuring other characters and not dealing at all with the first character's situation. One character tells another, "You hang on to your pain as though it were worth something. It's not." The younger of the two replies, "So what am I supposed to do?" The older says, "Anything you want to. You're alive." The younger says, "It can't be that simple." The older puts his arm around the younger and says, "What if it is?"

I think it is.

2:12 a.m.

Jim

October 4, 2004

When Maddie was little, Cec used to sing to her when she woke up. She would sing a variation on "Good Morning," from *Singin' in the Rain*: "*Good morning, good morning, you've slept the whole night through. Good morning, good morning to you. Good morning, good morning, I love the little girl. Good morning, good morning to you.*"

Cec always phrased it that way, "I love the little girl." I don't know why, but it was very Cec-like for her to do so. She was adamant that we start each day with Maddie in an upbeat and happy mood. She said that it would set the tone for Maddie's whole day. I, being one of those people who stumble around mumbling for half an hour after awaking, and one of those rare folk who don't drink coffee, was preternaturally disinclined toward merriment upon waking. But Maddie's temperament has always been so mellow, and she always responded so well to Cec's morning song, that I easily believe Cec was right. And now, when Maddie wakes up, I try to rouse myself to start the morning off with that song. It gives me a warm and happy ache in my heart to phrase that line in Cec's way, "I love the little girl." And Maddie, who often wakes with a bit of a whimper, bursts into smiles when I remember to sing the song. And when I finish she says, "Good *morning*, Daddy!"

If Cec only sees and hears, that's all I really need. I think the hole in my heart might actually heal if I could know, really know, with all doubts vanquished, that she sees and hears "the little girl."

Yesterday was seven months.

10:57 p.m.

Jim

October 5, 2004

Cec and I used to watch the play-offs and the Series most years. She didn't care much about baseball, but from our second autumn together, it became a bit of a tradition. That year, 1986, I'd made my first real money. My Social Security records indicate it was the first time I'd ever made more than $8,000 in a year. I'd been hired to write several episodes of a revival of the old *Alfred Hitchcock* show, and with my first check, I took Cec on a trip to New England. We visited friends in New York, toured West Point, and saw the place in Peekskill where Cec's mom and dad had lived. We drove through Vermont and across Massachusetts. We spent a glorious few days in a bed-and-breakfast on the beach in Gloucester, where I sketched and Cec took pictures and we walked on the grassy dunes and scraped messages to each other on the beach sand. And each night we would sit in the car and listen to the World Series on the radio and drive through the darkness of Massachusetts or New Hampshire or Maine villages and try to time our return to Gloucester with the final out. We had watched the play-offs in California and Cec had fallen madly in love with Dave Henderson of the Boston Red Sox, not because he was hunky or gorgeous, but because he played with such heart and had such a great smile. By the time we were listening to the Series in New England, Cec was as caught up in the drama of the games as any lifetime fan. I'm sure the natural trappings of the trees in that luscious fall and the lazy mornings kicking sand on the beach at Gloucester were the standouts of that trip for Cec, but her enjoyment of a little bit of baseball in the night, shared with me, is what I remember most about that trip. That, and the first morning we woke up in our extraordinarily cozy little room in Gloucester and luxuriated in the soft downy bed, listening to the cry of gulls on the beach, until at the exact same moment, both of us cried out to the birds, "Shut upppp!" And then we laughed hysterically.

Boston's back in the play-offs this year. But the roster's different, and it's not quite the same. Not quite the same at all.

12:56 a.m.

Jim

October 7, 2004

I said that most days the sadness and loss I feel is a dull ache inside. But every once in a while it takes on the character of a blade of steel stabbing through my breast. Today was like that. It was an odd sensation. No tears, no overt mournfulness, just an occasional feeling that someone had just chopped into my chest with an axe. And I would pause, as one does when perforated by an axe, and reflect on my loss and then move on. I've not had a day quite like it, in this regard. Apparently there's no end to the new ways one can experience such a cataclysm.

11:18 p.m.

Jim

October 8, 2004

Today's one of those days when I catch myself saying, "I'm never going to get over this, am I?" And then I remember the grief recovery proscription against projecting current feelings on the future. And so I allow myself the possibility of getting over this. Whatever that means.

I feel impotent and stupid and small tonight. I should have known something, I should have done something, I should have acted differently, and, oh, I should have been kinder. I'm well aware that these "should haves" are useless and detrimental to growth and recovery. If I had known the date and time Cec would die from the first time I met her, I could not have pulled off being the perfect husband, lover, friend, and supporter I wish so badly now I had been. I grant human fallibility and acknowledge my just share in it. The intellectual segment of my brain understands and forgives and tolerates this fallibility. But the limbic brain, where emotion rules and is ruled, is a tough taskmaster and not nearly so forgiving.

Have I mentioned lately that I loved her?

11:00 p.m.

Jim

October 9, 2004

Maddie and I looked at family pictures. She named all the people in the pictures she saw, including her aunts. She looked at a picture of my dad and said, "Where's Granddaddy?" I said, "He had to go away." She said, "With Mommy?" I said, "Yes." Mind you, this was not a painful exchange. Some sorrow is always involved in even cursory references to the two great gargantuan losses of my life. But I enjoyed the fact that Maddie was making these connections, and that she sensed that her granddaddy and mommy were together.

We talked about what we each did today and I told her I'd spent the afternoon working on taxes. She said, "I want to go to Taxes." I said, "Not Texas, taxes." She said, "Can we go to Taxes?" I said, "Texas is a place, taxes is about money, dollars." And, cross my heart, she said, "Can we go to Dollars, Taxes?" Now this is a routine right out of an actual Marx Brothers movie, but I haven't yet introduced her to the Marxes (oh, I will). So either she merely stumbled on the construction without construing its meaning, or I've just proven that bad puns are genetic. If the latter, I know my papa's smiling proudly, for there were few things he loved more than a bad pun. And as he always said, I'm a chip off the old blockhead.

11:31 p.m.

Jim

October 13, 2004

I watered the roses today, with special attention to the plant whereon I had placed the last residue of Cecily's ashes. It made me happy to see the green erupting from the thorny stalks, with promise of buds and blooms anew. And it made me smile to think how Cec would have chided me for letting too much time go by between waterings.

Thinking of how I might be chided by Cec for poor husbandry of these roses revived in my mind the question of whether she sees and experiences us in this world from her current vantage point, and, if so, what might she feel about what she sees.

She would, I'm sure, find amplification of whatever bliss she is in by dint of knowledge of how much she was and still is loved. The same goes for the joy she must have in the beautiful child she created. And, knowing Cec, I suppose she might have the odd critical note for me or others regarding how we've behaved without her here to tell us how. I would revel in the knowledge that she sees and hears and understands, even in the knowledge that she occasionally disapproves. Beyond the hopes and dreams I have for Maddie's health and happiness, I suspect nothing would give me greater joy than to know Cecily has consciousness of us still and that our love is transmitted to her.

12:11 a.m.

Jim

October 15, 2004

One of the complaints so many grievers have is, as I've mentioned, the comforting that takes the shape of an attempt to remove one's burden of grief, whether by giving reasons that things are not as bad as they seem or that the grief is outweighed by an abundance of blessings. Russell Friedman said that grief is a real-life experience, one that has value, and he would no more take away someone's grief than he would take away that person's happiness.

I was thinking about that when I ran across a letter written by the Episcopal preacher Phillips Brooks to a friend whose mother had died. He wrote:

May I try to tell you again where your only comfort lies? It is not in forgetting the happy past. People bring us well-meant but miserable consolations when they tell us what time will do to help our grief. We do not want to lose our grief, because our grief is

bound up with our love and we could not cease to mourn with-
out being robbed of our affections.

You tell 'em, Phil. (Brooks also wrote something a little better
known, a little ditty called "O Little Town of Bethlehem.")
   11:14 p.m.

Jim

October 16, 2004

A year ago tonight was our last night in our longtime home, the
house Cec had browbeaten me into buying with her in 1988. I just
knew buying that house was the wrong thing to do, that I was incapable of living up to the demands of home ownership, that it would
all be taken away from us and then what would we do? Fifteen years
later, there we still were, leaving only to move into a new and better
home, one with infinitely greater demands, but one which I looked
forward to with a joyous anticipation completely reversing the dif-
fidence I'd felt three lustrums earlier.

A year ago tonight, we were anxious about the move, about having it come off smoothly, but we were excited and despite enormous
stresses on us, I think we were happy underneath. How I wish I could
go back there to that night and treasure it in the moment more than
I did. Oh, how I wish.
   2:04 a.m.

Jim

October 17, 2004

A year ago today, the countdown began. We did not know it as
such, but in hindsight it's evident that that was the first day of a

recognizable beginning of the end of almost everything familiar in our lives. That Friday afternoon, a moving van showed up at our house on Rubio Avenue in Van Nuys and a crew began emptying our house of everything we owned. The beloved Ida was madly packing boxes, almost single-handedly preparing us for the move, because I was shooting *Deadwood* and running Maddie to therapy sessions and Cec was either at work or laid up in bed with this increasingly painful pulled muscle in her chest. She was in so much pain she couldn't do much about packing except make decisions. She would struggle to get out of bed and go to work, but it was increasingly difficult. She made frequent visits to a chiropractor, but these sessions seemed ineffective. Finally, upon the recommendation of her chiropractor, she'd met with a sports-medicine orthopedist. This doctor had taken X-rays and had seen nothing. He'd prescribed muscle relaxants and pain medication. Nothing had improved. So two days prior to moving day, he'd ordered a CT scan. We'd not had results yet. On moving day, Cec had some blood tests and visited Dr. Meth, our family doctor. Nothing seemed out of the ordinary. The orthopedist and Dr. Meth concurred that it was probably costochondritis, an uncomfortable but benign inflammation of the joints where the ribs meet the breastbone. The majority of cases occur in women, and every symptom matched what Cecily was experiencing. The one anomaly was that it didn't seem responsive to the standard pain medications.

Moving day was probably the single most stressful day I had ever experienced in my life. The valuables and the detritus of fifteen years in the same house were overwhelming. The movers started at 2:00 in the afternoon and were not finished putting everything into the temporary house we were renting from Debi Derryberry until 2:00 the following morning. I carried and loaded and unloaded almost as much as the movers, and made many trips from one house to the other, taking items that couldn't be entrusted to a moving van. I was still making such trips and cleaning out lamps and telephones and nightlights and curtain rods from the old house into the wee

hours. All through this, Cec suffered. She was forced by the circumstances of the move to get out of bed and stay out until our bed could
be reassembled in the new house. All the while she was trying, with
some help, to wrangle Maddie, who was underfoot and overwhelmed
by the changes being wrought in her life. Well after midnight, I
remember Cec begging me to make it all stop, to tell the movers to go
home with the truck still containing many of our belongings, so she
could sleep. But it was impossible. They had another moving job in the
morning and were unable to store our goods. In addition, they would
charge (another) bloody fortune to do so, even if they could. We pressed
on, and a little after 2:00 a.m., they finished and we went to bed.

It had been an awful day. Physically, I was exhausted beyond anything I think I'd ever known. Carrying furniture and boxes for twelve
straight hours, never sitting, never resting, had taken a toll on me. I
remember thinking at some point during the night that it might not
be possible for a person to survive the amount of stress I felt. (Little
did I know that in scarcely more than a week, I would have given
anything I owned to be able to return to the comparatively minor
stresses of moving day.) Cec was miserable, exhausted, fearful, and
in great pain. As she lay in her bed in the tiny house on Cartwright
Avenue, the pain in her chest competed with an increasing pain in
her lower back. Clearly, we thought then, she'd thrown her back out
again, for the hundredth time since I'd known her, probably by moving boxes or some other strenuous activity she should have avoided.

I think I was a little impatient with her, because she was always
hurting her back and never seemed to take precautions to keep from
injuring it. And thus, I had more to do—managing Maddie more on
my own, and doing things for Cec that she was unable to do for herself. I've no doubt that I was curt with her that night. My nerves
were shredded. So were hers. And everything familiar to us had suddenly slipped out from beneath our feet. Here we were in a house
much smaller than we were used to, uncertain how to control the
air-conditioning and therefore stifling, and we had only the vaguest

idea where anything we needed might be—in that box, or that one there, or maybe behind that one? It was, it seemed then, a hellish experience that could only get better. Ha.

Maddie still was not sleeping through the night, so there were frequent wakings for all of us before morning too soon arrived. But we'd made half the move—a month or so and we'd do it again, and be once and for all in our new dream home. Nevermore to roam. We had breathing space again. It was hard, but we'd done it, and now everything was okay.

Not so much.

Flash forward one year. I started to write that today was proof that no matter how bad things are, a year from now will probably be better. I draw back from committing to that statement, however. Yes, today was infinitely less stressful than this calendar date one year ago. But *the time is out of joint*, as our old friend Hamlet knows; something is wrong. As blessed as today was, it is nonetheless cursed with her absence. As wretched as that day was twelve sorry and sorrowful months ago, yet it shone brightly with her jewel-like presence. Be cautious what you say you cannot stand; fate may well feel compelled to teach you just how much more you can.

1:52 a.m.

Jim

October 18, 2004

A year ago today was a Saturday. All of us were exhausted by the move, which had concluded in the wee hours of this day. Cec was in a lot of discomfort, but none of us knew enough or suspected enough to worry us. I'm sure I was impatient. I remember being impatient with her a lot during that time, because her illnesses and aches and pains were so endless. At least I thought they were endless. I'd be proven wrong.

But for years, the carefree times had been islands, some large, some small, but mere islands, in an ongoing sea of physical ailments, few of which ever seemed to have any identifiable cause or resolution. They just came and they went, relentlessly. I know Cec was in real discomfort, in every case, but I confess I grew weary over the years, and I frequently believed she unwittingly aided and abetted her own illnesses and injuries by sort of leaning into them. Every cold was possibly pneumonia. Every headache was possibly an aneurysm. I'm no Job (though I think we went to the same school). I'm not a creature of endless patience. I look back now and know that many times over the years I treated Cec, not always consciously, as though I thought she were exaggerating her pains. I think sometimes she was. But a year ago, I know, I recollect being impatient with her as though these "muscle pains" that had kept her from pitching in on the move or even managing Maddie while the move was taking place were somehow an unconscious handing off of responsibility. And whenever Cec was in pain, she tended to be grouchy and to toss orders about like hand grenades. So here, on the last weekend before the world fell in on us, I squabbled with her and treated her like what she wasn't: a hypochondriac. I don't mean to imply that we were at great odds with each other throughout that weekend, just that, in hindsight, it's the things I regret that leap to mind. The things I wish I could do over differently. I can't do them over, and I realize that I know things now I didn't know then, and Cec and I both behaved like the humans we were. But if one is going to look back, as I'm doing now, one is bound occasionally to wish one had had one's head on straight. There's so much happiness and caring and love that could have filled some of those moments yet were instead subsumed by the pettiness of habit and stress.

I hope someday I get smart.

11:29 p.m.

Jim

FIFTEEN

October 19, 2004

Today, with Maribel out sick, a temporary nanny came to work. She's wonderful, much like Maribel. I'm such a clunker of a father in some ways—Maddie hadn't any cereal left for her breakfast, nor did she have the makings of the snack she was supposed to take to school. I'd meant, but forgotten, to go to the store last night. The new nanny waltzed in and whipped up eggs and beans and toast for Maddie, something I couldn't have done with a magic wand. Maddie had the best breakfast she's had in months, I'm sure. The hardest thing of the day was calling the nanny by her name—Cecilia.

Cec's name was not all that common. It was unusual enough that, she told me, as a child she had disliked it intensely. She hated the nicknames kids gave her: Cec-pool, Cec-quatch. With my last name, I only had limited sympathy for her. But I loved her name from the moment I heard it. It was a special name, one I adored, and one I was happy she shared with virtually no one of my experience. And then this morning I stood in this house and called someone else Cecilia. Close enough, it was. The hairs fluttered along my neck and my throat tightened as the name passed through it.

I'll get past that. It's the kind of thing one must lean into, and not flinch from or drag one's feet. It's the headlong leap into an icy stream that rushes you past the momentary shock and pain, then leaves you perhaps not comfortable but capable of tolerating the situation. It's just a name, yet the sound of my voice speaking it conjures up thousands upon thousands of echoes of the times past when I spoke almost exactly the same sounds to her, the girl with the chocolate eyes and an elegance Oscar Wilde could never have gifted his Cecily with.

Cecilia's good with Maddie, and though I hope Maribel's able to return soon, I'll be pleased to have Cecilia here for as long as she needs to be.

12:42 a.m.

Jim

October 21, 2004

I've never heard of a dog being as dog-tired as I am. Maybe I've never heard of it merely because dogs don't complain about it.

I was up and out before dawn, on my way to work. The only difficult part of the day, other than staying awake, was after I got home. Maddie was wired, for some reason, active and too rambunctious to go to sleep, so I watched a video with her while her bottle warmed up. I don't know what the trigger was, but I suddenly burst into tears while sitting with her. I was feeling a lot of regrets, a lot of shame and sadness, and so much missing. Maddie turned to me and looked with great interest and mild surprise and said, "Are you cwying, Daddy?" I told her I was and that I was sad and missing Mommy. She said, "Can we go see Mommy?" I told her no, that Mommy had to go away and we couldn't go, and I was sorry because her mommy loved her so. She said, "Are you sad?" I said yes, but that it was okay to be sad, that it doesn't feel good, but it's all right to be sad. And she said, "I hab something in my backpack to make you happy." I thought she'd brought something home from school yesterday that she wanted to show me, and I asked what she had. She repeated just that she had something in her backpack to make me happy. Then she said, "Say 'backpack.'" I realized she was talking about the magic backpack that Dora the Explorer wears in the video we were watching. I said, "backpack," and Maddie reached around behind her and pulled out a little invisible something and put it on my chest and said, "There, I made you all happy again." She had. I told her that I felt happier, but that she didn't *have* to make me happy, that it was okay to be sad sometimes. She said, "But, Daddy, I *have* to make you happy." The one thing I've tried so hard to inculcate in her is freedom from the notion that my happiness is her responsibility, yet somehow she picked it up anyway. I never tell her she "makes" me happy, I always say instead that I'm so happy when I'm with her. I'm utterly opposed to deliberately or unconsciously making kids "responsible" for the moods of their parents. Sure, a kid can tick you off or thrill you, but it's not their *job* to keep you on an even keel. So I told Maddie that I was happy she wanted to make me happy, but that she didn't have to and that there was nothing wrong with being unhappy sometimes, that sometimes that was the proper way to be. I can't imagine that any of this stuff sinks in deeply, but if I keep at it, maybe it will have a positive effect.

She was so wound up, though, that it took her until after 11:00 p.m. to get to sleep. She asked for the story of *The Three Bears*, which I got halfway through before she asked for the story of *The Three Little Pigs*, which I only got a few sentences into before she asked for the story of *The Three Cows*. That one stopped me cold.

A year ago today, Cec and I tried to carry on our lives as best as we could, with her in great pain and worry, and with me trying hard to prove that whatever was wrong with her was no big deal. It was all going to work out. The pain was sore muscles, the mass was an old dried-up and meaningless lymph node, and maybe some steroids for her muscles and rib joints would solve everything. Everything was going to be fine and worry was wasted on this.

Cec had a massively difficult time being an optimist, though she gave it effort. It wasn't her nature, not when life and death seemed part of the question. She never acted as though she thought worry was wasted. In retrospect, I would have wanted her free from the terror that invaded her in force a year ago, but it's clear she was not wrong about worrying. I can't say she ever really thought she would die soon, but I could not allow such a thought to cross my lips. I know she was afraid of it, very afraid, right from the first, while right from the first, I was convinced everything was going to be fine. It took a while for me to come around to her point of view, and I never fully achieved it, staying in some denial for a long, long time. As of October 21, 2003, I was only a little nervous—not deeply worried. Another day or so would change all that.

1:36 a.m.

Jim

October 22, 2004

"Confess yourself to heaven, Repent what's past, avoid what is to come,
And do not spread the compost on the weeds To make them ranker."

— *HAMLET*, ONCE MORE

The melancholy Dane of Shakespeare's play hath herein kindly broached the topic of tonight's missive. Confession. Open confession. Good for the soul, the Scots say.

Today is an anniversary. Certainly I've recorded a few in this year of nightly dispatches. Mostly birthdays, because the celebration of life is an important part of recovery from grief. But some of the noted anniversaries have had more exact pertinence to the topics at hand: survival, death, grieving, and survival again. And to tonight's other topic: guilt. Tonight is a special anniversary. It pales before the devastation of March 3, 2004, the single worst day of my life. But as a marker of pain, it has its own special seat in that circle of hell reserved for guilty sorrow.

I've written glowingly of the glories of my love for Cecily and the love she had for me. No one who has followed these pages can have missed the passion and solidity of that love. And, too, I've written about the difficult times, the moments when pain and fear and impulse and selfishness and reaction drove wedges between us, even at times when we most needed to cleave together. I've written of the void brought about by the loss of everything wondrous I had with her, the loss of all the joys we shared. And I've written of the regret and self-reproach I've felt over failures big and small, over derelictions and trespasses that smudged the gloss of our time together. I've written of ecstasies and agonies and tried to convey a scintilla of what it was to be with Cecily and what it was to lose her. But there's one thing I have not written or conveyed. One thing that could not quite be faced, yet which now, if I am to conclude this journal in the candor and veracity I have sworn to bring to it, must be faced and must be declared and made known. I have not yet written of the night I wished Cecily would die.

In denial I was, as I wrote yesterday or the day before. It did not feel like denial. (Does it ever?) I simply hoped and had confidence that Cec's worries were like all her worries before—ungrounded. I wanted so to believe and for her to believe that the odds were stacked in our favor, that every indicator of her condition leaned most heavily toward a benign circumstance that only faintly and innocuously resembled something dangerous. I grasped at every jot of suggestion that the mass showing in her chest was unimportant and that the pain she felt was a passing thing, no matter how much discomfort it carried. And in the course of clutching at these "probable" happy outcomes, I found myself growing increasingly impatient with Cec's fear. I felt that she often sabotaged herself with fear, and that she refused to take advantage of the good that could come with an optimistic outlook. She had told me on many occasions that the times she felt most cared for, most looked after, as a child were when she was ill. From infancy she'd had chronic kidney infections, with concomitant raging fevers. When she was sick, her mom would come flying to rescue her, turning on selflessness as with a switch. Cec relished these periods of intense loving care. But by the time I met her, Cec seemed to be sick half the time. After a few years of her seemingly endless cycling through one ailment or infirmity after another, I began to extrapolate a sense that perhaps when she needed emotional tending she would unwittingly make herself sick, recapturing those moments of highest nurturance. Though I understood instinctively then (and more clinically now) that she was not consciously undermining her own health and happiness, I was a little more frayed each time some new prostration reared its head.

In retrospect (that lovely vantage from which all mistakes are rectifiable), I know how scared she was when she was sick and how much pain she'd felt in that body of hers over her lifetime. Some of the treatments she'd had as a child made doctors in more recent times drop their jaws from the primitivity of those "remedies." She'd suffered great torment over the years, twice from being hit by cars and once from a car wreck. And the regimen required of her to conceive our daughter was far beyond anything I would have been willing to bear, no matter how I might have wanted a child. Shots, shots, and more shots, every day for months and months, each shot leaving her body tender and her mental and physical metabolism wracked. I knew all these things, yet after just a little impatience or temporary ingratitude from her, my own impatience would grow like Jack's bean stalk. One of the great shames of my life, long before I lost Cecily, was the knowledge of how many times I'd snapped at her when she was sick or in pain, and, worse, how many times she'd told me that the only times I'd ever failed her were the times she needed me most.

On Wednesday, October 22, 2003, I have no recollection of any impending doom. A bronchoscopy was scheduled for the next day, and I knew in my heart that this would put our fears to rest. A check back over my notes for that day shows that on Wednesday, October 22, I booked an airline ticket to Texas to spend the weekend with my dad. Clearly I was feeling free enough to leave town. We were still trying to settle in to the new temporary quarters, though Cec was too uncomfortable to do much herself. I had taken our beloved cats to board elsewhere, as we were in danger of losing Maribel because of her allergies. And Zully had come to work for us as a nighttime nanny, since Cec was hurting too much to do more with Maddie than sit and feed her. Cec was anxious and fretting, both about the things I now more clearly see were seriously frightening her and about the little things of getting settled into this new place and the increasing concerns over whether our new home would be ready by the time we were required to move back out of the temporary house. As the day wore into evening, she became testier and more pugnacious.

At our old house, our bed had been high off the floor, and as Cec's pain had increased, I often helped her in or out of bed without difficulty. But in the temporary house, we'd not assembled the bed frame, choosing instead to place the mattress and box spring directly on the floor. As a result, the bed was lower, and I was not able to hold Cec in my arms and lay her down in the bed the way I had when the mattress was at my waist level. The bed was too low for me to bend to with her full weight in my arms. As I was helping her back into bed that night, she shouted at me, angry that I wasn't being gentle enough, that I was shifting her about too roughly. I had gotten too used to her aches and pains and failed to see that this was different, that this was sharper, deeper pain than in times gone by. I was doing my best, though, in a physically awkward situation, to get her comfortably into bed. And it nettled me to be upbraided for not doing something well enough when I was doing my utmost to do it well. I got her settled, and then I went to tend to Maddie in some way or other. Something I did or did not do with Maddie bothered Cec, and she chastised me for not being more on top of the situation, of not giving Maddie's needs more thorough thought.

I said I was doing my best, and Cec tuned up a recurrent theme: that if something happened to her, I was going to have to take care of Maddie, and the care I gave Maddie would need to be a thousandfold better than what I was doing currently.

I said, "Nothing's going to happen to you," and she retorted, "You don't know that. This thing could turn out to be cancer tomorrow. You don't know. And if I'm not here, you will have to take care of Maddie, and 'I'm doing my best' just isn't going to cut it." I said something along the lines of "I don't know how to do better than my best," and she said, "If I'm dead, you're going to have to." The "conversation" ended in derisive anger on her part and stifled indignant rage on mine. I sat in the rocking chair at the foot of our bed, rocking and feeding Maddie her bottle in the dark.

My mind was seething. I knew that in the best times, I was indeed Cec's knight in shining armor, as she often reassured me. But I knew that when she was angry or afraid, she exhibited little or no trust in me. I knew I had failed her often in strained circumstances, but I also felt I had always tried my best and that my failings often followed being provoked. But Cec always agreed with *Star Wars'* Yoda: *"Do or do not. There is no try."*

I rocked Maddie, trying hard not to transmit my anger through my arms into the fussy little girl in my lap who, at that point, required an hour or more of rocking every night before she'd fall asleep. I kept thinking of the last part of Cec's remarks: "If I'm dead, you're going to have to." And I thought, "You're not gonna die. You've got torn cartilage, that's all. You're not gonna die. You're not gonna die. Quit holding that over my head. You're not gonna die. You're not gonna die. You're not gonna die. Sometimes I wish you would."

I'm certain few people in a marriage have not at one time or another had that thought flit through their minds. It wasn't the first time I'd had it skitter through mine, and I'd be utterly dumbfounded to learn it hadn't gone through Cec's mind about me. I know it had. That's where it ends, though, with most people.

That night, it didn't end there for me. Every night for almost two years I had sat in the dark with Maddie in my arms, rocking and thinking, rocking and thinking. I'd done some good and valuable thinking in those times. I'd even written a play in my head while rocking that baby, and seen that play produced on the stage. But on the night of Wednesday, October 22, 2003, I was not thinking good and valuable thoughts. I was thinking escape.

"You're not gonna die. You're not gonna die. Sometimes I wish you would," rumbled through my skull. And then the "sometimes" dropped away. "I wish you would." I didn't linger there. I didn't visualize or hope or pray or conjure up a spell for Cec to die. The thought just crossed my mind, and I was taken aback by how completely unemotional I was. I thought, "What if she did die?" And I was completely surprised that I didn't even feel guilty for thinking it. I just thought, "Hmm. What if she did? What then?" And I began to evaluate my feelings and predict how I would feel if, in fact, something happened to Cec.

And that night, as I rocked my daughter in my arms, I felt my anger and wounded ego subsume all other sentiments. I began to calm myself, not with loving thoughts or self-examination or rational remedy for this current rift, but with daydreaming. I began to walk, then canter, then gallop down the path of wish fulfillment. And for the next hour or so, with my baby in my arms and my dying wife lying tense and frightened a few feet away in the same room, I thought about how wonderful my life would be if Cec died.

It was not her death I desired or fantasized about. None of this, as contradictory as it may sound, had anything to do with desiring harm for her. The subject of my woolgathering was freedom. I thought about traveling. I dreamed about doing things I wanted to do, without the shackles of responsibility or disapproval or contravention. I envisioned life with someone else, someone who in this dreamy perfection would have no quarrel with me or anything about me. I began, rocking there in the dark, envisioning the women I would date, listing in my mind the persons I found most attractive in my world and deciding whom first to pursue. I thumbed through a mental Rolodex, giving weight and attention to every likely prospect, thoroughly enjoying the act of romantic window-shopping. Through it all, I found myself nonplussed and a bit taken aback by the utter lack of feeling I had about the circumstance that would set this fantasy life in motion. I kept thinking, "Hmm, what do you know about that? I'm thinking about Cec dying, and I don't feel anything." Except some excitement about how cool my life was going to be if something like that ever did happen. I rocked. Cec slept or ruminated or fumed, I don't know. Through it all, I envisioned and wished for the freedoms over which I had fantasized.

A wise man asked, *"How many of our daydreams would darken into nightmares, were there any danger of their coming true?"* Great teacher, my hand is up. I can answer that one now.

I'm not merely whipping myself. These are warnings, or suggestions for foresight. And I hope they're a help for those on similar journeys to know that the worst and best of their experiences are shared by others, that they are not alone in what they feel. I believe, utterly, that the only way out of such guilt is forgiveness—forgiveness of the ones we've lost and forgiveness of ourselves. So I've written these confessions tonight not to condemn or martyrize myself, but so it will be clear what a man is capable of and what a man is capable of forgiving, in himself and in others. I suspect in the end the forgiveness of self will prove the greater value.

I don't claim wisdom. And I cannot say whether I've made a point here or just a mess. I've spent five hours writing this tonight and many days thinking about it and planning it, so perhaps what I've failed to say in words can be inferred from the importance I placed on saying it.

Life, they say, is made up of successes and lessons. Take a lesson from me.

12:21 a.m.

Jim

October 23, 2004

Today is the anniversary of the day Cec first went into the hospital, and the first undeniable sign that something serious was really wrong with her. I remember calling Stacey and Nancylee from the hospital parking garage after the bronchoscopy, telling them that it was good news, that there weren't any tumor signs in her lung, and that as soon as she came out of the anesthesia we would go home. I remember being happy. I remember being relieved. I remember thinking that I had always known everything would be all right.

2:10 a.m.

Jim

SIXTEEN

A great day until the end, and even that was tempered with lessons and good fortune.

This morning, Maddie and I went to the pony rides at the farmers' market. We had a fine time, and I discovered something that'll make you a zillion dollars if you've got the patience and the gall: balloon yo-yos. It's a balloon with a small amount of water in it to give it weight, attached to a rubber band. Maddie *"needed"* a yellow one, so I bought it for her—for three dollars, a markup of probably 3,000 percent. Get yourself a $2 gross of balloons, some rubber bands, and a bucket of water, park yourself at a carnival or street fair, and watch the bucks roll in. Tell 'em Three-Dollar Jim sent you.

Tonight, after Italian food, I bathed Maddie and scrubbed a couple of pounds of spaghetti sauce off her. Then I took her up to bed. She fell asleep a mere two hours later.

It seems funny as I write it, but it wasn't funny while it was happening. She was hyper and frenetic and bouncy as a jeep rolling over a log. She wanted a tissue, she wanted water, no, in a cup not a bottle, she wanted to go to the bathroom again (and again and again), she wanted to watch TV, she wanted to look out the window, she wanted every single human activity a three-year-old could conjure up except one: sleep. I was exhausted and I just wanted her to go to sleep so I could write this e-mail and catch the tape I'd made of the World

Series and find out who won, and get to bed. But no. She preferred performing her one-person rendition of *Riverdance* in the bed.

I was angry. Not really at Maddie. After all, that's what three-year-olds do, and, frankly, she does a lot less of it than most kids her age. No, I found myself getting resentful, really resentful of Cec. I didn't immediately think of it as being directed at her. But I kept thinking that though I am fully equipped to love a little girl, I am completely unequipped to raise one. So why did she leave me here to raise this little girl by myself? The moment it stopped being amorphous and I realized it was Cec I was angry at, I reined it in, cooling the boil by reminding myself that Cec would *never* have left me here to raise Maddie alone if she'd had any choice in the matter, that in this regard, Cec had far the worst of the bargain—she'd lost her life *and* her daughter. Me, I'd just lost some peace of mind, which would surely return.

For a while, I was angry about the situation, and feeling sorry for myself, in a splenetic, fuming sort of way. I was also angry due to other emotions running high. I wanted badly just to curl up in bed and sob, either from pure grief or from mild grief alloyed with exhaustion. And as so often lately, I couldn't. I had to stifle the expression of those emotions because of Maddie. Though wracking sobs have become less frequent, they're still not something for Maddie's eyes and ears. And there haven't been many opportunities to get away from her sensibilities at those moments when I really need to let go. So frustration reigned in a multitude of ways tonight.

Finally, I gave up trying to get her to sleep and took her downstairs to watch some more of those tedious but invaluable videos she loves. We watched what seemed like a full season of *Little Bear* and *Dora the Explorer* before she finally said, "Daddy, what—" and fell asleep. Too worn out to move, I flicked off *Dora* and turned on the game and watched Boston take another one. I managed to relax a bit, though truthfully, just sitting with Maddie on the sofa had mellowed me out. And here's where the good fortune came in. If Maddie had gone to sleep right away, I'd have gone down, watched the end of the ball game, and been finished by 10:30 or so. Then I'd have gone upstairs to write tonight's e-mail, meaning I wouldn't have been downstairs at 11:45 p.m. when the hot-water hose to the washing machine burst and started filling the house with water. And I wouldn't have heard it happen. I would probably have gone to bed with water pouring onto the floor as from a fire hose, and not discovered it till morning. It is not unlikely that the entire downstairs floor would have been ruined. As it was, though, I was only a few feet away when the hose broke, and I caught the problem within seconds. So maybe tomorrow I'll give Maddie a blue balloon yo-yo like she wanted two minutes after I'd bought her the yellow one. If I do, I think I'll make it myself and save a few thousand percent.

A year ago today, Cec had the tests that would tell us what was wrong. The next day, the axe would fall.

2:10 a.m.

Jim

October 25, 2004

October 25, 2003. Now there's a date to live in infamy.

There are no adequate words to describe the sensation in the pit of my gut late Saturday morning, October 25, last year. The word "sinking" carries a whiff of the feeling, but to call what I felt in my stomach as I drove to Cedars-Sinai a "sinking" feeling is to call what happened to the *Titanic* a leak. Cec had called me, a tremor in her voice, to say that Dr. Meth, our longtime family doctor, had the results of her tests and wanted me to join them at the hospital to discuss the findings. I could tell Cec was terrified by the same thing I was: Dr. Meth's reluctance to tell her the findings until I arrived at the hospital. The nine-mile drive from North Hollywood to Cedars-Sinai in Beverly Hills was the longest car ride I've ever had. Every traffic light was agony. I felt as though I were desperately trying to get to my own execution. When I arrived in Cec's room, it was clear that Dr. Meth had been unable to keep the facts from Cec. He looked at me in deep pain, patently devastated, yet he said nothing at all that I can recall. Cec was composed and even in her tones, but fear danced in her eyes. "It's cancer," she said.

And that's almost all I remember of that day. Oh, Dr. Meth explained the details and recommended an oncologist. After a while, he left, seemingly battered by the experience. I'm sure he was. He was very fond of Cecily. Even with her tendency to cry wolf so many times before, he was enchanted by her, always delighted to see her. That this time there really was a wolf surely weighed mightily on him. It probably still does.

I do remember other doctors coming in, but most of it's a blur of vision, sound, and emotion, not unlike having a fire hose turned on in one's head. It makes me nauseous, recalling the sensations of that day.

I do recall Cec's sister Cathy getting the news and immediately flying in from Las Vegas. That's especially noteworthy because the preceding year there had been a contretemps between Cec and her sisters Cathy and Christine, and they had not spoken in sixteen months. When horror struck, though, every scrap of that disappeared, and Cathy was there extensively from then on, and Chris, who lived across the country, came whenever she could. The relationship between Cec, Chris, and Cathy was as volatile and mercurial as any I've ever encountered. Hate, laughter, sharing, anger, joy, compassion, pride, disdain, viciousness, and lionlike loyalty ricocheted off one another all the time I knew these three—the only constant being an axis of love that persisted however the flares spun around it. Cathy arrived that Saturday afternoon and, far better than I ever could, she centered and calmed Cec.

That's it. I can't remember anything else.

Except: As through a dark cloud, I see myself back home later in the day, lying on the bed, howling with a pillow stuffed in my mouth so as not to disturb Maddie. I do recall my amazement that one could cry so hard for so long. Little did I know.

11:40 p.m.

Jim

SEVENTEEN

October 26, 2004

Confessions, amends, the unbosoming of my heart in recent days, leave me concerned that fraction and contention may be the elements most prominently remembered by you who learn about my life with Cecily from these reports. That would be a false image, for this girl and I loved each other. We loved with power and rampant determination. We shared a tenderness with each other that redefined the phrase. We were friends, friends of the soul, we were pals. I've loved and been loved beyond measure in this life, so much so it's hard to believe one man could rightfully contain or feel so much. And with all that, I loved Cecily most. She was my morning and evening star, my partner, my lover, my heart mate. Every blessing I've ever received (save one) I would fling back in the face of fate to have her at my side, loving me again as she did for not quite nineteen years.

I received a note from Susan Morgenstern, a Theatre West friend and colleague. In it, a treasured gift, a reminder of how to deal with what's behind and what's ahead. She wrote about the love I've expressed in these nightly letters:

I always find myself thinking about Harold and Maude, *when Harold, weeping at Maude's deathbed, asks how he will survive*

and tells her he loves her. I have wanted so much to say this to
you. She says, "That's good. Go and love some more."

That's just what I plan to do.

For tonight, I'll leave you simply with words I wrote for her, on
occasions separated by our life together.

Prelude to my wedding vows,
spoken to Cecily at our wedding, May 7, 1989

In all my life, which has been filled with more joy and blessings
than I can describe, nothing has given me more happiness than
finding you. I can't imagine life without you now, Pie. Thank
you for coming down from your fences and opening the gate.
You know that line from *The Hasty Heart* that I love so much.
There's a reason that it's special to me. It's because it's true. I
offer you my heart because it does me no good without you.

My eulogy for Cecily, March 13, 2004

Come to the edge.
We might fall.
Come to the edge.
It's too high!
Come to the edge.
And they came,
and we pushed,
And they flew.

That poem by Christopher Logue was Cecily's favorite,
her mantra, her advice for herself and all others. Despite a

childhood not entirely devoid of Dickensian elements, and an innate anxiety and fearful nature, she pushed through her fears time and time again, bringing herself repeatedly to the edge, and, more often than not, stepping off and soaring like an egret.

My name is Jim Beaver, and for fifteen years I had the unutterable joy, the magnificent honor, the recurrent exasperation, and the staggering fun of being married to Cecily Adams.

Today I will do my best to get through this public part of the worst thing in my life. As a responsible actor, I have an understudy. We will hear from Cec's family, friends, and colleagues about a girl who brought an astonishing amount of vivacity into so many lives and whose departure has left bereft so many hearts.

Her birth certificate, an omen of indecisiveness to come, read "Baby Girl Yarmy." Cecily April Adams, as she was finally named, was born February 6, 1958 or 1965, depending on what the role called for. Her father, an up-and-coming comic named Don Adams, remarried and moved to Hollywood not long after her birth, and Cecily was raised in Silver Spring, Maryland, by her singer-dancer mom, Adelaide. The family came west eventually, and Cec attended Beverly Hills High and UC, Irvine, performing in plays and musicals. After college, she set out to be an actor. She liked to tell of her first restaurant job in Hollywood when, hearing a waiter mention an audition he'd gone on, she said, "Oh-my-God! You're an actor?! Me, too!"

She began to get gigs playing teenagers on *Quincy* and *Simon and Simon* and in commercials. Her aunt, Alice Borden, suggested she join Theatre West, the prestigious theatre company and workshop. She did, and remained an active and respected member for twenty years. That's where I met her.

I was an actor and writer, just beginning to get a few breaks. I had won an election to the theatre's board of directors, and Cec, whom I knew only in passing, came up to congratulate me. She surprised me by kissing me on the cheek. Then she sucker-punched me by saying, "That was nice," and doing it again on the other cheek. Then she left and got in her car.

I stood there a second, shook the stars out of my head, then ran to my car and chased her down the street till she caught me. It was Monday, August 26, 1985. For a woman who liked to look nine ways before crossing the street, those kisses on the cheek were a defining and glorious moment of impulsiveness for which I will be grateful all my life.

I proposed to Cec for four years before she gave me an answer. I don't mean before she accepted—before she answered. It was a question she was determined not to answer wrong, so she didn't answer it at all. Just acted as if I hadn't said anything. Every time. For four years. I admit that as a package, I could bear some inspecting. Finally in 1989, I guess I passed inspection.

She was afraid of marriage, never having seen it work and all too aware of the potential for sorrow and anguish when it failed. So, as with so many things she feared, she stepped off the edge, trusting in her determination to give her wings. Fifteen years later, we were still flying.

It was not always easy. I'm immature and undisciplined and she was harder-headed than Mount Rushmore. So we fought sometimes. Of course, she fought. She's Greek, Italian, Hungarian, and Irish. She could have done World War I as a one-woman show.

But she always fought *for* something, some goal, some betterment, never merely against. She had the passion and courage of her convictions to a greater extent than anyone I've ever known. She was a scared little girl who always stood up for herself.

She was wounded and angry and bitter at betrayal, and she

responded by being loving and charming and by embracing life and the community of her fellow man. She was the bravest scaredy-cat and the most spiritual misanthrope who ever lived. And what did she get for it? Simply more love, more friends, more unashamed adoration than she ever dreamed or could have dreamed.

You have to know how brave she was. Her daughter, Maddie, whom she struggled against Promethean odds and months of physical ordeal to bring into this world, was worth any sacrifice to her. When she learned of her illness, she told the doctors, "I don't care how much pain I have, I don't care how sick you have to make me to beat this, bring it on. I have a daughter to raise." It was far worse than she imagined yet she never retreated an inch for her own comfort.

So what memorial do we build for this brave girl? I challenge each of you who knew her, who admired her, who delighted in her, and who loved her, to examine those moments when fear pulls you back and then to hear the voice of a girl who, despite her conviction that disaster lay around every corner, always pressed forward. *Come to the edge.*
10:27 p.m.

Jim

EIGHTEEN

"Begin at the beginning and go on till you come to the end; then stop." Thus wrote Lewis Carroll. And if you can't take advice from *Alice's Adventures in Wonderland*, from what can you take advice? So tonight I end this journal of the plague year.

Today is my father's birthday. He would have been eighty today, had he lived, and I would have had him five months and eleven days more. *"A father, and a gracious, aged man,"* he was. Except for the year I was in Vietnam, this is the first birthday I have not talked with him, not told him how much I loved him, how much of my strength and whatever decency I have I took from him. Nothing in my life has made me prouder than being James Norman Beaver Jr. The date of his birth will always be one of my most cherished anniversaries.

Today is also another anniversary. One year ago tonight, I sat down to tell family and friends by e-mail of the terrible fate that had befallen Cecily and all of us who loved her. That first message went out to 120 households, a handful alongside the nearly 4,000 who would eventually receive these nightly tales of travail, woe, desolation, horror, and hard-won blessings. In the in-box I created for replies to these e-mails are more than 4,000 messages, from friends, family, acquaintances, and utter strangers who chose to board this vessel with me and Maddie and (for a while) Cec, to sail with us wherever the currents and trades and a trembling hand on the tiller took this little boat.

My sister Denise often says, "Look for the gift," but there was no need to look hard here. In the midst of heartache and despair beyond anything I've ever known or dreamed of knowing, there was bright, shining, and uneclipsed love, affection, and support from more people than Cec or I would have believed possible.

As I relayed the events of Cec's illness and treatment, I never imagined that it would ever go beyond reportage. Yet it has. I've tried to give an honest sense of what these events and emotions are like. I've attempted to flood the path with light where I could, and where I could not I've wanted at least to hold up a candle so that others coming this way might not stumble too painfully.

Progressing from frightened spouse to grieving survivor, I realized that a trait I'd often considered a liability, my predilection for telling what was in my heart, now gave me opportunity to do something few grieving people feel allowed by custom to do—to talk without restraint about the experience. I did it for my own good, my own survival, catharsis, and well-being, but that in-box precludes me from pretending it didn't find useful lodging in the hearts of others. I'm still not sure why my story should be particularly compelling, but if one word I have written has eased or enlightened the path for someone else on a similar journey, then this effort has been the crowning achievement of my life.

In school I was taught the correct narrative essay form: tell 'em what you're gonna tell 'em, tell 'em, and then tell 'em what you told 'em. This essay is hundreds of pages long and stretches over 366 leap-year days. And I failed miserably at the first part of the dictum. I started off telling 'em what I was gonna tell 'em, but I ended up telling 'em something different. I wrote on that first night, "Cecily's gonna beat this. You watch." I was wrong. When Germany attacked Poland in September of 1939, the Polish cavalry mounted up on their horses and defended their homeland by charging into the German tanks. My Cecily mounted her steed, too, and charged bravely into the maw of cancer's Wehrmacht. Not all cancers attack with tanks and dive-bombers, but this one did, and Cec, courageous to the end, like Poland fell. But who cheers for the victor in either of those fights? Who celebrates the triumph of monstrous bastardy over courage and devotion and selflessness? It is the brave, bloody, but unbowed, whose light we look to for inspiration, even in their ostensible defeat. It is my prayer and my belief that out of Cecily's fight and her loss will come, has come, some meaning beyond mere sorrow.

And so, to tell 'em what I told 'em, here is a recapitulation of some of what I've learned in 366 days.

Few things are as difficult as trying to convince someone not to be afraid of something you are terrified of.

To know dreadful secrets and to keep them from your soul's confidante is as torturous a task as any Hercules ever attempted. In my case, it was always hard to keep Cecily from living in the darkest possibilities, and when horror presented itself, it seemed my responsibility to prevent her from plummeting. Thus, and also for my own sanity, I tried to flavor every piece of information not with falsehood but with hope. I don't know whether that was right. It's not as though I left Cec to go through this experience oblivious to the terrible prospects. She didn't need me for that; she was fully capable of seeing them and completely incapable of ignoring them. I felt, though, that her fear should be tempered as much as I could do by hope, and that is what I tried so very hard to provide. But my own terror was wrenching and my greatest performances as an actor did not take place on a stage.

Be careful what you wish for.

I've touched recently on this. The turmoil of normal life in a relationship may cause you to daydream or hope or fantasize on some "better" picture of your life. Sometimes there are indeed better ways to live. But oh, take care. There are hotter places than frying pans. And this leads to the next:

You will never feel the way you think you will.

We humans are creatures of imagination. We thrive on images of what it would be like if some great fortune or misfortune occurred. I thought I knew, in past years, how I would feel if I were suddenly single again. I thought I knew how I would feel if Cecily died or if my father died or if I got a hit TV series or if, if, if. Not one of those thoughts would look familiar to me now. Everything I ever did or felt based on those predictions has proven to be without foundation, and the happiness or freedom or devastation or pride or horror I "knew" would come my way have all been melted and mutated in the cauldron of actual experience. Many apparently joyous prospects have turned into nightmares in actual experience. The reverse sometimes happens, too.

I've learned that everyone has a story like mine, or will have.

I'm continually amazed how little we humans know about the suffering that goes on around us. Only by writing and talking openly about *our* situation was it revealed to me how many thousands are going through just this, or worse, every day. Everyone has suffered or will suffer or knows someone who has suffered or will know someone, and some stories make even Cecily's and mine pale in comparison. Fifteen hundred people a day—a *day!*—die from smoking-related lung cancers in the United States. Add in the numbers dying daily from non-smoking-related diseases, accidents, and killings, and it is hard to understand why every person on the planet isn't currently mourning someone, or struggling to help someone survive. Both a blessing and a curse of my experience has been finding out how much pain is hidden in the lives of people I love, how much sorrow there is that I was oblivious to. I've learned that we are indeed a brotherhood of man, and that our strongest yet least known bond is that of pain.

I've learned that generosity is boundless.

It's strange that one of the greatest days of Cecily's life came during her darkest hours. When she saw the home she'd dreamed of but would barely be allowed to live in transformed into a holiday house lit and decorated like something from *Miracle on 34th Street*, she was speechless at the capacity of people to act out of love and generosity. That scores of people had come out in the middle of their own holidays to make a small miracle for Cecily's Christmas was something Cec marveled at all her remaining days. She called it her own *It's a Wonderful Life*. The house decoration was just the glowing star atop the tree of generosity that we experienced during those hard months. Cec drew people to her as a magnet draws iron filings, yet she never understood her own powers of attraction. She was astonished at the outpouring of love during her illness. I love that she kept being bowled over by the appearance at our door of people whom she believed didn't like her, that she once came home from chemo and found someone she *just knew* hated her in our bathroom scrubbing the toilet. But Cec was exceptional. She was lit from within and her glow reached out to many, many people. Conversely, I have not got her people skills and I am far more isolate. Yet this year, I've found people's bounteous love for Cec has overflowed onto me. Long after Cec was beyond the reach of human generosity, it has streamed my way without ceasing. Cec didn't care for the human race, but she loved everybody she met. It is those *individuals* who proved to her, in the end, the grace and bounty of that human race she'd been wary of so long. For that understanding, I'll be grateful forever.

I've learned that there are some things worse than death.

Watching one you love so deeply suffer, and, worse, seeing the terror in the eyes of that one, is in my mind easily worse than mere dying. If my own life could have been snuffed out in trade for Cecily's fear and pain, I'd have given myself over in an instant. This isn't bravery or self-sacrifice. Watching her hurting, seeing her fear, were the worst feelings I ever had in my life. If I could have traded my life for her freedom from pain and fear, I'd have jumped at it simply to escape the feelings I had seeing her like that. They were the closest things to torture I've ever known. With the exception, I suppose, of being left behind forever without her.

I've learned that profound sorrow knows no limits.

You can cry your heart and eyes out onto the carpet, dredge up every ounce and speck of pain and sorrow and weep it out of your wrung-out body, and then do it all over again five minutes later. Tears and anguish come up from a hole clear through the earth, flowing out onto the ground and washing around the world and coming up through the hole again, like a global fountain endlessly pumping sorrow round and out and round again. Sometimes respite comes for a minute or a day or an hour, and then without warning the flood resumes. And, too, it can relent, and will, eventually. Days will go by, then weeks, without that torrent rushing out and around. And on those days, you'll wonder what's wrong with you that you haven't cried or can't seem to cry anymore. And then you'll find out, for a minute or an hour, that you still can. Yes, you can.

I've learned that no one knows what to say.

When death claims the one you love, you are likely to be overwhelmed with attempts at solace and commiseration from those who love you. Often they won't know what to say, and their struggle to find something right and meaningful will present itself to you as a job, for you to comfort *them* in their discomfort at being unable to comfort you. There's nothing wrong with them for not knowing what to say, and nothing wrong with you for not knowing, either. A picture is worth a thousand words, it's said, but emotions comprise a thousand thousand pictures. How can we turn something as intricate as emotions into mere words?

I've learned that forgiveness of self and forgiveness of the lost one are vital to recovery and survival.

My grieving for my father was a gentle and tender thing, peaceful and scarcely even traumatic. This was due, in part, to the gentleness of his leave-taking, the ripeness of the time, and the preparation we'd been allowed. But most of all, I believe, it was a gentle, almost happy loss, because we had long since cleared all the air between us (not much to clear, really). There was utter understanding of what each of us meant to the other, the power and intensity of our love, and apology and forgiveness for every slight or pain caused one to the other. My dad and I had reduced the differences between us down to nothing but the direction love flowed when traveling from one of us to the other. This was miraculously unusual. The anguish following the loss of a loved one in most cases is because this resolution hasn't occurred. This is where apology and forgiveness still hold power. You can *still* have that conversation with the one you loved. You can *still* express your regret at pain you caused. You can *still* forgive the pain you received. Forgiveness is not something you do for someone else; it's something you do for yourself. To forgive is not to condone, it is to refuse to continue feeling bad about an injury.

For all that we shared, for all our openness, there was still much that I stifled or repressed during my life with Cecily. Nothing since her departure has brought me greater peace than telling Cec in death the sorts of things I was allowed to tell my dad in life. I have a peace now that I am convinced I would not otherwise have had. (Thank you, Russell Friedman.)

I've learned there are no stages to grief.

The famous stages of dying (denial, anger, bargaining, acceptance, etc.) apply to people who *are* dying, not grieving people. Grieving people don't deny for more than a moment that their loved one has died. They don't bargain with the universe; it's too late for bargaining. And anger, acceptance, all the other so-called stages don't come to a griever *in* stages. They wash over a griever, as though they were items of clothing in a washing machine, each rubbing and passing over the griever in turn, simultaneously, repeatedly. Anyone saying you are in a certain "stage" of grieving, or, worse, that you are "supposed to be" in a certain stage needs to be taken out and sh—well, needs to be nodded at and forgiven, I suppose.

I've learned that it feels different every day, sometimes every ten minutes.

The grief process is extremely unpredictable. You may find days, even early days, when you are able to go hours without even thinking of your loss. Other times, a hummingbird flitting by the window will topple you from a sense of well-being and send you plummeting into despair. You'll sometimes even feel relieved by your loss. This one in particular is hard to take, but it happens. You'll sometimes feel a *pleasantness* over the vanished responsibilities to your loved one or the new absence of obstacles to choices you might have differed over. Guilt will flood you at times like these, but guilt, the gift that keeps on giving, needs to be thanked for sharing and then ignored. Easy to say, I know.

I've learned that losing the one you love never ceases to be surprising.

It's nearly eight months since Cecily died. Yet fifty times a day, I am suddenly surprised that it's true. It's a penknife in the heart each time, a little aftertaste of the original realization that never seems to leave me. With surprise comes the equally recurring astonishment. How can this be true? That same fifty times a day it feels as though cows suddenly flew and the sun were green—how can this be true? And yet it is.

I've learned that there is a gift in everything.

Every moment of pain in this past year has brought with it in some tiny measure the recognition of a blessing. For Cec it was the realization that people were better than she imagined and that she was loved and adored and admired more deeply and more widely than she would ever have otherwise believed. For me, the gift was perhaps the knowledge that I could survive apparently anything and, perhaps, the awareness that I might, through suffering, be made useful in small fashion to the world. There are a multitude of other gifts, one of which is the very cognizance of the possibility of gifts in the midst of pain.

I've learned that in the midst of heartbreak, nothing on earth is more valuable than talking about it and having open hearts ready to hear it.

This year of writing has freed me from shackles I don't know I could have borne otherwise. I implore any who read this and find themselves in shoes like mine, to find those open hearts and pour yours out to them. Grief trammeled up is a slow poison. There is not only health and relief in talking about one's grief; there's the potential, the likelihood, of real joy springing from the roots so planted. The blessings I've received by being welcomed into the hearts of so many people, friends and strangers, reading these words every night are incalculable. I thank you, and some day my daughter will thank you.

And finally, I've learned the most important lesson of all: **Life's that way** →.

In a uniquely ironic turn of events, Cecily April Adams, my Cecily, my Cec, my Pie, was an ardent admirer of Gilda Radner. She could do an impression of Radner that was uncanny. When Radner married the idol of Cec's teenage years, Gene Wilder, it seemed cosmically right and cosmically cruel at the same time. And when Gilda Radner developed cancer following staggeringly difficult fertility treatments, Cec grew fearful that the parallels would continue. Once, I bought Cec an autographed photo of Radner, to go with the autograph I'd gotten from Gene Wilder for her when I met him once on an airplane. It was silly of me not to predict her response, for by that time Radner had died, not quite forty-three. Cec was grateful for the gift and for the thought I had put into it, but it was clear I had not put *enough* thought into it. She was then undergoing her own fertility treatments, and the medications were so harsh on her system that she spoke often of her fear that something like what had happened to Gilda would happen to her.

So she accepted my gift with graciousness, but she put the photo away in a spot where she didn't often see it. In Cec's last days, she frequently spoke of how ironic it was that she had indeed wound up in quite the same situation as her beloved Gilda. So I suppose it's not at all unfitting to include something Gilda Radner wrote, as I close out this journal. She wrote, *"I wanted a perfect ending. Now I've learned, the hard way, that some poems don't rhyme, and some stories don't have a clear beginning, middle, and end. Life is about not knowing, having to change, taking the moment and making the best of it, without knowing what's going to happen next. Delicious ambiguity."*

It's not the end, of course. I am beginning the next part of my life. I welcome it, with open arms and open heart. If no one minds, I will perhaps occasionally update you all on the progress Maddie and I are making, and I hope I'll continue to hear from as many of you as care to let me. But it's time to move on, not from these experiences, but from the procedure begun unwittingly a year ago tonight. Its purpose is served, I think. I hope it has been well served.

I'll let Johnny Mercer have the last words:

We're drinking, my friend,
To the end, of a brief episode.
Make it one for my baby,
and one more for the road.

Life's that way →.
2:56 a.m.
No bye-bye.

Jim and Maddie

EPILOGUE

Cecily's father, Don Adams, survived her by eighteen months. He died, aged eighty-two, on September 25, 2005.

Cecily's brother, Sean Adams, lost his fight against his brain tumor. He died June 28, 2006, at the age of thirty-five.

Tom Allard nearly lost his life in a motorcycle accident in 2008, but recovered well from serious injuries and has returned to his teaching duties in the theatre department of the Polytechnic School in Pasadena, California.

Russell Friedman continues to codirect the Grief Recovery Institute (www.grief.net) and to conduct workshops all over the United States and Canada. He and his life partner, Cecily's aunt, Alice Borden, live eight blocks from me and Maddie.

Maribel Elena is still Maddie's nanny. Maddie now calls her "Mommy."

Madeline Rose Beaver attends a mainstream elementary school and is no longer treated for autism-related issues. She reads and writes considerably above her age level. She has many friends and is extremely social, something once believed quite unlikely. She has no active memory of her mother, but she is wildly curious about her, and we talk often and openly about Cecily.

Maddie is such a typical youngster now that many people have expressed the belief that she must have been misdiagnosed. I am convinced she was not. The deterioration in her interactive persona between ages one and two was severe. I have no doubt that her near-miraculous progress thereafter was due to early diagnosis and intense, rapid intervention. Autism is a mysterious syndrome with few concrete answers. But if there are answers, I sincerely believe they are to be found in quick and early action. Not all children who are slow to speak, or who lose vocabulary or social interaction, are autistic. But such children should always be evaluated as quickly as possible. Maddie is living proof that miracles can happen if they are sought early enough.

I have continued my acting career, most prominently following *Deadwood* with a role on the *Supernatural* series. I occasionally send out e-mail updates on Maddie and myself.

I still live with Maddie in the house that Cec built. We expect to be here a long time.

Photo by Cecily Adams

ACKNOWLEDGMENTS

This book would not have been possible without my agent, Laney Katz Becker. Her passion and expertise were the pot of gold at the end of a writer's rainbow. Nothing in my professional life prepared me for her skill, her insight, or her goodness.

My thanks also go to Amy Einhorn, my editor at Putnam, for the honor she bestowed on me by selecting this book, and to Deborah Barylski and Ann Maney, friends of mine and Cecily's who first energized my hopes of bringing this to print. Were it not for them, and Lindsay Edgecombe and Beth Fisher, this journal would have existed only in a few thousand in-boxes.

Special thanks go to my editor at Berkley, Andie Avila, for her grace and unfailing and friendly encouragement. For their incomparable assistance in matters of publication and publicity, I thank my attorney, Jeffrey Arden Bernstein, Kate Travers, formerly of Folio Literary Management, Suzanne Gomez and Holly Ollis of the CW Network, Katie Barker of CBS, and Yvette Kelley, Erin Gloria Atwater, and Dr. Jane Jenab.

The original journal totaled around 265,000 words, three times the size of this book, and it was necessary to trim huge portions. In those portions were stories of kindness, generosity, even heroism by people who go unmentioned in this volume. So I wish to acknowledge some of those people: Jack Kutcher, Remi Aubuchon, Joanna Lipari, Jon Turteltaub, Sue Mullen-Germansky, Leonard Ross, Vivien Straus,

Pete Cunningham, Jerry Lambert, Jim Newman, Christian Malmin, Drew Katzman, Bill Anderson, Kelly Stables, Meg Liberman, Fred Pohl, Bridget Hanley, John Gallogly, Melanie Patterson, Pascal Van Dooren, Barry and Debbie Nulman, Robert and Kim Ulrich, Daryl Bolander, and Catherine Mary Stewart.

For their magnificent support during and after the events of this book, I thank my beloved sister-in-law Stacey Adams, and Nancylee Myatt, Ann Melby, David Milch, Edward Asner, G. Charles Wright, Winston Smith, Dayton Callie, Paula Malcomson, W. Earl Brown, Sean Bridgers, Ian McShane, Leon Rippy, Titus Welliver, Anna Gunn, Molly Parker, Robin Weigert, Timothy Omundson, Garret Dillahunt, David Burke, Maggie Murphy, Teresa Jones, J. Downing, Tina Carlisi, Chip Chinery, Catherine MacNeal, Carolyn Hennesy, Carol Kritzer, Larry Poindexter, Denny Sevier, Pam Braverman, Ginger Lawrence, John Terry, Amanda Sowards, Glenn Morshower, Dennis Haysbert, Jim Nolt, Michael J. Hayde, Gerald McRaney, Gordon Clapp, Kem Nunn, Robert Schenkkan, Maria Dahvana Headley, Jeff and Jackie Filgo, Armin Shimerman, Kitty Swink, Michael and Theresa Osment and their children, Emily and Haley Joel Osment, T. J. Miller, Ulrike de la Lama, Nancy West, Colby Jordan, Beth Becka, Arden Lewis, Charlie Mount, Maura Soden, Renee Lee Seals, Sharon Garnier, Eric Dawson, Roxann Dawson, Seemah Wilder, Paula Rhodes, Paget Brewster, Naomi Caryl, Nanci Christopher, Fredericka Miller, Will Gotay, Michael Helms, Bruce Tufeld, Lizzie Brixius, Robyn Rice Olmstead, Gil Olmstead, Linda Wallem, Debi Derryberry, Harvey Jordan, Andrew Parks, Betty Garrett, Brian Cox, Ed O'Neill, Valerie Landsburg, Will Forte, Jennifer Lutheran, William Wood, Jeanne Dougherty, Mary Lou Belli, Charles Dougherty, Dorothy Ferrante, John Puff, Eric Kripke, Robert Singer, the late Kim Manners, Jensen Ackles, Jared Padalecki, Lou Bollo, Anna Garduño, Colleen Reynolds, Kendra Cover, Mark W. Travis, Christopher Burns, Tina Cardinale, Adam Conger, Lanny Silva, Ken Jenkins, Judy Rich, Jonna Tamases, John Rizzo, my nieces, Wendy Stanley and Amy Schmitz, Steve Nevil, Frances Miller, Lisa and David Jacobs-Pontecorvo, Dr. Leo Orr, and my friends on the Balcony, on Rara-Avis, alt.obituaries, alt.fan.cecil-adams, and rec.arts.movies .past-films.

The sacrifices and dedication of Steve Lee and his wife, our treasured Ida, cannot go unnoted. Nor can those of my daughter's beloved nanny, Maribel Elena, her husband, Mario Elena, and their children, Krystal, Danny, Debby, and Abby, whom Maddie now considers her brother and sisters. To Cecily's family, especially her sisters, Carolyn Steel, Christine Adams, Cathy Metchik, Beige Adams, her cousins, Claudia Yarmy, Eileen Kane, Kathleen Kane, Colleen Fitzpatrick, Demi Dunne, Maria Brennan, Rose Kelly, Steve Efantis, and Dino Efantis and his wife, Amy Chevalier, our niece, Rebecca Nowlen, and Cecily's aunt, Alice Borden, and uncle, Russell Friedman, go my love and thanks for their devotion and unmitigated support. Special thanks go to the entire company of Theatre West, the cast and crew of *That '70s Show*, the cast and crew of *Deadwood*, and to Yarmy's Army.

To my father, Norman Beaver, my mother, Dorothy Beaver, and my sisters, Denise Beaver, Renée Blum, and Teddlie Everett, I offer thanks to God for giving me the gift of their lives in mine.

And finally, while this book is and must be dedicated to my wife and daughter, my greatest thanks must go to my best friend through four decades, Tom Allard, who gave the book its title and, more important, taught me what it meant.

ABOUT THE AUTHOR

Jim Beaver is an actor, playwright, and film historian. Best known as Ellsworth on the acclaimed HBO drama *Deadwood* and as Bobby Singer on *Supernatural*, he has also starred in such series as *Harper's Island, John From Cincinnati,* and *Thunder Alley,* and has appeared in nearly forty motion pictures. His plays, including *Verdigris, Spades, Sidekick,* and *Semper Fi,* have won numerous awards and been produced internationally. Beaver was a critic and columnist for *Films in Review,* and his book *John Garfield: His Life and Films* will be followed by a biography of TV Superman George Reeves. He lives with his daughter, Madeline, in Los Angeles.

Visit the author at www.jim-beaver.com or at www.lifes thatway.com.